REWRITING THE BIBLE

Rewriting the Bible

Land and Covenant
in Post-Biblical Jewish Literature

Betsy Halpern-Amaru

TRINITY PRESS INTERNATIONAL
Valley Forge, Pennsylvania

Trinity Press International
P. O. Box 851
Valley Forge, Pennsylvania 19482

Library of Congress Cataloging-in-Publication Data
Amaru, Betsy Halpern.
    Rewriting the Bible : land and covenant in post-Biblical Jewish literature / Betsy Halpern-Amaru. — 1st ed.
        p.   cm.
    Includes bibliographical references and index.
    ISBN 1-56338-091-9
    1. Apocryphal books—Criticism, interpretation, etc. 2. Land tenure—Religious aspects—Judaism. 3. Covenants—Religious aspects—Judaism. 4. Jews—History—
168 B.C.-135 A.D. I. Title.
BS1700.A57 1994
229'.91—dc20   94-7383 CIP

A version of chapter 4 on the *Testament of Moses* was previously published in Ellen Spolsky, ed., *Summoning: Covenants in Law and Literature: Essays in Honor of Harold Fisch* (Albany: SUNY Press, 1993). Chapter 6 is an expanded version of "Land Theology in Josephus' *Jewish Antiquities*," *JQR* 71 (1980-81): 201-229.

Scripture quotations are from *Tanakh: A New Translation of the Holy Scriptures According to the Traditional Hebrew Text*, copyright 1985, Jewish Publication Society of America, and are used with permission.

This book is printed on acid-free paper and was produced in the United States of America.

94   95   96   97   98   98   6   5   4   3   2   1

To the memory of my Parents ז״ל
and
To the joy of Sara Elisheva and Ariel Sara

Contents

Acknowledgments

I became interested in the treatment of biblical Land theology in post biblical Jewish literature a number of years ago. Sparked by W. D. Davies' *The Gospel and the Land* and subsequently enriched by his *The Territorial Dimension of Judaism*, that interest first began to acquire a scholarly focus in the context of my participation in a National Endowment for the Humanities Seminar during the summer of 1980. Directed by Professor Louis H. Feldman of Yeshiva University, the seminar was the occasion for my first examination of the treatment of the Land concept ("Land Theology in Josephus' *Antiquities of the Jews*," *Jewish Quarterly Review*, N.S.71:4 [April 1981], 201-29). Even more significantly, the NEH experience reopened the door to active scholarship that I had closed during the early childhood years of my four children. I am most grateful to the National Endowment for the Humanities for providing the impetus for that return. I cannot begin to acknowledge the extent of my indebtedness to Louis Feldman who, over the course of years, has remained my teacher and became my friend. He has been a steady source of encouragement, has given generously of his time, and has shared his knowledge of *Pseudo-Philo* and Josephus.

I am also deeply indebted to Devorah Dimant of Haifa University who not only helped me to define the limits of this project, but also read and critiqued much of the manuscript. Her wealth of knowledge and her wonderful eye for critical detail have been invaluable.

Much of the research on *Jubilees* was done during a sabbatical year spent in Jerusalem. I wish to thank Professor Chaim Rabin for his help in working with Ge'ez and Professor Michael Stone for the invitation to participate in his graduate seminar where I presented the first draft of the material on *Jubilees*. The final version (multiple drafts and several years later) benefited not only from the comments of the members of the seminar, but also from Mike's wise counsel "to live a few years with *Jubilees*" I also want to acknowledge the benefit of working during that year and in subsequent summers in the Judaica Reading Room of the National Library in Jerusalem. The Library provided a marvelous collection, a resourceful staff, and a quiet and friendly environment for work.

I am indebted to colleagues and students at Vassar College, in particular to Deborah Dash Moore and Mark Cladis for their enthusiastic support and constructive readings of parts of the manuscript; and to student research assistants, Celina Grey and Kanitra Strong, for their help with editing and checking the many source references. The chore of final editing, of course, lay with the staff at Trinity Press International. They have done their work with a knowledgeable, but kind hand that reflects the spirit of the publisher, Dr. Harold Rast, who made what could have been a tedious task a most pleasant one.

More personally, I would like to thank Aliza Rosenberg who came to visit and stayed to index. And to my daughter Rebecca, who shared the difficult moments and offered the ultimate in encouragement, my love and deep gratitude.

Translations and Abbreviations

Translations

All biblical citations are from *Holy Scriptures*, 3 vols., Philadelphia: Jewish Publication Society, 1962-1968.

Unless otherwise indicated, all citations of *Jubilees* are from the translation by O. S. Wintermute in *OTP*, II; the citations of *Testament of Moses* are from the translation of J. Priest in *OTP*, II; and the citations of *Pseudo-Philo* are from the translation of D. J. Harrington in *OTP*, II.

All citations of *Antiquities* are from the Loeb Classical Library edition of Josephus' *Works*, H. St. John Thackeray, et. al., eds., Cambridge, Mass.: Harvard University Press and London: Heinemann, 1926-1965.

Abbreviations

BA	*Biblical Archaeology*
BASOR	Bulletin of the American Schools of Oriental Research
CBQ	Catholic Biblical Quarterly
CBQMS	Catholic Biblical Quarterly Manuscript Series
HDR	Harvard Dissertations in Religion
HTR	*Harvard Theological Review*
HSM	Harvard Semitic Monographs
HUCA	*Hebrew Union College Annual*
IDB	Interpreter's Dictionary of the Bible
JAOS	Journal of the American Oriental Society
JBL	Journal of Biblical Literature
JJS	Journal of Jewish Studies
JQR	Jewish Quarterly Review
JSHRZ	Jüdische Schriften aus hellenistischromisher Zeit
JSJ	*Journal for Study of Judaism in the Persian, Hellenistic & Roman Periods*
JSP	Journal for the Study of the Pseudepigrapha
JSS	Journal of Semitic Studies
JTS	Journal of Theological Studies
OTP	Old Testament Pseudepigrapha, James Charlesworth, ed., 2 vols.
PAAJR	Proceedings of the American Academy of Jewish Research
SBLSCS	Society of Biblical Literature Septuagint and Cognate Studies

CHAPTER 1

Introduction

There is a hierarchy of values in Judaism, and...those who fail to distinguish holiness from holiness will in the end fail to distinguish between the holy and the profane. We must consider the relative priority of three values: [the people of] Israel, Torah, and the Land of Israel. The interest of the people of Israel precedes that of the interest of the Land of Israel.

Yehuda Amital

The value of the Land of Israel exceeds that of peace....We are commanded to conquer the land by war, even at a high price.

Hanan Porat[1]

F ew ideas in Judaism have been so tenaciously held, so defined and redefined, and so intricately woven into the fabric of Jewish history and self-expression as the Land concept. Indeed, the idea of the Land is an integral aspect of Judaism that has accompanied the Jewish-religious tradition from its biblical origins to its most contemporary formulations. The nature of that accompaniment, however, has not been static. Standing at the core of the biblical covenant that informs the central theological, historical, and literary myths of Israel's beginnings, the Land concept has undergone multiple transformations as Jews have reinterpreted its meaning and significance in each epoch of their changing historical circumstances.

A meeting ground between theology and history, religion and politics, the Land concept has been exaggerated, minimized, allegorized, idealized, rationalized, and polemicized. In the expansionist era of the Hasmoneans, the biblical Land idea was formulated in geo-political terms. With the growth of large diaspora communities in the early rabbinic period, it became a spacial benchmark for the development of Jewish law. And, displaced from its central position in Jewish thought in the course of diaspora history, it was then transformed in idealized form into a temporal symbol of redemptive hope. Nineteenth-century political Zionism retranslated the concept into a signpost of cultural and political normality; and the return to sovereign nationhood in the twentieth century provoked renewed efforts to determine its religious significance. The interpretive encounter with the biblical concept of Land has not ended. As the conflicting interpretations of Rabbis Amital and Porat indicate, the contemporary encounter is even more intense, for the experience of return to sovereignty has been accompanied by the history of its interpretation.[2]

This study is concerned with the treatment of the biblical Land concept in the post-biblical period—an early chapter in that history of interpretation, but the first one in which the experience of return required reformulation of the biblical Land concept. In contrast to the contemporary one, this era was not preceded by a prolonged exile distancing it from the scriptural perspective. To the contrary, the provocation for reinterpretation of the Land concept in the post-biblical world came from its proximity to the biblical notion of a covenantal relationship between God and Israel that is played out on an historical stage. The idea of the Land—promise, acquisition and retention, exile, and return—functions within that history as the central motif for defining the covenantal relationship. In fact, within the scriptural narrative the character and quality of the relationship between God and Israel are recorded and monitored primarily in the language of Land theology. Given that perspective, how did Judeans living in the Land long after the return from Babylonian exile understand biblical Land theology? What context did they find for an extended post-exilic continuation of covenanted history in the Land? How did they place their own historical situation within the parameters of the biblical theological system?

In the following chapters I address these questions in the context of an analysis of the treatment of the biblical concept of covenanted Land in four post-biblical works: *Jubilees*, *The Testament of Moses*, *Pseudo-Philo*, and Flavius Josephus' *Jewish Antiquities*. Deliberately choosing texts that rewrite narratives involving covenant and Land, I view the author of each as a reader responding to the sacred source text, and approach each reinterpretation as an interplay among the biblical text, the ideological concerns of its author, and the post-exilic historical context of its composition.

The works I have selected have received significant scholarly attention, but the reinterpretations of the biblical concept of Land contained within them have not.[3] The neglect relates not so much to the nature of the subject as to the sources of scholarly interest. Frequently placed in the context of an inquiry related to New Testament writings, the post-exilic (intertestamental) period has been treated as the background to early Christian thought and literature, rather than as an extension of biblical history and a continuation of Jewish life in the Land.[4] As a result, the literary texts were viewed in relationship to what followed rather than to what preceded them, and the question of the relationship between post-biblical and biblical concepts of the Land was lost in the process.

With a few notable exceptions, historians of post-biblical Judaism who have worked on this literature have not focused their attention on the Land theology embedded in the texts.[5] Instead, they have concentrated on two interrelated areas: form-critical literary analysis that attempts to classify various types of texts, and historical-critical scholarship focused on identifying the circumstances and date(s) of composition. The work of these scholars provides an invaluable background for this study which focuses not on the texts *per se*, but on the treatment of one particular biblical motif within the texts.

That motif has received attention from scholars of the history of Judaism, particularly those interested in the sources that have fed into modern Zionism. But like the intertestamentalists, their focus has also been on later periods. The loss of the Land at the end of the Second Jewish Commonwealth and the development of rabbinic Judaism are of such import in the history of Judaism that rabbinic responses to the disasters of the first and second centuries of this era have overshadowed earlier reinterpretations of the biblical concept of Land. Consequently, surveys of the territorial concept in Judaism have tended to move from Scriptures to the rabbinic period and onward, with little, if any, attention paid to treatments of the subject in the literature of the Second Temple period.[6]

The purpose of this endeavor is, first and foremost, to fill that significant lacuna. The treatment of the biblical Land concept in all four of the texts calls into question the commonly-held belief that the displacement of the Land in favor of the centrality of Torah and peoplehood in Judaism had its origins in the rabbinic effort to accommodate the consequences of loss of sovereignty and exile. Moreover, the eschatological perspective in two of the works cautions against too intimate a connection being made between the preoccupation with eschatology in modern Land theology and the transformation of the Land into a messianic symbol over the course of diaspora history. Aware that the encounter with biblical Land theology in modern Israel makes a study of its reinterpretation in Second Temple texts all the more alluring, I refrain from ahistorical comparisons between the earlier works and the considerations that engage the minds and hearts of the present. The value of this study to the understanding of the contemporary debate over the significance of the Land lies not there, but in the extent to which it informs the broader history of interpretation that nourishes that debate.

THE "REWRITTEN BIBLE"

The four works that provide the subject matter for this study have been classified under the rubric of the "Rewritten Bible," a term coined by Geza Vermes more than two decades ago[7] that in recent years has become a subject of scholarly controversy. Some use it rather loosely as a designation for a type of literary technique, process, or activity, and apply it to the corpus of post-biblical literature in an inclusive way that covers any number of writings that begin from a biblical base.[8] Others, often treating the term as a designation for a specific genre of literature, limit its application to rewritings that are closely integrated into the biblical framework.[9] Since the works used in this study fit into even the most narrow application of the term, no purpose is served by engaging in the details of the controversy over classification and genre. For purposes of clarity, I will, however, offer a description of the understanding of the term "Rewritten Bible" as I employ it.

First, "Rewritten Bible" uses narrative structure as an exegetical medium for reinterpretation. Hence the key to unraveling the rewritten text lies in its implicit as well as explicit relationship to the sacred one.

Second, the rewritten narrative is not offered as a substitute or replacement for the biblical narrative. To the contrary, with the possible exception of Josephus, who wrote *Antiquities* primarily for a gentile audience, each author not only assumes but requires that the reader relate the rewriting back to Scriptures.

Third, the purpose of the rewriting is to "actualize a religious tradition and make it meaningful within new situations."[10] Hence, insofar as the reconstructed text involves a major motif in the biblical narrative, the rewritten version reveals some sense of the historical circumstances that motivate the rewriting.

Fourth, although not developed as a theological treatise, the reconstruction that replaces biblical theology in each text is systematically developed and internally consistent. Moreover, the exegetical methods by which the various reconstructions are achieved have their own internal logic. Embedded, like the theology that it reconstructs, in the biblical narrative, the logic may not be as succinct or obvious as that of rabbinic midrash or Qumran pesher. Yet there are sufficient similarities in the reconstructions of the various texts to warrant an effort to uncover a general exegetical approach.[11]

The authors and/or redactors of the four rewritings lived in Judea; except for Josephus they wrote in Hebrew; and together, their works span at least the period from the first half of the second century BCE to after the Jewish war in the second half of the first century CE.[12] Only the work of

Josephus can be firmly set in time and place. The historical settings of the three pseudepigraphic texts continue to be subjects of debate. Since it is focused in a different direction, this study does not directly engage in that debate, but it does offer an additional dimension for consideration in the ongoing study of pseudepigraphic texts.

Paleographic data on the Qumran fragments of *Jubilees* has set 100 BCE as the latest possible date for its composition,[13] but no consensus has been reached on the earliest possible date for the work. Struck by the halachic emphasis in "Little Genesis," R. H. Charles identified it as Pharisaic and placed composition during the reign of John Hyrcannus (135-104 BCE).[14] This remained the most widely accepted date until the appearance of Gene L. Davenport's claim that the work as we have it is the product of three different periods, one pre-Maccabean, one produced during the Maccabean conflict, and a third during the reigns of Simon and John Hyrcannus.[15] Davenport's thesis of separate redactions was based on the assumption that eschatological theology could be used as a measuring rod for textual analysis. The approach explained away certain inconsistencies, but critics argued that the work in fact showed "greater harmony of viewpoint than one usually finds in Palestinian documents."[16] Moreover, many scholars felt that the author of *Jubilees* was far more involved in his own present than in the drama of a future time.[17] Working on that assumption, James VanderKam analyzed key passages and established the Maccabean period (163-40 BCE) as the earliest date of composition.[18] VanderKam's historical analytical approach to the text was generally accepted; the 163-40 date was not. Indeed, the same passages which VanderKam associated with the late Maccabean years other scholars identified with both earlier and later periods.[19] Still far from a consensus, there remains today a range of possible dates that goes full circle with a recent study arguing for the Hyrcannean era originally set forth by Charles.[20]

Consequently, one begins an examination of the land theology in *Jubilees* without the benefit of a specific, certain date for its composition. There is, however, the biblical text. By combining VanderKam's technique of focusing on how that text is reworked in *Jubilees* with Davenport's thematic approach and applying them to Land theology—a far more central theme in Hebrew Scriptures than eschatology—it becomes possible to extract a theological perspective that adds another piece to the puzzle of *Jubilees*. That piece does not firmly resolve the question of a Maccabean or Hyrcannean date of composition for the work. But the nature of the reconstruction of biblical Land theology does suggest that *Jubilees* was written during an expansionist era in opposition to a complacent, automatic anticipation of the end-time, a characteristic that favors the later dating.

Determination of the historical circumstances of the composition of the *Testament of Moses* is even more complex. In this case, the question of date is combined with a more generally held but still contested opinion that the text is the product of a process of redaction that extended from the Maccabean to the post-Herodian period. The earliest effort to establish a date of composition was again that of R. H. Charles. Attributing the document to a single author, he placed its date around the turn of the era (7-30 CE) on the basis of internal references to Herod and his sons and an attack on the Jews by Varus in 4 BCE.[21] Subsequently, this view was challenged by Jacob Licht, who, on the basis of form criticism, argued that the work was originally composed in the time of Antiochus IV Epiphanes and later material (chaps. 6-7) was added by a post-Herodian redactor.[22] This view is accepted by a number of scholars, albeit, in one case, with the proviso that the earlier base was significantly reworked by the first-century redactor.[23] On the other hand, several scholars continue to hold to a single author, some of whose material "may have had considerable prior history in either oral or written form."[24]

In their concern for dating the work, the proponents of both opinions focused their analyses almost exclusively on evidence of historical milieu and, hence, authorship. In contrast, the approach I take to the work emphasizes the relationship between the "rewritten" (pseudepigraphic) text and the "written" (scriptural) one. In the *Testament of Moses* that relationship is intricate and particularly significant. Treating the text as an intertextual play on biblical passages—a play that presumes great familiarity with Scriptures on the part of the reader—highlights biblical allusions and clues that provide substance and cohesion to a work which otherwise appears most disunited. Such an approach demonstrates a cohesive unity in the *Testament* that supports an argument for a single hand or for a redactor who so finely interwove traditions that his contribution would warrant attribution of authorship.

Although the historical setting for the composition of *Pseudo-Philo* has not been firmly established, the range of possibilities is far narrower and less complex than in the cases of the other two pseudepigraphic works. Using internal evidence, scholars place *Pseudo-Philo* in the first century CE before or after the destruction of the Second Temple.[25] Particularly intricate are the questions of the purpose for which the work was composed and its relationship to *Jubilees*.[26] Scholarship on these issues has usually involved comparative analyses of the pseudepigraphic texts in and of themselves rather than in relationship to their respective treatments of major motifs in the biblical narrative. The latter approach clarifies the internal logic operating within *Pseudo-Philo*, adds another dimension to the question of its relationship to comparable rewritten narratives, and, by emphasizing the major concerns of its author, offers added insight into the circumstances under which the work was composed.

My interest in the treatment of biblical Land theology in pseudepigraphic literature developed out of a study of the treatment of the Land concept in Flavius Josephus' *Jewish Antiquities* undertaken some years ago. Because the circumstances of the author and the setting of the work were firmly set and known, it was possible to focus solely on the play between the written and rewritten texts. In subsequently turning to the three pseudepigraphic works, I have made every attempt to maintain that focus, for therein lies the key to treating rewritten narratives as they were composed, as interpretative commentaries that permit new life situations to be encompassed within the biblical structure.

This scriptural structure is so significant that each author creates a formula that places the interpretive rewriting within its context: *Jubilees* is a revelation conveyed by the Angel of the Presence to Moses on Sinai; the *Testament of Moses* is a private communication from Moses to Joshua set within the context of Deut. 31:15; *Pseudo-Philo* provides insights into the intent and mind of God that are set within the biblical narrative; and *Antiquities* is presented as a translation of the Jewish holy books. The key text for understanding each of them is the biblical one whose fullness of meaning unfolds in a reformulation that accommodates the exigencies of historical time and circumstance.

CHAPTER 2

Reading the Bible: Land and Covenant

L and is so central to biblical theology that one might describe it as the major theme in Hebrew Scriptures.[1] The promise of eternal possession of the Land serves as the pivot for the patriarchal covenant that introduces the biblical history of Israel. Recollecting that covenant, the narrative of the exodus then connects liberation from enslavement to a promise of future redemption characterized by acquisition of the Land. This Land is not only superabundant; it also possesses certain metaphysical attributes, not the least of which is a special relationship with the deity. When the covenant is nationalized at Sinai, Torah legislation links Land and Law, particularly by locating fulfillment of specific commands in the Land, and more generally, by making retention of the Promised Land contingent on fidelity to the covenant and adherence to certain types of commandments. Ultimately the tension between such conditional tenure and the earlier promise of eternal possession of the Land becomes the foundation for the development of the theme of restoration, and "ingathering of the exiles" emerges as a central motif in the eschatology of the classical prophets. Thus, in all the major aspects of biblical theology—covenant, metaphysics, law, and eschatology—the concept of Land has particular significance.

Before turning to how that concept was interpreted and/or reinterpreted in reworkings of biblical narratives during the Second Temple period, it is first necessary to examine how the Land concept functions within the text that presented itself to the post-biblical reader. Such an overview of the biblical presentation of the Land concept offers not only a point of departure, but a comparative point of reference for subsequent examination of the treatment of biblical Land theology in post-biblical texts. Given that the basic elements of that theology are set forth in the Torah books, and that, of the four authors we will be dealing with only Josephus goes beyond Early Prophets (and then with minimal attention to prophetic literature), the primary focus here will be on the Pentateuch, Joshua, and Judges, with significantly less attention paid to the Land concept in prophetic literature.

PATRIARCHAL HISTORY

Serving as the contextual focus for the initial encounters between the patriarchs and God, the promise of the Land is one of a triad of assurances (the other two being God's blessings and future peoplehood) that comprise the patriarchal covenant. Within the covenantal context the Land promise may appear without direct reference to the promises of special blessings and/or peoplehood. Never, however, is the patriarchal covenant presented without some reference to the promise of the Land.

Abraham is promised the Land on five occasions, two of which occur before the covenant is actually formulated. The first, after the patriarch has obeyed the command to leave his birthplace (Gen. 12:1, 7), and the second, after his return from a sojourn in Egypt and his separation from Lot (Gen. 13:14-17), set the stage for two covenant-making scenes on the occasions of the predictions of Abraham's sons (Gen. 15:7, 18-20; 17:7-8). A fifth scene, reconfirming the covenantal relationship, follows the *Aqedah* (Gen. 22:16-18). Variously expressed in the different passages, the assurances of God's blessings, of peoplehood, and of acquisition of the Land are consistently interwoven in all five of these promissory scenes. Within the triad, however, the Land holds a primary position. God's relationship with Abraham begins with the dramatic, unexplained divine command for the patriarch to leave birthplace and family and move to the land "that I will show you" (Gen. 12:1). When that relationship is stated in covenantal terms and extended to the patriarch's seed, its context again is a landed one (Gen. 17:8).

Moreover, each time the first patriarch is assured of future progeny, the Land is either the context or the reference point for the assurance. The command to migrate to the Land provides the first occasion for presentation of the promise of peoplehood (Gen. 12:1-2). The first sighting of the Land prompts a repeat of it (Gen. 12:7), and a third version is embedded in the description of the patriarch's tour of the Land after his separation from his nephew (Gen. 13:14-17).

Even more significantly, in the two narratives where one would most expect an emphasis on progeny—the predictions of the births of Abraham's sons (Genesis 15 and 17)—it is the promise of the Land, not seed, that defines the covenantal relationship. In the first instance, the assurance that Abraham's "very own issue" would be his heir (Gen. 15:3-5, with the text temporarily permitting the erroneous assumption that it will be Ishmael) is followed by a formal covenant-making scene in which the Land promise is dominant and where the term "covenant" is applied with specific reference to the Land:

> On that day the Lord made a covenant with Abram, saying, "To your off-spring I give this land, from the river of Egypt to the great river, the river Euphrates, the Kenites, the Kenizzites, the Kadmonites, the Hittites, the Perizzites, the Rephaim, the Amorites, the Canaanites, the Girgashites, and the Jebusites." (Gen. 15:18-21)

The same emphasis appears on the fourth occasion for the promise, the prediction of the birth of a son by Sarah. Again the major theme of the narrative is progeny, and again the passage clearly associates the covenant with the Land promise. The annunciation is preceded by a promissory passage that presents possession of the Land, not progeny, as eternal like the covenant itself. Indeed, overall, the language used to characterize the covenant is strikingly parallel to that used to describe the promise of the Land.

> I will make you exceedingly fertile, and make nations of you; and kings shall come forth from you. I will maintain My covenant *between Me and you and your offspring to come as an everlasting covenant* throughout the ages, *to be God to you and to your offspring to come.* I give the land you sojourn in *to you and your offspring to come,* all the land of Canaan, *as an everlasting possession. I will be their God.* (Gen. 17:6-8)[2]

This presentation of the covenant is prompted by no casual event in biblical literature—a change of name—which here, as in two other significant name changes, places particular emphasis on the promise of the Land.[3] Moreover, in specifying that Ishmael would be fertile and father a great nation but that the covenant would be fulfilled through Isaac (Gen. 17:15-21), the text clearly indicates that the line of descent for the covenant is defined by possession of the Land: the heir to the Land, not the first of the progeny, carries the covenant.

The renewal of the covenant at the scene of the *Aqedah* (Gen. 22:16-18) again demonstrates the centrality of the Land idea within the covenant. The restatement is prompted by the dramatic evidence of Abraham's faith in the endurance of the covenantal line through Isaac. Yet, even in that context the renewed promise of progeny is counterpoised by an assurance of land conquest ("your descendants shall seize the gates of their foes") that momentarily shifts attention from reassurance of Isaac's seed to a foreshadowing of future involvement with the Land.

Well laid out in the promises to Abraham, the fundamental components of the covenant are repeated, albeit in much less detail, with each of the succeeding patriarchs. Isaac, confirmed in the covenant before his birth and again at Mount Moriah, receives the promise directly at Gerar where, in spite of a local famine, he is told to remain in the Land and not go to Egypt (Gen. 26:1-5). Jacob first hears of the promises by way of blessings from Isaac when, in flight from Esau, the future patriarch goes to the home of Laban in Mesopotamia (Gen. 28:3-4). En route to Paddan-aram and again upon his return years later, Jacob receives the promises directly from God (Gen. 28:13-15; 35:11-12). All of these covenant-making encounters incorporate aspects of Abraham's experiences of the promise. The recipient is assured God's blessings, multiple seed, and the Land; but in every instance the Land is the point of reference for the triadic blessing.

Paralleling the first patriarch's covenantal encounters upon entrance to the Land and return after a sojourn in Egypt (Gen. 12:7; 15:4-7), the covenant-making with both Isaac and Jacob is related in some fashion to migration. The single covenant-making scene with Isaac is initiated by divine discouragement of a contemplated move from the Land and specifically equates transfer of the Abrahamic covenant with the promise of the Land.

> Reside in this land, and I will be with you and bless you; I will give all these lands to you and to your offspring, fulfilling the oath that I swore to your father Abraham. I will make your descendants as numerous as the stars of heaven, and give to your descendants all these lands, so that all the nations of the earth shall bless themselves by your offspring. (Gen. 26:3-4)

The equation is reflected in Isaac's own understanding of the covenant for, in a subsequent demonstration of faith after digging a well at Rehovoth, he states: "Now at last the Lord has granted us ample space to increase in the land" (Gen. 26:22). Thereafter, the other two aspects of the triad—God's blessings and great numbers—are confirmed in a dream vision (Gen. 26:24).

Actual leave-taking is the context for the two occasions on which Jacob enters directly into covenant-making. In the first instance, the transfer of the covenant upon Jacob's departure to Laban, Isaac presents the promise of fertility (Gen. 28:3), but defines the "blessing of Abraham" specifically as possession of the Land (Gen. 28:4).[4] In the second instance, the first of Jacob's two covenantal encounters with God, the patriarch is commanded to emigrate, and the promises are directly linked to a divine assurance of return to the land that has been promised to him (Gen. 28:13-15). When that return in fact comes, like Abraham's return from Egypt (Gen. 13:14-17), it occasions a renewal of the covenant and a name change. Again paralleling a similar scene with Abraham (Gen. 17:4-8), the change of name involves a covenantal blessing with the promise of the Land as its closing climax. Moreover, here, as in the earlier blessing Jacob received from Isaac, only the Land aspect of the covenantal triad is specifically identified with Jacob's forefathers.

> You whose name is Jacob, You shall be called Jacob no more, But Israel shall be your name....I am *El Shaddai*, Be fertile and increase; A nation, yea an assembly of nations, shall descend from you. Kings shall issue from your loins. The land that I gave to Abraham and Isaac I give to you; And to your offspring to come will I give the land. (Gen. 35:10, 11-12)

The major difference between the later patriarchal covenants and the one with Abraham lies in the matter of merit. With the first patriarch the covenantal promises are presented as unconditional gifts in spite of references on two occasions to Abraham's fidelity.[5] In the first instance, the covenantal scene is preceded by Abraham's refusal of material rewards from the king of Sodom out of concern that when the divine promise of prosperity would be fulfilled the Sodomite king would usurp the credit due to God (Gen. 14:23). In the second instance, Abraham does not hold back his son Isaac out of fear that the promise of Land and nation through him could not otherwise be fulfilled (Gen. 17:19; 22:16-17). However, in both of these cases fidelity is defined in terms of the patriarch's surety that God would keep promises that had initially been made without reference to the merits of the recipient. Hence, in the biblical narrative Abraham's merit does not elicit the covenant so much as offer justification for it after the fact.

In contrast, with the last two patriarchs there is no question of personal merit or reward. The covenant with Isaac is explicitly rooted both in the promise to and the merit of his father (Gen. 26:3-5).[6] Isaac in turn conveys "the blessing of Abraham," that he "possess the land which God gave to Abraham" (Gen. 28:4) to his own son. And in the subsequent covenant-making encounters between Jacob and God, the first two patriarchs again serve as the point of reference for transmission of the Land promise.[7]

The issue of merit aside, the biblical text makes a point not only of repeating the Land promise with each patriarch, but also of explicitly transmitting that promise to the post-patriarchal generation. Immediately before his death Jacob tells Joseph of the promises he had received at Bethel ("making of you a community of peoples," and giving "this land to your offspring to come for an everlasting possession") and assures his son that God would bring him "back to the land of your fathers" (Gen. 48:4, 21). In turn, upon his deathbed, Joseph, referring to the land that God had sworn to Abraham, Isaac, and Jacob, conveys the covenantal promise to his brothers. Significantly, this first of several bridges between the patriarchal and exodus narratives is set forth entirely in terms of the Land aspect of the covenant (Gen. 50:24).

In similar fashion, the transitional recollections of the patriarchs which follow in the early chapters of Exodus focus exclusively on the Land promise. At the divine renaming scene of the Burning Bush, Moses is twice told that the "God of your fathers,...of Abraham...of Isaac...of Jacob" has come to take the Israelites out of Egypt "to a land flowing with milk and honey" (Exod. 3:6-8, 15-17). When these implicit references to the covenant are made explicit, once in response to Moses' expression of doubt (Exod. 6:2-4) and again in response to the people after the apostasy of the Golden Calf (Exod. 33:1-3), the patriarchal covenant again is presented solely in terms of the promise of the Land.[8]

Recollections of the covenant with the patriarchs appear throughout the Hexateuch. At times recollective phrases preface legislative passages: "When the Lord brings you into the land which He swore to your fathers, Abraham, Isaac, and Jacob, you shall...";[9] at other times they are placed within narrative descriptions of the wilderness and early conquest years. The commandment-associated recollections appear both in the context of specific legislation (the observance of the Passover festival, the commandments regarding firstlings, sabbatical years, tithing, affixing of the signpost, and the prohibition against idolatry) and, especially in Deuteronomy, as a structural aspect of general admonitions to maintain the Law. In all the instances where the recollection is associated with a particular commandment, only the promise of the Land to the patriarchs is mentioned. In several of the admonitions in Deuteronomy the promises of fertility and divine blessing also appear. But, when reference is made to an oath sworn to the fathers, the referent is always the Land promise.[10] In one instance (Deut. 7:8), a recollected oath does refer back to redemption from bondage. The exception has little significance, however, for in the pentateuchal narrative redemption from Egypt is consistently associated with settlement in the Land, be it in the context of the initial prophecy of slavery and redemption conveyed to Abraham (Gen. 15:13-16) or in the early scenes of Exodus when Moses is told of the coming redemption and of the Land "flowing with milk and honey" (Exod. 3:6-8, 15-17).

The numerous recollections which appear within the narratives of the post-exodus and early conquest years follow the same pattern as those in the earlier narratives: they focus almost exclusively on the Land aspect of the covenant. The single exception is the recollection of the promise of great numbers in Moses' intercession on behalf of the Israelites at the time of Golden Calf. In the context of the divine threat to destroy the Israelites, such a recollection is most fitting. Given that context, however, it is particularly notable that the appeal includes not only a recollection of the promise of the Land, but one which is expressed in the strong promissorial language of "whole land" and eternal possession.

> Remember your servants, Abraham, Isaac and Jacob, how you swore to them by Your Self and said to them: "I will make your offspring as numerous as the stars of heaven, and I will give to your offspring this whole land of which I spoke, to possess forever." (Exod. 32:13)

Moreover, in the narrative of the intercession at Kadesh Barnea where the major issue is entry into the Land, there is no comparable recollection of the promise of numbers; only the Land aspect of the promises is mentioned (Num. 14:22-23; 32:10-11). Similarly, the recollections of the patriarchal covenant in Moses' review of Israelite history (Deut. 1:7-8, 35; 4:37-38; 10:11), in his preparation of the people for conquering and living in the Land (Deut. 8:18; 9:5),[11] and in God's own final words with Moses (Deut. 34:4) all share the single focus on the Land aspect of the covenant with the forefathers.

The pentateuchal recollections almost always associate the covenantal promises with an oath to the forefathers.[12] In contrast, the narrative descriptions of the conquest in Joshua and Judges do not extensively recall the patriarchs. Never mentioning the forefathers by name, the author of Joshua three times recollects an oath to the "fathers" (1:6; 5:6; 21:41). But in only one instance (5:6) is the reference clearly to the patriarchs. In the other two, the "fathers" refers, as in Judges 2:1, to the exodus generation that had received the covenant at Sinai. Save for these passages and several references to fulfillment of God's word to Moses (Josh. 1:3; 11:23), the narrative perspective of both books is more involved with the immediate working of the covenantal relationship—God's immediate role in the conquest and the issue of Israelite fidelity—than with recollection of the original covenant.

THE NAME AND CHARACTER OF THE LAND

The term "Land of Israel" is not used in the Pentateuch or in the first books of Early Prophets.[13] Instead, the Land is referred to in descriptive terms that are experiential, geographic, metaphysical, or reflective of ownership either by natural or divine right. Experiential descriptions appear in the promises to all three patriarchs. Abraham is promised the "land I will show you" (Gen. 12:1), "this land" (Gen. 12:7; 15:7), "all the land that you see" (Gen. 13:15) and the "land you sojourn in" (Gen. 17:8). Isaac is assured "all these lands" which have been pointed out to him (Gen. 26:3);

and Jacob, instructed to return to "your native land" (Gen. 31:13), receives "the ground on which you are lying," together with a prediction of geographic expansion (Gen. 28:13-14). When the promise to the patriarchs is subsequently recollected to the enslaved Israelites, the Land is described in terms of the patriarchal experience of living there (Exod. 6:4).[14] And paralleling the experience of the patriarchs, at the onset of the conquest the Israelites are twice assured of acquiring "every spot on which your foot treads" (Deut. 11:24; Josh. 1:3).

The geographic dimension is strongest in the promises to Abraham, where they are progressively specified, from the vague "this land" of the first encounter (Gen. 12:7) to "to the north and south, to the east and west...all the land you see" (Gen. 13:14-15) to "from the river of Egypt to the great river, the river Euphrates" (Gen. 15:18). For Isaac, Jacob, and Joseph the spatial delineation of borders is replaced by a temporal definition employing recollection of the promise to progenitors.[15] But when the covenant is nationalized and its context becomes the conquest, anticipated or actual, the geographic description reappears, either with geographic detail (Exod. 23:31;[16] Num. 34:1-12; Deut. 11:24; Josh. 1:4)[17] or with conscious repetition of the explicit promise of "the whole" or "all the land" (Exod. 32:13; Josh. 2:24; 11:23; 21:41).

The most common term for the Land throughout the narratives involves acknowledgment of the presence of indigenous populations, either by enumeration of resident peoples—land of the Canaanites, Hittites, and so on—or, more frequently, by the name "land of Canaan."[18] Because it connotes ownership, the naming invokes a certain tension, particularly in passages in which the Land is being promised to the patriarchs and/or their descendants. In fact, the issue of indigenous populations is originally addressed in just such contexts. By explicit or implicit statement all the promissory passages with Abraham acknowledge the presence of indigenous peoples. On three occasions this acknowledgment comes from the narrator. When Abraham is first told of the Land promise, the patriarch is described as traveling with his entourage to "the land of Canaan" and notation is made that "the Canaanites were then in the land" (Gen. 12:5-6). After the separation from Lot, the notation is "the Canaanites and Perizzites were then dwelling in the land" (Gen. 13:7). On the third covenanting occasion, acknowledgment of the presence of the indegenous peoples shifts from the mouth of the narrator directly to that of God (15:19). At the announcement of Isaac's birth, the patriarch is told that "all the land of Canaan" will be given as an "eternal possession" to him and to his offspring (Gen. 17:8). More obliquely, perhaps because of a shift from a promissory tone to a predictive foreshadowing of conquest history, at the scene of the

Aqedah Abraham is assured that his "descendants shall seize the gates of their foes" (Gen. 22:17).

The background for the transition from narrator to divine perspective regarding the contemporary occupants of the Land is laid at the *Brit ben ha-Betarim,* where God tells the patriarch that the actual fulfillment of the Land promise would be delayed because "the iniquity of the Amorites is not yet complete" (Gen. 15:16). The same covenantal scene opens with an acknowledgment of Abraham's merit (Gen. 15:6), which consequently stands in direct contrast to the character of the Canaanite peoples. Nonetheless, the forfeiture of the Amorite right of possession, a right implied by priority of occupation if nothing more, is rooted in the moral quality of the occupants' life in the Land rather than in the patriarch's merit. Neither the association between the right זכות to occupy this particular land nor the obligation חובה to live by a moral code is clarified at this point:[19] Indeed, as the narrative moves on to the stories of Isaac and Jacob,[20] the phrase "land of Canaan" disappears from direct dialogue (as opposed to narrated description), only to reappear on numerous occasions in the context of the sojourn in and exodus from Egypt.[21]

Moses and the enslaved Israelites first hear of the promised territory as "the home/land of the Canaanites, the Hittites, the Amorites, the Perizzites, the Hivites, and the Jebusites" (Exod. 3:8, 17). From the exodus through the conquest years, the Land is referred to variously as "the land of Canaan,"[22] "the land of the Canaanites" or of some particular Canaanite people, and even more possessively, as "their land."[23] Used in the context of the covenantal promise of the Land, such descriptions frequently serve to deny the Israelites a claim to the Land by right of conquest and to affirm the extent to which their right of tenure is conditioned by fidelity to the covenant.[24]

On the other hand, on at least two occasions (Num. 18:13, 20) one finds "their land" used, with the Israelite tribes as the clear referent. Moreover, in a number of legal passages "your land" appears, reflecting the intimate connection between the Land and Law in the biblical narrative. In some instances that connection involves anticipation of life in the Land;[25] in others it appears in enumerations of rewards and punishments.[26] In both contexts the claim for ownership is moved from possession by right of occupancy to possession by right of the covenant. Sometimes this transfer is simply implied; other times, such as in Exodus 23 and Leviticus 20, it is clearly spelled out.

> I will send forth My terror before you, and I will throw into panic all the
> people among whom you come...I will drive them out before you little by

little, until you have increased and possess the land...You shall make no covenant with them and their gods. They shall not remain in *your* land. (Exod. 23:27-33)

You shall possess *their* land, for I will give it to you to possess, a land flowing with milk and honey. (Lev. 20:24)[27]

Yet another notion of ownership, that ultimately the Land belongs to no occupant, Canaanite or Israelite, but rather to God himself, is explicitly stated in Lev. 25:23.[28] Although Joshua 23 has been understood as God gaining possession of the Land through conquest,[29] the biblical narrative more strongly conveys that the promise of the Land to the seed of the patriarchs, the dispossession of the populations dwelling in the Land, and the ability of the Israelites to overcome superior odds all reflect God's ownership of the Land.[30] God himself lives in the Land (Num. 35:34); it is "the Lord's own holding" (Josh. 22:19), a place upon which God "always keeps His eye" (Deut. 11:12). "Flowing with milk and honey," it is an "exceedingly good" and "spacious" land[31] with mineral deposits in its rocks, multiple springs and brooks, a place of superabundance (Deut. 8:7-10). Yet, unlike Egypt, it is immediately dependent upon God for its yearly water supply (Deut. 11:11-12).

Indeed, because of God's involvement the Land acquires a personality, a distinct character and a sacred quality of its own.[32] It needs its sabbath years (Lev. 25:18-22; 26:34); it is peculiarly susceptible to defilement and pollution (Lev. 18:25; 19:29; Num. 35:33-34); it withholds its fruitful abundance (Lev. 26:20) and ultimately ejects occupants who would defile it (Lev. 20:22).[33] Personification of the Land and portrayal of its unique relationship to God is far more vividly developed in the writings of the classical prophets than in the Pentateuch.[34] The presence, albeit limited, of such poetic description in the Torah book appears primarily in the context of the Law.

THE LAND AND THE LAW

Much as the promise of the Land serves as the contextual focus for the patriarchal covenant, so anticipation of the conquest and life in the Land girds the socio-religious legal order envisaged by the Sinai covenant. Specific laws are often linked to the Land by phrasing indicative of the land-based context in which the Law is to be observed. "When you come into the land" or "when the Lord has brought you into the land" is a common preface to a wide range of legislation, from the commands to observe the Passover festival (Exod. 12:25; 13:5) and the sabbatical year (Lev. 25:2) to injunctions regarding first fruits (Lev. 19:23; 23:10; Deut. 26:1-2), firstlings and the meal and *challah* offerings (Exod. 13:11-12; Num. 15:2-3, 18); from a series of prohibitions against imitation of Canaanite worship and customs (Lev. 18:3; 19:26-31; Deut. 12:2-4) to regulations regarding leprosy (Lev. 14:34), kingship (Deut. 17:14-17), and a miscellany of ethical injunctions involving justice and treatment of the sojourner in the Land (Lev. 19:33-37).

Whereas the worthiness of the recipient of the Land is a subtle factor in the patriarchal contexts,[35] in the covenant theology of Sinai the connection between the Land and obedience to the Law is explicit. Acquisition of the Land, quality of life in the Land and, ultimately, retention of the Land all depend upon adherence to the covenantal law. Stated in positive as well as negative terms, each aspect of Israel's relationship to the Land is coupled either with a general admonition to maintain fidelity or with specific injunctions and prohibitions.

Nowhere in pentateuchal law is the ultimate acquisition of the Land as promised to the patriarchs brought into question. Rather, the link between obedience and acquisition is expressed in terms of delayed or diminished fulfillment of that promise. This linkage is developed both in the exposition of the Law and in the narrative of the conquest. Each time the Land promise is presented to the Israelites with full specification of territorial borders, the geographic description is accompanied by a reference to destruction or explusion of the indigenous population (Exod. 23:27-33; Num. 33:50-34:12; Deut. 11:22-24). Consequently, such passages imply a relationship between acquisition of the Land in the fullest sense of the promise and fulfillment of that command.[36] A similar connection is made, but in positive formulation, with the assurance of enlarged borders preceding a description of the duty of thrice-yearly pilgrimages (Exod. 34:24).

It is in the narrative of the conquest, however, that the relationship between full acquisition and adherence to the commandments is most explicitly developed. When the exodus generation fails to demonstrate the fidelity demanded by the Sinai covenant, fulfillment of the promise is delayed until all but two of that generation have died in the wilderness (Num. 14:22-23; 32:10-11; recalled in Josh. 5:6-7). In his testamentary addresses to the next generation of Israelites, Moses repeatedly connects success in the upcoming conquest with general fidelity (Deut. 4:1; 8:1; 11:8, 22; and recalled by Caleb in Josh. 14:9).

In spite of repeated affirmations of God's role in the conquest,[37] the full dimensions of the Land as promised to Abraham (Gen. 15:18), as recollected by Moses at Sinai (Exod. 32:13), as reiterated to the Israelites (Exod. 23:31; Num. 34:1-12; Deut. 11:24), and as supposedly conquered in

Joshua's time (Josh. 2:24; 11:23; 21:41) are not in fact achieved. The generation that enters the Land fails to drive out all the Canaanites. Consequently, the sin of incomplete conquest becomes the punishment that compromises the original Land promise (Judg. 2:2-3). The flawed nature of the fulfilled promise does not go unrecognized in the biblical narrative. Immediately after the description of the incomplete conquest, a new interpretation is offered for the continued presence of the Canaanite nations in the Land: they have been left as a divine test of Israelite fidelity (Judg. 2:20-3:4). The resolution it offers is a superficial one. Ultimately the problem is not divine constancy, but rather that conquest of the Land is at one and the same time absolute and conditional. It is both a divine venture in fulfillment of the promise to the forefathers and an Israelite venture in response to divine command.

The quality of Israelite life in the Land is also law-linked in the theology of Sinai: obedience achieves the rewards of prosperity and peace, disobedience brings their opposites. The flow or restraint of dew and rain, the fulfillment or denial of the earth's potential for abundance, fertility or infertility of flock and person, peace or non-peace of mind and body: all reflect the extent to which the Israelites adhere or do not adhere to the Law.[38] Frequently involving natural occurrences, such phenomena are sometimes presented as the Land's personal response to Israelite behavior,[39] sometimes as rewards or punishments executed by God's will,[40] and, on at least one occasion (Lev. 26:19-20), as a response from both. The commandments to honor sabbatical and jubilee years (Lev. 25:2-19) and the rules of tithing (Deut. 26:12-15) are particularly associated with the Land's fertility or lack thereof. But imitation of the Canaanites and general infidelity to the commandments have a comparable impact on the capacity of the Land to provide for its inhabitants.[41]

In its most extreme form, the conditional covenant involves the possibility of Israel's own dispossession from the Land.[42] One formulation of the relationship between covenantal fidelity and Land retention focuses largely on specific actions which pollute the Land, regardless of their perpetrator—be it Canaanite or Israelite. Proscribed as imitation of the behavior of the soon to be disinherited Canaanites (Leviticus 18), incestuous relations, harlotry, adultery, various violations of sexual purity, and the sacrifice of children in worship of Molech[43] so violate the soil that either God or the Land itself ejects (or "spews forth") its desecrators. The shedding of innocent blood and permitting the body of a criminal executed by impalement to remain unburied overnight are also seen as pollutive,[44] but their impact on retention of the Land is not explicitly stated.[45]

Other types of tenure-linked legislation are peculiar to Israelite settlement in the Land. God's land, like his people, is in need of its sabbaths, and when that need is ignored, when the sabbatical and jubilee laws are violated, the response is "measure for measure." The Land's resources are withheld, and its sabbaths regained by exile of those responsible for the deprivation.[46] Another formulation of the conditional covenant focuses on the long-range consequences of violation of the command to dispossess the inhabitants of the Land. Their continued presence not only results in diminished territory, but becomes a "snare," an invitation to imitation, intermarriage, and ultimately idolatry. This is the sin most associated with exile in Moses' final discourses on the plains of Moab, the most extensive presentation of the conditional covenant in pentateuchal literature.[47] In those addresses the relationship between covenantal fidelity and land tenure is expressed in terms of length of time (life) in the Land.[48] Unlike Joshua and Judges, where issues of full acquisition and insecure tenure dominate, the major theme of the Land theology in Moses' final discourses is a vision of dispossession.

THE LAND AND ESCHATOLOGY

Maintaining the centrality of the Land, biblical eschatology retains the tension between the patriarchal covenant, with its promise of eternal possession of the Land, and the conditional Sinai covenant, with its threat of loss of the Land, by projecting both forms of the covenant onto an historical stage. In this projection the linkage of Law and Land moves from the realm of theoretical admonition to the reality of exile, with visions of future redemption and restoration to the Land marking an end-time. Tied to prophecies regarding the House of David in early prophetic literature, in latter prophets this historical eschatology has "ingathering of the exiles" and restoration of the Land in an idealized condition as its cardinal features.[49]

Although primarily developed in prophetic literature, the structural underpinnings of this eschatological perspective are present, albeit in embryonic form, in certain pentateuchal formulations of the conditional covenant, where description of the consequences of violation of the covenant shifts, more and less subtly in tone, from a theoretical consideration ("if") to a predictive vision ("when") of what will follow the destruction and loss of the Land. Each of these formulations or admonitions (*tochachot*) sets forth some version of a paradigm in which sin (violation of the covenant), punishment (destruction and exile from the Land), reconciliation (usually conceived of in terms of repentance), and restoration (usually ingathering of exiles and return to the Land) present future stages in Israel's history.

Cast in a contingency framework of rewards and punishments, the first such passage, the *tochacha* of Lev. 26:3-45, sets forth elaborate warnings about the conditional nature of Israel's tenure on the Land culminating in a predictive vision of Israel's destiny after the violations have occurred: the Land will be made desolate and the Israelites scattered among the nations (vv. 32-33). The exiled will waste insecure in the land of their enemies (vv. 35-38) until "they shall atone for their iniquity. Then will I remember My covenant with Jacob; I will remember also My covenant with Isaac, and also My covenant with Abraham, and I will remember the Land" (vv. 41-42).

Presented solely within the theoretical realm of the conditional "if you do not obey Me...," the description is barely eschatological. It conveys minimal if any sense of future history, little detail about the process whereby the Land is lost or about the nature of life in exile, and no conception of an historical end-time. Most significantly from the perspective of Land theology, the ingathering and return of the exiles to the Land is only implied in the divine recollection.

> Yet, even then, when they are in the land of their enemies, I will not reject them or spurn them so as to destroy them, annulling my covenant with them; for I the Lord am their God. I will remember in their favor the covenant with the ancients, whom I freed from the land of Egypt in the sight of the nations to be their God: I, the Lord. (Lev. 26:44-45)[50]

The description of mutual rejection, atonement, reconciliation, recollection, and restoration of the covenantal relationship remains metaphysical. But within that metaphysical structure there is a perception of an ongoing encounter between God and Israel, an encounter in which covenantal instability (sin/punishment) coexists with metaphysical surety of God's commitment to "the covenant with the ancients" whom he had freed from Egypt (reconciliation and restoration of the covenantal relationship).

The theological pattern of sin/punishment/reconciliation/restoration assumes a more finite character and an historical frame of reference on the three occasions that it appears in Deuteronomy. The first and most concise formulation (Deuteronomy 4) opens with a review of Israelite history from the time of the exodus (vv. 1-24). The four-staged pattern follows (vv. 25-31), and then the focus shifts back to the Israelite present, with an exhortation to obedience and an elegy to God's faithfulness (vv. 32-40). The presentation of the four stages is set within the conditional covenant of stipulations—"should you do such and such, then..." (v. 25)[51] as opposed to the absolute voice of a future history—but the veil of the conditional language is a thin one. The positive formulation of the rewards for covenantal fidelity is missing; only the sin—making "for yourselves a sculptured image in any likeness" (v. 25)—and its consequence of exile (vv. 26-27) are mentioned. Thus the issue at hand appears to be not so much a choice of alternatives with their respective consequences as a warning against a foreseen future.

The presentation of the pattern evidences a clear indication of sensibility to historical time. Framed on one side by a subtle allusion to Israelite vulnerability to idolatry in the past[52] and by a warning to beware of it in the present time on the other, the sin and consequent exile are set in a future time of "when you have begotten children and children's children and are long established in the land" (v. 25), with atonement and reconciliation eschatologically projected into an "end of time" (v. 30). The description of the future includes a relatively concrete conceptualization of exile (vv. 27-28).[53] On the other hand, the ingathering of exiles and return to the Land in the reconciliation/restoration stage is only alluded to in an assurance, as in Leviticus 26, of God's recollection of the covenant sworn to "your fathers" (v. 31). The allusion is clarified at the close of the address by a succinct restatement of the dual facets of covenantal Land theology: tenure of the Land is contingent on obedience to the commandments, but the promise of the Land is "for all time" (v. 40).

The paradigm appears again in Deuteronomy 28-30, where it is presented in the context of a formal covenant renewal ceremony preceded by a recitation of blessings and curses consequent to a conditional covenant. This time all four stages are fully developed: the sin, generally stated (28:15) then specified in the anticipated recollection (29:24-25); the punishment, a detailed description of deprivation, destruction, and exile (28:20-68) that is summarized in the anticipated recollection (29:21-27); repentance and reconciliation in exile (30:1-2); and a restoration involving the ingathering of the exiles, return to the Land, and renewal of the covenantal relationship (30:3-10).

The presentation opens with a conditional (Deut. 28:1, 15) that in fact covers only the first half (sin and punishment) of the paradigm. Recollection of the destruction presented from the future perfect perspective of later generations (29:21-27) then acts as a transition for a shift in tone. The descriptions of repentance/reconciliation and restoration to the Land that follow float free from the contingency language[54] and move into an explicit prediction of a return that is both physical (restoration to the Land) and metaphysical (renewed covenant) (30:1-10).

Partially described in a straight narrative (31:16-18, 20-21) and then fully laid out in poetic form (32:15-43), the last rehearsal of the paradigmatic cycle is a divine revelation to Moses totally devoid of conditional language and tone. After they enter the Land the Israelites will break the covenant by worshiping foreign gods (31:16, 20; 32:15-18, 21a). In response God will abandon them and hide his countenance, bringing upon them both natural evils and the sword of an invader nation (31:17-18; 32:19-20, 21b-26). But because Israel's enemies will attribute her downfall to their own hand rather than to that of God (32:27-33), God will turn his anger against them, avenge his people and "cleanse" their land (32:36-43).

In spite of its predictive voice, the presentation lacks the interactive "God-Israel" historical focus of prophetic eschatology. The sin remains the worship of foreign gods, but the punishment for that sin reflects the absence of God's protective custody rather than the direct presence of the hand of divine avenging anger. Even more significant from the perspective of Land theology, the punishment that is predicted includes no reference whatsoever to dispersion and exile. Consequently, there is no mention of the ingathering of exiles in the parallel description of reconciliation/restoration. The single explicit reference to the Land appears at the end of the poem: in the final stage God "will avenge the blood of His servants, wreak vengeance on His foes, and cleanse the land of His people" (32:43).[55]

The reading is unusual.[56] No context for the idea of the Land being in need of atonement has been established within the poem.[57] The Israelites have no role at all in the final stages of this version of the paradigm. Just as there is no physical return, there is no spiritual one. Instead of being activated by Israelite repentance, the restoration is provoked, along the lines of Moses' argument at the intercessions of Sinai and Kadesh Barnea, by divine concern over the assumptions of Israel's enemies. The omission of the stages of exile, repentance, and return creates a new constellation. In this version of the paradigm tenure of the Land is not an issue; life in the Land is presumed throughout all the stages. Loss and recovery of the Land cease to function as the nadir and apex of the paradigm. The disharmony between the patriarchal promise of eternal possession (regardless of history) and the Sinai stipulations of conditional tenure (played out within Israel's history) is gone and God's ultimate relationship with Israel and with the Land is assured by theocentric rather than historical processes.

The model is not the one that stimulates the dominant eschatological voice of biblical prophecy. There, as in the most of the Pentateuch, possession of the Land functions as the ultimate barometer for the covenantal relationship between God and Israel. However, as we shall see, for certain post-exilic writers this particular version of the paradigm is rich in interpretive potential—be it to set their own history within the context of an assured covenant theology or to account for the delay of the eschaton.

Modern scholars approach the complexities and internal contradictions within biblical Land theology with the tools of critical thought: comparative studies of ancient near eastern texts, critical dating of texts, and analyses of various source documents.[58] Such historically critical resolutions would be neither apparent nor appealing to the post-biblical authors we will be examining. To them, the biblical text was whole and holy. Even more significantly, it was viewed as dynamically relevant to understanding their own post-exilic experience in the Land. Hence, rewriting the biblical narratives to reflect that experience became both a mode of biblical exegesis and a way of explaining the present in light of the sacred text. For some such exegists the various presentations in the biblical text called out for resolution and reconciliation; for others they provided a textual environment rich in possibilities for interpretation and reinterpretation. For all, the covenantal relationship between God, Land, and people remained immediately relevant and ongoing.

CHAPTER 3

The Metahistorical Covenant of *Jubilees*

J*ubilees* is a composite of a number of genre[1] set within the biblical framework of Genesis 1 through Exodus 12. With that base, one would anticipate first finding the concept of covenanted land in the author's presentation of the patriarchal narratives. In fact, the reader encounters both covenant and land long before any reference is made to Abraham. Presenting his rewritten text as a revelation of past and future narrated by an angel speaking to Moses on Sinai, the author retrojects the election of the seed of Jacob and the allocation of the Land to Abraham's line into his rewritten version of the cosmic narratives of Genesis 1-11.

The first of the retrojections involves a forecast of Israel's election inserted into the Creation story:

> Behold I shall separate for myself a people from among all the nations. And they will also keep the sabbath. And I will sanctify them for myself, and I will bless them. Just as I sanctified and shall sanctify the sabbath day for myself thus shall I bless them. And they will be my people and I will be their God. And I have chosen the seed of Jacob from among all that I have seen. And I have recorded him as my firstborn son, and have sanctified him for myself forever and ever. (2:19-20)

Constructed around a select set of phrases abstracted from Exodus,[2] the covenant described here focuses solely on the relationship between the elected seed and God. There is no land component; the paraphrased biblical passages the author selects to support the description either include no reference to the Land, or such references have been excluded in the process of abstraction and relocation.[3]

The Land concept appears in another context of the *Jubilees'* rewriting of Genesis 1-11. Allocation of the Land to the patriarchal line, descriptions of the Land, and associations between Land and Law abstracted from various biblical passages are all retrojected into an extensive set of narratives depicting Noah as a kind of cosmic forefather who, like the patriarchs in *Jubilees*, adheres to the Sinai covenant.[4]

The allocation of the Land is placed, in nonpromissory form, into a created narrative that links the Land promise given to the patriarchs to an initial division of the earth in the prepatriarchal era. Immediately after the Flood the earth is apportioned "by lot" (8:11)—a mode of division not mentioned in Genesis, but clearly the method by which the land of Canaan was apportioned among the tribes of Israel. Not only does the allotment that falls to the house of Shem "to possess it forever"[5] include the territory promised to the patriarchs in the biblical narrative, but within the house of Shem that particular territory is assigned to Arpachshad, the ancestor of Abraham.[6] Having thus placed the Promised Land within the allotment of the patriarchal progenitor (in contrast to the biblical narrative[7]), the author then creates an account of how "the land of Lebanon as far as the river of Egypt,...eastward and westward, from the bank of the Jordan and from the shore of the sea" was subsequently illegitimately seized by Ham's son, Canaan. Acting against the counsel of his father and brothers and in violation of an oath sworn "before the holy judge and before Noah" (10:32), Canaan brings upon himself the curse against any who would seize territory not within his assigned lot "forever in their generations until the day of judgment" (9:14-15).[8] No motive is provided for the usurpation, but the descriptions of Shem's portion provide their own motivation. Incorporating the four places on earth which belong to God (4:26), the Promised Land is the place where Noah prays God will dwell (8:18), a "blessed and wide land," a "very good" land (8:21; 10:29)—descriptions of the Promised Land drawn from multiple biblical passages.[9]

The inventive insertions serve a number of functions. First, the specific territory promised to the patriarchs, the descendants of Shem through Arpachshad, is set within the esteemed ancient world of Noah. Second, the retrojected allocation is buttressed against other claimants for all future times by the oath Noah required of his heirs. Third, as the writer himself informs, the tale of Canaan's illegitimate seizure of Shem's portion accounts for how "that land" came to be called "Canaan" (10:34). Last and most significant, as a whole unit the rewriting makes acquisition of the Land in the subsequent patriarchal narratives a "return" rather than a theologically complex, if not troubled, claim to a land inhabited by others.

Given the importance of the Land in the lives of the patriarchs and the Land connection in much of the Sinai legislation, it is not surprising to find that the author of *Jubilees* also retrojects aspects of the biblical link between Land and Law into his portrait of a Noah who lives in accordance with Torah Law. This type of retrojection, however, is particularly troublesome, for the Noah story is universal in context, whereas the biblical association between Land and Law presumes a particular understanding of land. In fact, when the author of *Jubilees* retrojects an halachic concept associated with the Promised Land in the biblical text into the cosmic, prepatriarchal setting, frequently the particularity of the land reference is confused, if not lost.

After the Flood, Noah builds an altar and offers thereon a sacrifice to make "atonement with blood for all the sins of the *medr*" (the Ge'ez equivalent for ארץ [6:2]).[10] The sins which precipitated the Flood and necessitate this offering—"fornication, impurity, and injustice" (defined as the shedding of innocent blood) (7:20-25)—appear in Torah legislation as sins which "pollute" or "defile" not the earth, but the Promised Land, such that it will no longer contain its inhabitants.[11] Moreover, in his final testament Noah instructs his sons and grandsons not only to avoid the Flood-related sins, but also to reserve firstfruits, to keep sabbatical years (7:35-39), and particularly to guard carefully against pollution of the earth by blood (7:28),[12] all legislation associated with the Land in biblical literature. The regulations regarding firstfruits and sabbatical years have clear counterparts in Leviticus, where they are prefaced by the phrase "when you come into the land,"[13] a phrase that appears only once in *Jubilees* and then in conjunction with the construction of the tabernacle and the celebration of the Passover festival (49:18).

Although undoubtedly rooted in the concern with blood in the Noah story of Genesis 9:4, the injunctions against pollution of the *medr* by blood in *Jubilees* are developed through an intricate interweaving of specific levitical commandments regarding blood with paraphrased versions of verses that, in their biblical contexts, involve Israelite life in the Land.

> And let no blood from any of the blood which is in anything be seen upon you on the day when you sacrifice any beast or cattle or what flies upon the earth. But do a good deed for yourselves by covering that which will be poured out upon the surface of the earth. And you shall not be like one who eats with blood, but beware lest they should eat blood before you. Cover the blood, because thus I was commanded to testify to you and to your children together with all flesh. (7:30-31)

> And you shall not eat living flesh[14] lest it be that your blood which is your life be sought by the hand of all flesh which eats upon the earth. For the earth/land will not be cleansed of the blood which is poured out upon it, because by the blood of one who poured it out will the earth/land be cleansed in all of its generations. (7:32-33)

By interpretive paraphrase the first set of verses (30-31) equates not covering the blood spilt in sacrificial slaughter (a version of Lev. 17:13)[15] with permitting the eating of blood (Deut. 12:23).[16] Paraphrasing Num. 35:33, the second set of verses (32-33) associates the eating of blood with the flesh (the prohibition of Lev. 17:14)[17] with the spilling of human blood (Num. 35:33).[18] Addressed to Noah's sons in the *Jubilees* context, the prohibitions are clearly universal, and the punishment for their violation is "being blotted out from the surface of the *medr*" (7:27-28). But the biblical verses which the author paraphrases in each case deal specifically with Israelite life in the covenanted Land. The prohibition against the eating of blood in Deut. 12:23 appears in the context of permission being granted to the Israelites to eat meat outside of the setting of the sanctuary when they come into the Land. And the scriptural context for the prohibition against the shedding of innocent blood in Num. 35:33-35 involves the peculiar nature of the Land and its inability to tolerate moral pollution. Violators of that tolerance are threatened with ejection from the Land, not, as in *Jubilees*, with destruction from the face of the earth.

Without clarification, the term used for earth or land—*medr*—in these passages as well as in the story of the division of the earth by lot among Noah's sons (8:10-11), presents the reader with a double association. In the overall context of the flood, *medr* is understood as "earth," but in the contexts of the biblical reference points it refers to the Promised Land.[19] The meaning of *medr* as earth or land is further complicated by the fact that the narrator, an angel at Sinai, is speaking from a recollective perspective. Within his narrative he interweaves the immediate future—the various instructions which Moses is to give to the children of Israel—with the past—the story of Noah and his testament to his sons. The Israelites also are to keep the "feast of the first fruits" (6:21) and refrain from the eating of blood (6:12-14). Yet no explicit reference is made to the Land even when the angel is speaking of the future Sinai legislation directed to the Israelites. The prohibition against blood is accompanied by the warning that any Israelite who violates the blood legislation will be "uprooted, he and his seed from the earth/land" (6:12, 14).[20] Thus we have concepts and commandments associated with the particular Israelite Land covenant inserted into the context of the cosmic Noah covenant, and Land-based commandments directed to the Israelites presented without specific reference to the covenanted Land.

Clearly the author of *Jubilees* wishes to establish a close, if not singular, relationship between the Noahite, patriarchal, and Israelite covenants. He retrojects the blessing language of the covenant with Abraham to the Noah context: "increase and be multiplied upon the earth and become many upon it, and become a blessing upon it" (6:5).[21] Conversely, he makes reference to the covenant with Noah when he later describes the one with Abraham (14:20). Moreover, not only is Noah cited as one of the cosmic forefathers in the Abrahamic testaments appended to the biblical narrative of the first patriarch (19:24, 27; 21:10; 22:13), but the testament created for Noah structurally parallels those the author creates for the biblical patriarchs: each contains a warning against some form(s) of pollution, a blessing (promise) of planting and/or a curse (threat) of uprooting.[22]

From the perspective of biblical Land theology, the planting imagery is particularly intriguing. Noah urges his sons to be just and upright so that they "may be planted in righteousness on the surface of the whole earth (*medr*)" (7:34). In prophetic literature, such language of uprooting and planting (either separately or together) is generally associated with warnings about the possibility of exile from and/or promises of return to the Land.[23] In post-biblical literature, "righteous plant" usually appears as a metaphor for the righteous, the patriarchs, and/or Israel, without any association with the Land.[24] Such is not the case in *Jubilees*. With one exception (16:26),[25] the "righteous plant" metaphor is used in contexts which employ the predictive tone of prophetic literature that associates the planting with the Land (1:16; 21:24; 36:6). However, in none of the *Jubilees* passages is the site of the planting clarified. To the contrary, in one case (1:16) where the author paraphrases Jer. 32:41 ("I will plant them in this land faithfully with all my heart and soul"), he omits the words "in this land," which would provide just such clarity.[26]

The contrasting image, being plucked out or uprooted,[27] a verbal form with and without the noun *medr*, appears throughout *Jubilees*, always in sections the author has added to the biblical narrative, and usually in association with violations of *halacha*. When the warning is directed toward the Israelites in the prepatriarchal narratives, the specific issues involved are violation of the Sabbath (2:27) and the eating of blood (6:12). Although the Israelites are specified and the phrase "from the *medr*" is used in both instances, in neither passage is an effort made to indicate the particularity of the noun *medr* either by the biblical mode of inserting a modifying phrase such as "from the land which the Lord is giving you" or by any other manner. Consequently, the passage involving violation of the Sabbath in particular could be understood as threatening death—"uprooting from the earth"—as the punishment.

> And everyone who pollutes it let him surely die. And anyone who will do any work therein, let him surely die forever, so that the children of Israel

might guard this day for generations and not be uprooted from the earth/land[28] because it is a holy day and a blessed day. (2:26-7)

Such an understanding would be supported by the biblical penalty of death for the Sabbath violator (Num. 15:35). On the other hand, the choice of syntax could recall the concern with Sabbath observance in Isa. 56:1-8 and Ezek. 20:12-14, 23-24, in which case the appropriate penalty would be exile from the Land.[29]

The lack of clarity, I would suggest, is a deliberate technique adopted to facilitate the smooth placement of Israelite and Noahite covenants into a common context. The technique links the two covenants, giving a cosmic perspective to the Law and, consequently, releases it from the limitations of historical particularity. Methodologically, the treatment is not unlike that of the Chronicler, who takes the promise of the Land out of its biblical historical context in order to project it into a future time.[30] Insofar as that writer is projecting from an earlier biblical narrative into a later one, the ahistorical treatment is more interesting than problematic. However, when, as in *Jubilees*, rewriting involves retrojection, the achievement of "timelessness" is more complex, for the biblical Land promise is both spatially and temporally particularistic.

The author of *Jubilees* handles that particularity in several ways. He simply deletes the spatial component from the description of covenantal election that he inserts into the Creation narrative. When he includes Land-linked legislation in his cosmic narrative, he is deliberately vague about the specific sense of *medr*, thus achieving a sense of the timelessness of the Law. His handling of the temporal dimension is more complex. On the one hand, when he retrojects the allocation of the Land from the time of the patriarchs to that of their antediluvian progenitors, he transforms an event in concrete time into an ongoing condition from time immemorial. On the other hand, he preserves the biblical particularity by inserting two crucial additions into his narrative: Arpachshad is made heir to the particular portion of Shem's territory that will come to the patriarchal line, and the tale of Canaan's usurpation of the Land accounts for its status at the opening of the patriarchal story. Its origins thus successfully rooted in Noah's division of the earth, the Land promise floats free from its patriarchal context and achieves the desired timelessness. At the same time, the stage is set for presenting the history of the patriarchal acquisition of the Land as a restoration story.

PATRIARCHAL HISTORY

The author of *Jubilees* presents all five of the biblical covenant-making scenes with Abraham in full, altering each narrative so that it echoes the metahistorical past he developed in his rewriting of Genesis 1-11. Although he paraphrases significant blocks of the scriptural promissory passages, by slight alterations and additions to the wording of the divine promise and by substantial changes to the context in which the promise is presented he shifts the focus in each encounter such that the special relationship between God and Israel replaces the Land promise as the integral theme in the covenant-making.

Whereas the encounter with God in Haran introduces Abraham as a story character in Genesis, in *Jubilees* that encounter is preceded by a series of tales presenting the first patriarch as a spiritual protege of Noah and as the worthy progenitor of Israel whose election has been foreordained.[31] Before his death, Noah had been taught how to restrain the workings of Mastema and his demons. Although he had passed these teachings on to Shem, his eldest and favorite son (10:7-14), by the time of Abraham's birth Mastema and his evil spirits had seduced even the descendants of Shem into idolatry. In contrast, Abraham not only is aware of the Creator (and hence, avoids idol worship) from early childhood, but possesses Shem's knowledge of how to thwart Mastema, who has sent crows to devastate the seed crop of the land (11:11-22). Lacking his son's powers over Mastema, Terah is aware of the futility of the idols he ministers to, but fears to speak out lest he be killed. Only after Abraham destroys the house of idols does Terah move his family to Haran, where Abraham rejects astrological signs and recognizes that it is God alone who controls everything. This awareness leads him to beseech God to protect him "from the hands of evil spirits" and "to establish me and my seed forever" such that they never depart from the correct belief. Within this context Abraham asks whether he should return to Ur of Chaldees or remain in Haran (12:16-21). The directions to go to "the land which I shall show you" follow as God's response.

The addition totally alters the tone of the biblical story. Not only does the earlier metahistory guide the narrative—the move from Ur to Haran is made "so that they might come into the land of Lebanon and into the land of Canaan" (12:15)—but Abraham's expressed concern that God establish him and his seed forever hints, if obliquely, at an awareness of what long before had been divinely recorded as the destined future of that seed.[32] Moreover, Abraham is no longer suddenly approached with the direct command to leave all that is familiar in order to go to an unidentified land. The prayer and the inquiry on the part of the patriarch transfer the initiative from God to Abraham, and diminish the dramatic impact of a "context-free" divine command to migrate. Consequently, the promise that follows appears as a reward for Abraham's knowledge of and fidelity to God, rather than as a gratuitous gift.

In presenting the subsequent covenantal encounters between God and Abraham, the author of *Jubilees* retains the essential form of the biblical text. However, in each instance he makes two significant alterations to the content and/or the context of the promise scene: the special relationship with God is always included, and Israel's future history is foreshadowed and its roots in the metahistorical past are recollected.

On the first promissorial occasion, the special relationship is introduced in a substantial addition to the divine promises that accompany the directive to move to Canaan:

> And I shall be God for you and your son and for the son of your son and for all of your seed. Do not fear henceforth and for all the generations of the earth, I am your God." (12:24)

A minor change to the Land promise follows: "to *you and to your seed* I will give this land" (13:3).[33] The changes serve not only to strengthen the election aspect of the covenant, but also to establish Abraham's role from the outset as the link between that which had been foredetermined and that which would be realized in the future.

That linking is the major motif in the reconstructed scene that follows. In the Genesis narrative the patriarch moves southward into the Land, where he acknowledges the divine promise with a sacrifice (Gen. 12:8). In *Jubilees*, however, the move is accompanied by a description of the Land which foreshadows a future one by Moses in Deut. 8:7-8.[34]

> And he saw, and behold the land was wide and very good and everything was growing upon it; vines and figs and pomegranate trees, oaks and ilexes and terebinths and olive trees and cedars and cypresses and date trees and every tree of the field, and water was upon the mountains. (13:6)

Concomitantly, a look backward is provided by the sacrifice scene which closes the encounter. Proclaiming "You [are] my God, the eternal God," Abraham presents an offering "so that he [God] might be with him and not forsake him all the days of his life" (13:8-9)—elaborations that echo the divine relationship with Abraham's progeny announced in the Creation story (2:19) as well as the patriarch's own prayer before departing from Haran (12:19).

The same theme—Abraham as mediator between the time-bound historical and the timeless metahistorical—appears with various degrees of emphasis in the rewriting of each of the subsequent covenantal encounters. Prefaced by an elaboration on "Abram invoked the Lord by name" (Gen. 13:4), the promissory scene after Abraham's return from the sojourn in Egypt opens with the patriarch subtly prefiguring his descendants' blessing of gratitude (Joshua 24) after returning from a future sojourn in that country. "Blessing the Lord his God who brought him back in peace," he declares his commitment to the covenantal relationship: "You, O God, Most High,[35] [are] my God forever and ever" (13:16).[36]

With no mention either of the Canaanites living in the Land or of the division of land between uncle and nephew, and only a casual reference to the separation from Lot (Gen. 13:5-12)—deletions justified by retrojection of the allocation of the Land to the time of Noah and his heirs—the Land promise follows. The promissory language is that of Gen. 13:14-16,[37] but two significant alterations have been made to the accompanying directions. Abraham is told not only to walk about in the Land, but to "see all [of it]" because God will be giving it not "to you," as in Gen. 13:17, but "to your seed" (13:21).[38] Although the changes appear to be minor ones, they shift the focus of the giving from Abraham to his future descendants. The author has the patriarch assume symbolic possession of the Land on behalf of that future by a viewing, not unlike that of Moses immediately before the Israelites begin their conquest of the Land. Skipping the building of the altar at Mamre (Gen. 13:18), the narrative moves to the war of the Sodomite kings, where the patriarch's tithing of firstfruits is explicitly connected to the tithes to be offered by future generations of Israelites (13:25-27) even as it recalls the earlier command by Noah to his sons (7:34-39).[39]

The same emphasis governs the rewriting of the covenant-making that accompanies the annunciation scenes of Abraham's two sons. In each case the wording of the covenant includes assurance of a special relationship with God, and contextual elaborations establish Abraham as a link between the Israelites and the prepatriarchal cosmic past. The first requires an addition to the divine words at the announcement of Ishmael that makes the substance of the promise parallel to the one preceding the conception of Isaac:

> I am the Lord who brought you from Ur of the Chaldees so that I might give you the land of the Canaanites to possess it *forever and [so that I might] be God for you and for your seed after you.* (14:7)[40]

The consequent implication of equal status for the two sons is immediately clarified by the substitution (as in the Septuagint) of Isaac for Sarah as the carrier of the blessing of nationhood in the name change scene that immediately follows (15:16)[41] and by repeated emphasis on Isaac's primacy in three additional passages relating to his birth.[42]

As for the metahistorical past and historical future, a notation at the close of the scene foretelling the birth of Abraham's first son indicates that the covenant was made in the same month as the one with Noah, and that Abraham, like his covenantal progenitor, commemorated the occasion by renewing the celebration of the festival of Shevuot (14:20). The brief comment recalls the history of the holiday attached to the description of Noah's commemoration of it. Established as an ordinance for all time at Creation, Shevuot had been "celebrated in heaven" until "the days of Noah." Commemoration lapsed from the death of the cosmic patriarch to the time of Abraham. It would be kept by Isaac, Jacob, and his sons, only to be forgotten again until the time of Moses when it would be recalled for the Israelites on Sinai (6:17-19).

Elaborations to the Isaac annunciation and birth narratives offer another opportunity to develop the election aspect of the covenant concept. A discourse on circumcision connects the command to the election of Israel at the time of Creation. Sanctified like the Sabbath at the close of Creation, Israel is now to be sanctified like "the angels of the presence and the angels of sanctification" who, circumcised "from the day of their creation," had witnessed the prehistorical recording of Israel's election (15:27). Like the sanctified angels (and, not coincidentally, like Noah and Abraham, who are immune to the powers of Mastema), circumcised Israel stands immediately under the protection of God, who guards and blesses them that "they might be his and he might be theirs henceforth and forever" (15:32)—a paraphrase of "they will be my people and I will be their God," the description of the election in the *Jubilees* Creation narrative (2:19).

Election of future seed is also the theme of Abraham's celebration of Succot (16:20-27, 31), an addition that the author presents as an expression of the patriarch's gratitude "to the Lord who delivered him and who made him rejoice in the land of his sojourn." The connection to future Israelite commemoration of the festival is explicit (16:25-30). More subtly, the link back to Israel's election at Creation is expressed in the patriarch's blessing of the "Creator who created him" and the angel narrator's acknowledgment that Abraham now knew that "from him there would be a righteous planting for eternal generations and a holy seed from him such that it would be like the one who made everything" (16:26).

The workings of God's special protection is the major point in the rewriting of the last covenantal scene. Attributing the test of the *Aqedah* to Mastema's goading of God, who is quite confident of Abraham's faithful response, the angel describes how he was instructed by the deity to stand in front of Mastema and prevent Abraham from harming Isaac. Recollecting the comparable power against Mastema that Noah had passed on to Shem, his firstborn (10:7-14), a twice-repeated reference to Isaac as "firstborn" (18:11, 15) draws attention back to the original metahistorical election when God recorded Israel as His "firstborn son" (2:20). On the other hand, the added notation that the patriarch established the festival of Passover to commemorate the "seven days during which he went and returned in peace"[43] looks ahead to the redemptive consequences of election, much as the wording of the Land promise in the biblical text looks to the future conquest. In contrast to the contextual embellishments to the scene, save for the use of "firstborn" instead of "favored" and an added acknowledgment of Abraham's merit (19:16),[44] the language of the divine promise closely follows that of Gen. 22:17-18.

With one significant exception, the same fidelity to source text is found in the presentation of the divine promises on the single occasion for the establishment of the covenant with Isaac (24:8-12).[45] Notably, in the rewriting of this scene there are no contextual additions—no particular emphasis on the special relationship with God and no linkage either to the cosmic fathers who preceded or to the children of Israel who will follow this patriarch. The covenant with Isaac remains, as in the parent text, Land-centered both in formulation and context. However, a telling closure—"And now, obey my voice, and dwell in this land" (24:11)—is added to the covenantal blessing.

The addition is particularly striking when viewed within the context of the blessing of Isaac in the testamental narratives that the author creates for Abraham. Isaac receives his father's testamental blessing twice: once as one of many of the first patriarch's children and grandchildren (chap. 20), and once alone (chap. 21). In neither of these final testaments is there recollection of the covenant or an explicit reference to its transference. Instead, like the addition to the covenantal promise in 24:11, both testaments focus on obedience to divine command.[46] Presented in the conditional voice of "if..., then...," the two testaments are structured like the *tochachot* of Deuteronomy rather than like a promissory scene. The one addressed solely to Isaac does close with the prayer that God would "bless all of your seed and the remnant of your seed for eternal generations with all righteous blessing so that you might be a blessing in all of the earth" (21:25). But that same blessing, a paraphrase of the biblical one Abraham received at Haran, also appears in the address to all of Abraham's children and grandchildren.[47] Moreover, prefaced by "May...my God and your God strengthen you to do to his will," it still echoes the exhortative tone of the call to obedience added to the covenant at Gerar.

Isaac, the biological intermediary, is of significantly less stature than his father, and, as we shall see, than his son, Jacob. Even at the annunciation of his birth, he is presented as a transitional figure:

> And through Isaac a name and seed would be named for him [Abraham]. And all of the seed of his sons would become nations. And they would be counted with the nations. *But from the sons of Isaac one would become a holy seed and he would not be counted among the nations* because he would become the portion of the Most High and all of his seed would fall into that which God will rule so that he might become a people to the Lord, a possession from all people and so that he might become a kingdom of priests and a holy people. (16:16-18) *(emphasis mine)*

This patriarch is never the direct bearer of the embellished covenant of *Jubilees*, of the special relationship with God extending back to Creation and Noah and forward to the Israelites. The promises conveyed to him are the unaltered biblical ones, accompanied here by an exhortation to obedience more appropriate to the testaments the author creates than to the promises he cites.

Moreover, Isaac cannot transmit that which he never received. Developing Isaac's inability to include his own covenantal experience in blessing his offspring from the wording of Gen. 28:4 ("May He grant the blessing of Abraham to you and your offspring"), the author has him refer to "Abraham, my/your father" on three blessing occasions (26:24; 27:11; 36:6).[48] Almost perversely, only when he believes that he is addressing Esau is the Isaac of *Jubilees* able to include himself as a covenantal reference point, and then, only with the content of the blessing expressed in the most general of terms.[49] When knowingly addressing both sons in the created final testament, he refers back to the Lord, "the God of Abraham, your father," whom, parenthetically, "afterwards I, too, worshipped and served...properly and sincerely" (36:6).[50] Then, using the admonitory tone with which the covenant had been transmitted to him, he urges his sons to be just and upright so that "the Lord will bring upon you everything which the Lord said that he would do for Abraham and for his seed" (36:3). Indeed, in that final testament he is portrayed as unaware of the covenantal line, for in dividing his property, that is, "everything which Abraham acquired at the Well of the Oath," between his sons (36:12), he attempts to allocate the larger portion to Esau, "the one whose birth was first."[51]

Thus, Jacob first hears of the covenant, not from his father, Isaac, but from his spiritual progenitor, Abraham, who loves him "more than all [his] sons" (19:20).[52] The heritage Abraham transfers to him, as opposed to Isaac, is consistently expressed in terms of the themes developed in the rewriting of the narratives of the Abrahamic covenant: emphasis on the special relationship with God as a key aspect of the promises, and development of the patriarchal role as a connective between the metahistorical past and Israel's future.

Encouraging Rebecca's favoritism for her second born (19:16), Abraham, whose life story overlaps with that of Jacob, assures her "that the Lord will choose him as his own people [who will be] special[53] from all who are on the surface of the earth" (19:18). Through Jacob the name of Abraham, as well as those of the cosmic forefathers, "Shem, Noah, Enoch, Mahalelel, Enos, Seth, and Adam" (19:24), will be blessed. Not only does the context for the created passage have no biblical counterpart, but Abraham's vision of his grandson's destiny is far more expansive than anything in the biblical promissory scenes. The seed of Jacob will "establish heaven," "strengthen the earth," and "renew all the lights which are above the firmament" (19:25). Except for the generalized blessing—"All the blessings with which the Lord blessed me and my descendants will be for Jacob and his descendants for all time" (19:23) (included also in Isaac's blessing of Jacob disguised as Esau [26:24])—no reference is made to the Land promise which provides the central focus for the biblical presentations of the patriarchal promises. Instead, Abraham tells Rebecca that the seed of her favored son will be so numerous that "his descendants will fill the entire earth"[54] (19:21), a foreshadowing, albeit subtle, of the expansion of the Land promise that Jacob will receive in the *Jubilees* reworking of Gen. 28:13-15 and 35:11-12.

When Abraham conveys the blessings directly to Jacob, the cosmic forefathers are again the point of ancestral reference: "May he give you all of the blessings with which he blessed Adam and Enoch and Noah and Shem" (19:27). And again the promise of the Land is not mentioned save insofar as it is implied in the general "everything he said that he would give me may he cause to cleave to you and your seed"(19:27). The emphasis is placed on the father-son relationship that will exist between God and Jacob and the people who descend from him. Jacob is destined to inherit the power against Mastema earlier granted to Abraham, Shem, and Noah (19:28), and in fulfillment of the decree "recorded" at Creation (2:20), he and his seed will be God's "firstborn son" (19:29).

The same themes appear in Abraham's final testament to Jacob. Parallel to the two other testaments created for Abraham (one addressed to all his children and grandchildren and one to Isaac), this one includes an extensive warning to keep separate from the gentiles (22:16-22). However, unlike the other testaments, the exhortative here in no way impinges on the promissory. Abraham not only prays that God bestow on Jacob the blessings granted to him and his forefathers "Noah and Adam" (22:13) and protect him from error (22:19), but also explicitly seeks transfer of the covenant to his grandson:

> May He renew His covenant with you, so that you might be a people for him, belonging to his inheritance forever....And renew Your covenant and Your mercy with him and with his seed with all Your will in all the earth's generations. (22:15, 30)

The transfer is a personal one. Describing Jacob as "My son...in whom I rejoice with all my heart and all my emotion" (22:28), Abraham sees his grandson as the one who will "build my house" and "raise up my name before God forever" (22:24). Cosmic in proportion, the petitions on behalf of Jacob are neither temporally nor spatially limited by the biblical base text: He should "rule over all the seed of Seth" (22:12),[55] "inherit all of the earth" (22:14), and parent a "holy people" who, enduring "in all the earth's generations" (22:24), would have a special relationship with God "throughout all the days of the earth" (22:10-11a, 12, 28b, 29).[56]

There is only one clear reference to the biblical promise of Land in the blessings: an addendum to a salutation to an explicitly cosmic God[57] that recollects the election of Israel in the *Jubilees* Creation story.

> God Most High, the God of all, and Creator of all[58] who brought me out from Ur of the Chaldees so that he might give me this land to inherit it forever and to raise up a holy seed so that the Most High may be blessed forever. (22:27)

The recollection is in fact a paraphrase of the author's own rewriting of Gen. 15:7,[59] a rewriting that adjusts the focus of the divine promises such that they incorporate and emphasize the special relationship, "a holy seed," that is the central theme of the covenant in *Jubilees*. It is that special relationship that Abraham stresses when he immediately thereafter blesses Jacob. No particular significance is given to the Land promise. It remains just a recollection and is transferred to Jacob only as incorporated in "bless him with all of your blessings" (22:28-30).

In his encounters with God, Jacob receives even more than he had in the blessings from his grandfather. Just as the author had developed the prepatriarchal Genesis narratives such that they foreshadowed the first patriarch's story, so he creates an unusual forecast for his dramatic alterations to the promises at Bethel. The conveyor is Rebecca.[60] Assured of her son's future by Abraham, after that patriarch's death she reveals Jacob's destiny in a blessing that interweaves the biblical formulation of the covenant, its rewritten complement, and a forecast of the promises the author creates particularly for her. The triadal terms of the biblical covenant are heard in her prayer that Jacob be blessed "more than all the generations of man," that his sons be "more numerous and greater than the stars of heaven and more than the sand of the sea," and that he and his descendants be given "this pleasant land…to hold [it] as a possession forever" (25:15-18). On the other hand, the author-created revelation by Abraham of the special people Jacob will father is echoed in "a blessed and holy seed, may all your seed be" (25:18) and "may your name and your seed stand for all the ages; and may God Most High be their God" (25:21).

The most striking feature of Rebecca's blessing, however, is her own addition, which prefigures Jacob's two covenant-making encounters at Bethel:

> *Increase and spread over the earth,*[61] and may your seed be perfected in every age in the joy of heaven and earth . . . . And may the God of Righteousness dwell with them [your seed]; and with them may his sanctuary be built in all ages. The One who blesses you will be blessed, and all flesh which curses you falsely shall be cursed (25:20, 21-22).[62]

While the first line can be read as a development of the prediction in Abraham's created testament that "his seed will be one which fills all of the earth" (19:21), the particular choice of verbs is suggestive of several biblical blessings. On one hand, it recalls the cosmic blessings of Adam and Eve in Gen. 1:28 ("Be fertile and increase, fill the earth and master it") and of Noah in Gen. 9:1 ("Be fertile and increase, and fill the earth"). On the other, it looks ahead to the blessing Jacob receives at Bethel in Gen. 28:14 ("You shall spread out to the west and to the east, to the north and to the south"). In the Genesis 9 passage ארץ clearly refers to "the earth"; in the later patriarchal one (Gen. 28:14), neither "earth" nor "land" is specified, but, insofar as the language of the promise to Jacob replicates a parallel promise to Abraham (Gen. 13:14), "land" would be indicated. However, for the author of *Jubilees*, the absence of the word "land" in the biblical promise to Jacob (Gen. 28:14) becomes an exegetical basis for expansion of that promise.[63]

Taking advantage of the lack of specificity in Gen. 28:14, the author first inserts the line suggestive of cosmic beginnings ("increase and spread over the earth") into the prescient blessing he creates for Rebecca. Then, laying the groundwork for his reconstruction of the second Bethel scene into a covenant of cosmic proportions, he shifts the blessing presented at the second Bethel encounter in Genesis to the first scene at Bethel with a seemingly small change to its wording: the biblical "you shall *spread out* to the west and the east and north and south" (Gen. 28:14) becomes the recollective "You shall *increase* in the..." (27:23).[64] Simple but significant, the change is clearly no accident. Immediately recalling Rebecca's telling use of both words (25:20), by its very singularity the "you shall increase" shifts the emphasis from the Land to a cosmic future for the patriarchal seed.

It is that perspective which dominates the author's rewriting of the second covenant at Bethel when Jacob's name becomes Israel.

> I am the Lord who created heaven and earth. I will increase your numbers and multiply you very much. Kings will come from you, and they will rule wherever man has set foot. I will give your descendants all of the land that is beneath the sky. They will rule over all the nations just as they wish. Afterwards, they will gain the entire earth, and they will possess it forever. (32:18-19)[65]

Breaking away from his pattern of maintaining a level of fidelity with God's words in biblical promissory passages, the author makes substantial alterations at every level of the divine address. God identifies Himself as the "creator of heaven and earth" instead of as "*El Shaddai*." The biblical promise of fertility is maintained, but the blessing focuses on sovereignty, power, and territory, not future numbers. The seed of Jacob will include not simply kings, but kings whose dominion will extend to "everywhere where man has set foot" and "over all the nations just as they wish." The territory promised to that seed is no longer just Canaan, but "all of the land under heaven." Moreover, the day will come when Jacob's descendants "will gain the entire earth" and "possess it forever."

Starkly contrasting with its biblical counterpart, the restructured covenant is in fact grounded in an interpretive reading of biblical sources. The biblical version of the fertility promised to Jacob is modelled after a parallel promise to Abraham when he was engaged in covenant-making at Bethel (Gen. 17:4-8). Both scenes involve name changes; both stress patriarchal fertility with promises of kings and assurances of a progeny of many nations. More interested in the quality than in the numbers assured to Jacob's seed, the author of *Jubilees* deletes the reference to future nations and selects another Abrahamic model for his version of the blessings for Jacob: the final testament he created for Abraham's transfer of the covenant (chap. 22).

All the promises of power that appear in the rewritten Bethel scene are forecast in that earlier blessing by Abraham: the servitude of the nations (22:11), the dominion over others (22:12), and the most dramatic, possession of "all the earth" (22:14).[66] But the promises themselves are drawn or developed from biblical prooftexts. While assurance of sovereignty over the nations appears in Isaac's blessing of Jacob in Gen. 27:29 ("Let peoples serve you, and nations bow to you"), the transformation of the Land promise requires more creative textual manipulation. Deleting the particularizing, geographical modifier from "Every spot on which your foot treads shall be yours; *your territory shall extend from the wilderness to the Lebanon and from the River—the Euphrates—to the Western Sea*" (Deut. 11:24), the author transposes the verse to his rewritten version of the Jacob covenant and establishes a textual basis for inheritance of the earth.[67]

The extravagant promise of territory in the blessing does not nullify the promise of the Land. Although not explicitly stated here, as opposed to Rebecca's blessing where the promise of the Land and inheritance of all the earth are both predicted (25:17, 20), possession of the Land is presumed in the Bethel narrative as it is throughout *Jubilees*. The closure to the Bethel blessing deals with construction of the sanctuary that Rebecca had predicted in her blessing of Jacob (25:21). Developing the pillar-building and vow-taking by the patriarch when he first came to Bethel (Gen. 28:20-22) into a David-like desire to build the house of the Lord (27:27), the author brings the scene to an end with a revelation of the future that implicitly assumes the life and worship in the Land (32:21-24) spelled out by the angel narrator at the close of the book.[68] Immediately thereafter, Jacob confirms his place in the covenantal line by adding, much as his encounter with God had added to the promises, an eighth day to the Succot festival (32:27-29) Abraham had established to acknowledge his joy "in the land of his sojourn" (16:20).

Unlike his biblical counterpart, the author of *Jubilees* has no need of recollective transitions in his covenantal history. Foreordained from Creation, the connection between the patriarchs and the generation that will stand at Sinai is structured into the very metahistorical nature of the covenant. Deleting the recollective transitions that focus on the Land aspect of the covenant, the author uses the Jacob/Joseph narratives to highlight the revelations at Bethel which portray Jacob as a metaphorical embodiment of future Israel.[69] Foretold at Bethel that he would die in Egypt but be buried "in this land...with Abraham and Isaac" (32:24), Jacob is reluctant to join Joseph until reassured by a second theophany citing God's words in Gen. 46:2-4 (44:2, 5-6). Similarly, his deathbed testament (to all his sons, not just to Joseph), relates only the vision of the future he had received at Bethel (32:21; 45:14). Joseph's deathbed recollection of the Land promise (Gen. 50:24) also is deleted; only the request for removal of his remains when the Israelites go out of Egypt, evidence of Joseph's own knowledge of the future, is retained (46:5).

When he comes to the narrative of the exodus, the author omits all the Land-focused recollections that interconnect the patriarchal covenant, the redemption from Egypt, and the future acquisition of the Land. The scene of Moses' encounter with God at the burning bush scene is totally deleted from the angel narrator's brief recollective summary of the leader's early life.[70] Just as the recollections that closed the Jacob/Joseph story served to highlight Jacob's spiritual prowess, so this summary focuses on the attribute Moses shares with his spiritual forbearers: divine protection from Prince Mastema's machinations to intervene on behalf of the Egyptians (48:2-3, 9-10). The entire story of the redemption from Egypt that follows, summarized into nine verses (48:11-19), is presented from the same metahistorical perspective: the first manifestation of the comparable protection from Prince Mastema that God will be providing for the elected Israelites.

THE NAME AND CHARACTER OF THE LAND

Having allocated the land "where God dwells" to the descendants of Shem through Arpachshad and accounted for the presence of the Canaanites in the Land by the tale of Canaan's usurpation of his cousin's territory in his rewriting of Genesis 1-11, the author of *Jubilees* has prepared the way for a relatively straightforward description of the Land in the patriarchal period. He repeats the experiential descriptions of the biblical text (12:22; 13:3, 19; 14:18; 15:10; 24:10; 27:11, 24),[71] adding a detailed description of the Land's resources to Abraham's first viewing (13:6) and an elaboration to his first touring (13:21), both of which foreshadow Moses' and the scouts' experiences of the Land in Deuteronomy.

He maintains a similar fidelity to the base text with the geographic descriptions of the Land as promised to the patriarchs (13:19; 14:18; 27:23)[72] until the second covenant with Jacob at Bethel. Then, as described above, he expands the territorial dimension to the grandiose proportions which mark his creative development of the covenant with Jacob.

The story of usurpation (10:28-34) having eliminated the problematic implications of the name "Canaan," the author of *Jubilees* uses the phrase freely throughout the patriarchal story. Following Gen. 12:5, the angel narrator describes Abraham coming to the "land of Canaan" (13:1). God enumerates the indigenous peoples, as in Gen. 15:18-21 (14:18),[73] refers to the promised land as the "land of Canaan" (15:10) as in Gen. 17:8, and, adding to the biblical text of Gen. 15:7, makes specific reference to giving Abraham the "land of the Canaanites" (14:7). "Land of Canaan" also appears repeatedly in the various rewritten and created stories of Jacob's children.[74]

The tale of usurpation has other consequences for this rewriting. In *Jubilees* the oath of Noah's children at the first division of the earth remains the basis for the Israelite rightful claim to ownership of the Land. No longer necessary, informative phrases such as "the Canaanites were then in the land" (Gen. 12:6, 13:7) are set aside. More significantly, none of the tension embedded in the biblical descriptions of the Land remains. The implicit biblical position that the Amorites had a just claim to the Land that eventually would be forfeited because of their behavior (Gen. 15:16) is deleted. A revelation of the future to Jacob added to the dream vision at Bethel (32:21-24) takes its place as an explanation for the delay in fulfillment of the Land promise to the patriarchal seed. The Land is nowhere described as belonging to the indigenous population. Neither, for that matter, is there any indication of it belonging in a special way to God, which would justify a transfer of ownership comparable to that developed in such biblical passages as Exod. 23:27-33 and Lev. 20:24. God's relationship with this particular territory (divine presence in certain sites or special qualities attributed to the Land) is mentioned only in the context of the division story in 8:12-21. In his patriarchal stories the author of *Jubilees* betrays no interest either in ascribing metaphysical properties to the Land or in personifying it as a moral force.

The absence of such attributions is not striking because metaphysical description is not characteristic of biblical Genesis. However, the omission marks a departure from biblical Land theology because the author of *Jubilees* retrojects biblical halachic concepts into his "Little Genesis" without developing divine ownership of the Land as a conceptual link between the right of occupancy and the Law.

THE LAND AND THE LAW

In spite of the absence of a concept of divine ownership and repeated assurance of eternal possession of the Land in the patriarchal covenants,[75] *Jubilees* evidences a clear predilection for a covenant defined in terms of adherence to stipulated law. In his narration of the Noah story, the author shifts the focus back and forth from the present tale to the Israelite future, in each period connecting "uprooting from the land/earth" to Sabbath and blood legislation. The same type of shifts in perspective and comparable connections appear in his narratives of the patriarchs and their children. However, these connections do not involve a succinct biblical association between violation of particular commandments and loss of the covenanted Land. Instead, like the connections in the Noah narratives, in the patriar-

chal context the particularity of the Land concept frequently is contextually clouded or lost.

The commandment to Abraham to circumcise the males of his household is initially presented in the context and terms of the biblical text.[76]
But immediately thereafter the author moves into an exposition of the law
in which circumcision is presented not as a mark of the covenant and the
Land promise, but rather as a sign of Israel's similarity to the sanctified angels who had been circumcised "from the day of their creation" (15:27).
Moreover, whereas the author included the threat of being "uprooted
from...family" as the punishment for violation of the commandment
(15:14), when he shifts to circumcision as an ordinance for the future sanctified Israelites the threatened punishment for violation becomes the familiar, unclear "uprooted from the land/earth (15:26, 28, 34).[77]

The stories of Dinah and the Shechemites, of Bilhah and Reuben, and
of Tamar and Judah each provide an occasion for discussion of some aspect
of the levitical laws of גלוי עריות. Presented as morality tales exemplifying a
levitical principle pertaining to future Israelite purity, each narrative con-
cludes with a statement of, or an allusion to, future ordinances, violation of
which would result in "uprooting."[78] Developed around the theme of defilement by intermarriage, the Dinah story is linked to Lev. 18:21, the father
who would give "some of his seed to Moloch" (30:10). Such a desecrator of
Israel's purity is to be stoned, his daughter burned ("uprooted from Israel"),
and, as a general ordinance all defilers of Israel's purity are to "be destroyed
with those who will be uprooted from the *medr*" (30:22).[79] The levitical
prohibitions against defilement by incest are cited in the Reuben/Bilhah
and the Judah/Tamar narratives.[80] But whereas Leviticus warns that incestuous relationships (as well as Moloch worship) so defile the Promised
Land that it vomits forth its inhabitants (Lev. 18:27-28; 20:22), the author
of *Jubilees* avoids personification. Even when he shifts from story line to future ordinances for the Israelites, he makes no connection between pollutive acts and covenanted Land. The general principle that violators of
Israelite purity will be uprooted from the *medr* set forth at the end of the
Reuben/Bilhah narrative (33:19) is not particularized with specific reference to the Land. In fact, contextually the threatened punishment is most
readily understood as destruction from the earth, not exile from the Land.[81]
In the context of Judah and Tamar, the ordinance is described without reference to the *medr*. Explaining that Judah's descendants were not "uprooted" because his two sons had not slept with Tamar, he specifies death
as the appropriate punishment for those who in fact do violate the prohibition (41:27).

In spite of the clear references to the Land-connected purity laws of Leviticus 18 and 20, the issue for *Jubilees* is not defilement of the Land, but rather, like Leviticus 21, defilement of the people of Israel, God's holy nation, "his own possession," the nation that "he owns."[82] Just as the author had substituted the assurance of a special relationship with God for the Land promise as the contextual pivot for the patriarchal covenant, so he ignores the Land-focused context of the levitical laws of purity and shifts the point of emphasis from desecration of the Land to desecration of the people. Indeed, all the biblical techniques for creating a Land context for the legislation are omitted in the morality tales developed around Jacob's children. There is no personification of a Land rejecting its violators. The insertions of ordinances pertaining to Israel's future obedience never include the biblical phrase, "when you come to the Land," and, its meaning consistently kept murky, the threat of uprooting from the *medr* most often contextually connotes destruction from the earth rather than exile from the Land.

The omissions and absence of clarification are deliberate. Not only is the threat of exile from the Land undeveloped in these narratives, but the language used in place of that threat—"uprooting" (with or without *medr* as its object)—is also used in contexts unrelated to the biblical concepts of covenant and Land. Esau's intermarriage with Canaanite women is condemned with "neither he nor his seed is to be saved for they will be destroyed from the earth, and they will be uprooted from under the heaven" (35:14). Moreover, a paraphrase of Amos 9:2-4 predicting Israel's exile from the Land for violation of the covenant is transposed into the noncovenantal context of a curse predicting "destruction and uprooting and removal from the earth" for the Philistines (24:28-32).[83]

When the author of *Jubilees* inserts legal material into his created testaments, he again uses the phrases and structures that associate adherence to the Law with retention of the Land, without in fact establishing any linkage between the Law and the Land. Admonitions to obey God or adhere to specific commands appear in four of the six blessing scenes, two addressed to biblically inappropriate covenantal heirs—Abraham's testaments to all his children and grandchildren (chap. 20) and Isaac's blessing of Jacob and Esau together (chap. 36)—and two to appropriate ones—Abraham's testaments to Isaac (chap. 21) and to Jacob alone (chap. 22).

Both addresses to inappropriate covenantal heirs are set in *tochacha*-like structures and employ the language of covenantal promise without the Land element central to the biblical context. Following the structural style of Deuteronomy 28, Abraham's address to all his heirs, progenitors of the Israelites and not,[84] begins with exhortations to keep certain commandments, followed by threatened punishments (curses) and promised rewards (blessings.) Like Moses addressing the children of Israel on the plains of Moab, the first patriarch particularly warns against idolatry and intermarriage with the seed of Canaan which "will be rooted out of the earth/land" (20:4).[85] If the warning is ignored, his children, like the future Israelites, will make their "name a curse" and all their "life a hissing" (20:6).[86] The punishment predicted for violators of these injunctions, however, is not the exile destined for Israelite violators in Deuteronomy 28, but rather the fate of the primeval giants destroyed in the Great Flood and of the Sodomites (20:5). On the other hand, the rewards for adherence—rain, fruitfulness of womb, herds and flocks, and fertility of land—are exactly those described to the Israelites in Deut. 7:13 and 28:8.[87] Addressed to all the heirs and thus displaced from its particular covenanted Land context, this reward is set in parallel opposition to a curse that totally ignores the punishment most associated with admonitions against intermarriage and idolatry in the *tochacha* source text: exile from the Land.

Similarly, in his blessing of Jacob and Esau (chap. 36), Isaac urges the two brothers to love each other and avoid idolatry, assuring them that if they do so, God "will multiply you and increase your seed like the stars of heaven with regard to number and...will plant you on the earth as a righteous planting which will not be uprooted for all the eternal generations" (36:6). Then, recalling the ancient oath of Noah's sons to honor the division of the earth's territory (9:14) and foreshadowing the Israelite commitment to fidelity to the covenant before entering Canaan (Deut. 29:9-14), Esau and Jacob are enjoined into an oath by the "mighty name which created heaven and earth together" that the one who would plot evil against the other will "be uprooted from the land of the living,"[88] and on the day of judgment God will "burn up his land" just as he burned Sodom (36:9-10).

In the two created blessing scenes, where it would be contextually appropriate, there also is no evidence of the biblical link between Land and Law. The scene in which Isaac alone is blessed opens with the old theme of the Noahite covenant, the spilling and/or eating of blood. Significantly, there is little if any difference between the counsel Noah gave his sons in that context and that which Abraham gives his son Isaac here. Both cite from Lev. 17:13 and Num. 35:33; both note how blood pollutes the earth; and in neither narrative is *medr* identified as the Land promised to the patriarch's descendants. The second half of the Isaac blessing opens with a warning against the "defilement and corruption and contamination" which characterize the "deeds of all mankind." Should Isaac imitate their ways, God will "hide His face," will "uproot" him "from the land/earth," his "seed from beneath the sky," and his "name" will "perish from all the land/earth"

(21:21-22)—terms and phrases associated with the blessings and curses and the loss of the covenanted Land in the *tochachot* of Deuteronomy, but used here without any reference to the Land promise.[89]

Abraham does recall the Land promise in his final blessing of Jacob, the covenantal heir. That recollection comes as an aside, and is in no way connected to the halachic concern with idolatry and intermarriage voiced in the admonitory section of the testament (22:16-23). Instead, the covenantal blessings being transferred to Jacob and his seed are linked back to the cosmic forefathers, Noah and Adam (22:13),[90] and the fate of violators of the injunctions is likened to that of Ham, whose "seed is destined for uprooting from the earth," and that of "the sons of Sodom" who were "taken from the earth" (22:21-22).[91]

Only at the close of his work does the author of *Jubilees* present a succinct connection between Land and Law, and then in a context that is eschatological rather than exhortative. Twice employing the equivalent of the biblical "when you come into the Land..." as a preface to legislation that is Land-related in the biblical text, he retains the Land connection with its particularity not only intact, but specifically emphasized. Set in the context of a description of the prescribed Passover offerings, the first involves the deuteronomic regulation limiting sacrificial worship to a single select place:

> And whenever the children of Israel enter into the land which they will possess, into the land of Canaan, they will set up the tabernacle of the Lord in the midst of the land, in one of their tribes, until the sanctuary of the Lord is built upon the land...And in the days when a house is built in the name of the Lord in the land of their inheritance. (49:18-19)

No reference is made to covenantal promise, but the striking repeated references to the Land, the emphatic specification of "the land of Canaan," and the assurance of "the land which they will possess...land of their inheritance" are clear evidence that it is presumed. The subject matter is future Passover worship in the Land that, in accord with the ruling of Deut. 16:5-7, must be centralized. But whereas prescription of the Passover legislation holds the focus of the Deuteronomy text, in the full *Jubilees* narrative (49:18-21) prediction overwhelms prescription, and the focus shifts from the festival to the tabernacle and subsequent "House of the Lord" that will be built in the land the Israelites possess as their inheritance.

Immediately thereafter the angel narrator turns to the subject of the sabbatical years. Informing Moses that the exact year of the jubilee will not be revealed "until you [the Israelites] enter into the land which you will possess," he affirms that once the Israelites are dwelling in it, "the land will keep its sabbaths" (50:1-2). The shift from the biblical context of the sab-batical legislation is not subtle.[92] There is no promise of fruitfulness should the sabbath years be kept and no warning of rejection should they be vio-lated. Instead, the angel turns the prediction of Lev. 26:34, "Then shall the land make up for its sabbath years throughout the time that it is desolate and you are in the land of your enemies," on its head. The biblical vision of future pollution, ejection, and exile is replaced by a portrait of fidelity and of the Land being nourished by the Israelite presence.

Clearly eschatological rather than historical, the vision is developed by projections into the future end-time that parallel the retrojections used in the rewriting of the prepatriarchal narratives.[93] The technique is much the same, but this time there is no lack of clarity about *medr*. Specifically desig-nating the "land of Canaan" (50:4), the angel employs the terminology used in the biblical context of the years preceding conquest of the Land ("when they come into the land which they will possess") to describe an end-time when the Israelites "will dwell in confidence in all the land." Here, as in the witness poem of Deuteronomy (32:43), the mark of that eschaton is that "the land will be purified from that time and forever" (50:5).

THE LAND AND ESCHATOLOGY

The author of *Jubilees* devotes two chapters of his work specifically to es-chatology. The first, the chapter that introduces the work, has the external setting of Moses on Mount Sinai receiving the revelation of past and future from the angel. Internally, however the author reconstructs the biblical perspective of the end of Moses' leadership and retrojects it back to the be-ginning of his career. The chapter opens with Moses being instructed to re-cord a revelation of past and future "in a book" (1:5) which will serve as a "testimony" (1:8) against Israel in future generations. The "book," of course, is *Jubilees*. Set forth in witness terms parallel to those used to de-scribe "the book of the law" and the poem of redemption in Deuteronomy, the revelation of *Jubilees* replaces the poem of Deuteronomy 31.[94] However, the author gives a significant twist to the "witness" concept he adopts. Whereas the Deuteronomy poem is to justify God's hidden face in the fu-ture time of Israel's rebelliousness (Deut. 31:19), the object of *Jubilees* is to provide a revelation of future history "so that their descendants might see that I have not abandoned them" (1:5).

Jubilees encompasses both the Law and the revelatory poem. The two are interwoven within the work such that revelation of the Law (the past Moses is recalling in Deuteronomy) and revelation of the redemption (the future he is predicting in Deuteronomy) both have their roots in Creation. Hence the author chooses a rewriting of Genesis as the textual frame for unfolding the dual revelation. The ultimate point of reference, however, is not Genesis but Deuteronomy, and "Little Genesis" opens with a deuteronomic preview of future history.

Prefaced by a traditional recollection of the promise of the Land to the patriarchs (1:7), the preview draws its language from a variety of biblical *tochachot*[95] but its structure is that of Deuteronomy 28-30[96]—a full paradigm, cast in predictive voice. The primary sin is idolatry: imitating the gentiles and forgetting the commandments (1:8-12).[97] The punishment, mentioned only this one time in *Jubilees*, is exile from the Land (1:13-14). Repentance and a restoration that is both physical and spiritual follow (1:15b-18). However, unlike any of the Deuteronomy models, in this paradigm the repentance stage is split so as to create a double-tiered restoration.

> And afterward they will turn to me from among the nations with all their heart and with all their soul and with all their might. And I shall gather them from the midst of all the nations. And they will seek me so that I might be found by them. When they seek me with all their heart and with all their soul, I shall reveal to them an abundance of peace in righteous (15). And with all my heart and with all my soul I shall transplant them as a righteous plant. And they will be a blessing and not a curse. And they will be the head and not the tail (16). And I shall build my sanctuary in their midst and I shall dwell with them. And I shall be their God and they will be my people truly and rightly. And I shall not forsake them, and I shall not be alienated from them because I am the Lord their God (17-18).

By inverting the sequence of events paraphrased from Jer. 29:13-14[98] in verse 15 and omitting the words "in this land" from an otherwise direct citation of Jer. 32:41 (16a),[99] the author gives the primary place in the eschatological drama to the relationship between God and Israel. As in Deuteronomy, Israel's initial repentance in exile (15a) effects the ingathering of exiles (15b). But return to the Land no longer is the culminating point in the cycle. It is followed by a second, more intense repentance (15c) that brings restoration of the special relationship with God (16-18) that is the focal point of the covenant throughout *Jubilees*.[100] Now only a starting point, return to the Land no longer serves as an eschatological signpost.

The purpose behind this departure from the traditional paradigm is made abundantly clear in an intercessory scene which interrupts the revelation. Confronted with the revelation of future history, Moses begs that the predicted cycle not even be permitted to begin:

> O Lord, let your mercy be lifted up upon your people, and create for them
> an upright spirit. And do not let the spirit of Beliar rule over them to ac-
> cuse them before you and ensnare them from every path of righteousness so
> that they might be destroyed from before your face. But they are your peo-
> ple and your inheritance, whom you saved by your great might from the
> hand of the Egyptians. Create a pure heart and a holy spirit for them. And
> do not let them be ensnared by their sin henceforth and forever. (1:20-21)

Given the restoration and return that the angel has just described, the intercession seems inappropriate. Unlike its pentateuchal models, it is not
preceded by a threat of final destruction, and no recourse is made either to
the merits of the fathers or to the promise of the Land.[101] Instead, building
on the absence of penitence in the poetic cycle of Deuteronomy 32, the
author has Moses express a lack of confidence in Israel's capacity to repent
and self-reform through historical experience. Consequently, the intercession seeks what is tantamount to an end effected solely by supernatural
means. Replacing the angel delegate, God responds directly with a rejection of the plea. God reconfirms the relationship between history and eschatology set forth in the traditional paradigm and restates the necessity
for full repentance and Israel's potential to achieve it.[102] Only thereafter
will divine intervention effect the change of nature that characterizes the
end-time and closes the cycle.

The historical perspective of the revelation is a broad one that spans all
of Israel's history. The intent is not to present a detailed eschatological portrait, but to develop an all encompassing theology of history which employs
a deuteronomic paradigm redesigned such that the post-exilic period *in the
Land* is within its perimeters. The task is not a simple one. In setting, substance, and perspective, the eschatology of Deuteronomy is Land-centered:
entry into the Land, exile from the Land, and restoration to the Land are
the milestones of Israel's history. By placing the revelation of *Jubilees* at Sinai as opposed to preceding the entry into Canaan, the author avoids the
Land setting which envelops Deuteronomy, and consequently is able to develop a theological framework for Israel's history which does not have the
Land at its center. He does not ignore the Land; indeed, he uses the traditional frame of reference up to the point of the intercession. The most significant aspect of that intercession is its strikingly unbiblical outright
rejection.[103] It marks the author's departure from the eschatology of Deuteronomy, a departure the author legitimates by having it come directly
from God rather than being voiced by the angel who, up to that point, has
been the annunciator for the revelation.

In the new theology, the Land is not the key to Israel's history. Release from exile is not the sign of the end-time, and return to the Land does not indicate completion of the cycle. Israel's history continues. Before the cycle will end, there must be thoroughgoing repentance and reform. This reform has nothing to do with Land. Land was the critical issue in the first part of the cycle, which from the perspective of the end-time is the past. In describing the preconditions for the second restoration the author is no longer dealing with that past. He is retrojecting *his own present* into Moses' future. Spiritual regeneration and total repentance, not Land retention, is the crucial issue in the author's present. From the perspective of the past, Land promise, acquisition, and retention are the markers of Israel's history. From the author's present, purity of heart and fidelity to the covenant become the new eschatological markers.

Whereas the scenario that introduces *Jubilees* is painted with a broad brush that covers the span of Israel's history, the second presentation of eschatology, occasioned by Abraham's death (chap. 23), narrows the focus to a detailed description of a post-exilic period.[104] The author again uses a deuteronomic paradigm, but this time the source model is Deuteronomy 31-32 with its doubled scheme and interplay of poetry and prose. Using the techniques employed in earlier narratives—deletion of the territorial-specific phrases and deliberate vagueness with the term *medr*—the author attempts to give the end-time events in the post-exilic period cosmic significance by placing them in universal contexts and/or on an historical continuum that relates back to Noah.

The central motif of the eschaton is developed around a reconstructed version of the deuteronomic concern with prolonged life in the Land. Taking advantage of the use of the more general אדמה in lieu of ארץ in the warnings of Deuteronomy,[105] the author extracts the warning of "you shall not prolong your days upon the soil/land" out of the particularizing context of "which you are crossing the Jordan to invade and occupy"[106] and develops a universal history around the theme of longevity of lifespan. Until the Flood, the days of "the ancients were nineteen jubilees" (23:8), but after Noah,[107] because of the evil of their ways, human lives were filled with suffering and drastically shortened. The impact of that human Fall was so great that even Abraham, who was "perfect in all of his actions with the Lord" (23:10), died far short of his warranted jubilees because of the evil around him.

With the notation of lifespans now limited to seventy or eighty years of misery (23:15), the narrative moves immediately (and awkwardly) on to a paradigmatic description of a future time immersed in sin. The cycle, like the one in the macro-view in chapter 1, is doubled. However, adding a repentance stage to the paradigm of Deuteronomy 31-32,[108] this *Doppel-schema* is a more substantial one: sin (14-17); punishment (18-19); failed restoration (20); sin (21); punishment (22-5); repentance (26); restoration (27-31).[109] Whereas the purpose of the doubling in the earlier chapter was to reconstruct the biblical paradigm such that it would incorporate a return to the Land that had not borne the predicted eschatological fruit, the doubling here has nothing to do with the Land. Rather, with a lens focused on closer historical events, the new cycle provides a frame of reference for interpreting a happening that otherwise might be mistaken as a fulfillment of the promise of restoration.[110]

It is the language and content of the paradigm, not its doubled structure, that point to the author's reinterpretation of the place of Land in biblical eschatology. Although the covenant and the people are mentioned (23:16, 19, 23), in none of the stages is there a clear reference to a specific Land[111] or any indication of a particular geographic site in which the eschatological drama unfolds. The word *medr* appears only in contexts (vv. 14, 18, 20, 23) that are notably vague in particularity.[112] No distinctions are made between universal and Israelite history. The sins which characterize the "evil generation which sins on the *medr*" are "pollution and fornication and contamination and abomination" (23:14) (in the doubling pollution of the holy of holies, corruption and deceit in pursuit of wealth are added). Here committed by those who "forsake the covenant which the Lord made between them and himself" (23:16-17), these are the very sins the author earlier attributed (without reference to a sanctuary) to the generation of the Flood (7:20-21), to Sodom (20:5), and to the ways of the gentiles (22:16). Moreover, although the concern with purity here is levitical in tone, the levitical theme of a polluted Land expelling its inhabitants is never mentioned.

Since the author is developing this paradigm as an internal post-exilic cycle within the larger panoramic cycle of the first chapter, there is no mention of the traditional biblical connection between violation of the covenant and loss of the Land. The biblical consequences which do appear are loss of fertility (23:18) and the shedding of so much blood "upon the *medr* that there "will be no one who will gather and no one who will bury" (23:23). Neither consequence is Land-focused. In and of itself, infertility is not Land-specific, and the phrases in the *tochachot* of Leviticus and Deuteronomy that would provide such specificity ("your land," "the land promised to the fathers") do not appear in *Jubilees* 23. Moreover, the infertility includes as one of its dimensions the destruction of animal life such as occurred in the era of the Flood.[113] The description of the blood shed "upon the *medr*" by avenging "sinners of the nations" in 23:23 also does not include an explicit spatial delineation. Indeed, enriching his description with a phrase drawn either from Jer. 8:2 or 1 Macc. 7:17, the author omits the very precise place context (Jerusalem) identified in both texts.[114] The geographical vagueness seems a purposeful, resourceful use of the dual sense of ארץ/*medr* that gives a cosmic perspective to the end of history, much as the retrojection of the covenant into prepatriarchal narratives gave to the beginning of that history.

Without exile as a punishment, there clearly is no rationale for return to the Land at the end of the cycle. In its place the author sets another kind of physical return as the key feature in a multifaceted restoration: mankind gradually regains the longevity it had lost at the Flood such that by the end of time, when righteousness is totally restored, the "days of man" again "approach a thousand years" (23:28). Satan and the power of evil will be destroyed, God's servants will be empowered to "drive out their enemies," and, thereafter, will "rejoice forever and ever with joy" (23:29-30). The substitution is a significant one. Awkward in the context of the death of the patriarch who was perfect but whose lifespan fell far short of the prediluvian nineteen jubilees, the introduction of the longevity theme as a preface to the cycle now makes sense. It provides the means for preserving the biblical motif of a "paradise lost and regained," while avoiding the biblical Land theology that is inappropriate to the writer's post-exilic perspective. Moreover, with its origins ("promise") traced back to the cosmic forefathers, and its achievement ("fulfillment")—a variation on the divinely administered vindication described in Deut. 32:36-43—redesigned without the particularity of the biblical context,[115] the restoration acquires the mythic, universal proportions that mark the rewriting of covenant theology in *Jubilees*. Thus, taking advantage of the absence of an explicit reference to the Israelites and the weak development of the Land theme in the poem of Deuteronomy 32, the writer of *Jubilees* has reinterpreted the biblical text to construct a vision of an imminent end-time that fits the perspective of his own day—a time when return to the Land no longer can be viewed as a signpost of the end-time, yet a period of expansion when there is reason to perceive the promise of Land from its origins to its fulfillment in mythic, cosmic proportions.[116]

Jubilees cannot be understood as an attempt to develop a theology which excludes the biblical promise of Land. Were that the case, the author would not have paraphrased substantial Genesis passages in which that promise is affirmed. Nor, for that matter, would he have ended his work (chaps. 49-50) with explicit references to Israel's destiny in the Land. Rather, the writer is attempting to extend the perimeters of biblical covenantal history to encompass the years after the return from Babylonian exile. In order to attribute covenantal significance to the post-exilic period, he must free the covenant from the Land-tied context of the biblical narrative. Rooting his effort in biblical text, the author of *Jubilees* redefines the essential component of the covenant,[117] relocates its origins, and from that new perspective rewrites its history within the biblical narrative. In that rewriting God's relationship with Israel, not the Land promise, becomes the pivot for the covenant which originates at Creation rather than at Abraham's entry into the Land. The biblical links between the exodus, Sinai, and the Land are deleted. Acquisition, eventual loss, and subsequent recovery of the Land become single rather than singular events in an ongoing redemptive history. The eschatological closure to that history can then be marked by restoration of the primeval human condition and total fruition of the covenantal relationship ordained at Creation, not by return to the Land.

CHAPTER 4

Covenant and *Aqedah:* The *Testament of Moses*

W hereas the various aspects of biblical Land theology are embedded within a complex fabric in *Jubilees*, superficially the *Testament of Moses* appears to be a far less intricate document. Identifying the scope of the work as "the prophecy which was made by Moses in the book of Deuteronomy" (1:5), the author uses Moses' imminent death, the transfer of leadership to Joshua, and the prediction of Israel's future history in Deuteronomy 31-32[1] as a substructure for the testament.[2] The acknowledgment of the base text is deceptive, however, for the *Testament* is an intricately interwoven document whose full meaning unfolds only in the context of certain allusions—clues, so to speak—to biblical passages outside of Deuteronomy.

Structurally, the *Testament of Moses* has two major sections: a dialogistic frame which introduces and closes the work (1; 10:11–12:13), and, inserted within that frame, a revelation composed of an historical preview of Israel's history from the conquest of Canaan to the reigns of Herod's sons and an apocalyptic poem describing an imminent end-time (2:1-10:10). These major sections of the work are connected by virtue of their mutual relationship to Deuteronomy 31-32. The opening frame is developed along the general lines of Deut. 31:1-8, 14-15, 23-26. The closing one involves Joshua's reaction to the revelation he has just heard and Moses' response. These last chapters are not as closely tied to Deuteronomy 31-32, but the transfer of leadership is the point of departure for the dialogue which sets forth the theological perspective of the work. The historical revelation and apocalyptic poem which comprise the central part of the *Testament* respectively replace the prose of Deut. 31:16-21 and the poem of Deuteronomy 32.

In order to develop his own covenant theology the author makes several changes to the biblical frame. Whereas in Deuteronomy God is the source of the prediction of Israel's violation of the covenant and the subsequent divine wrath (31:15ff.), in the *Testament* Moses (speaking to Joshua) conveys the prediction. The revelation attributed to God is a more positive one, reaffirming the promise of the Land in accord with "the covenant and oath" (1:9). This reaffirmation involves the first of several explicit recollections of the covenant expressed either in terms of a promise to the "fathers" (1:8; 2:1; 4:2-3, 5; 11:11) or in terms of God's "covenant and oath" (1:9; 2:7; 3:9; 11:17; 12:13).[3] Not surprisingly, the recollections are found only in the frame and first half of the historical revelation, that is, in those sections which chronologically parallel the historical period covered within Hebrew Scriptures.

PATRIARCHAL HISTORY

The first type of recollection, that of the promise to the fathers, refers, like comparable recollections in Deuteronomy, either explicitly or contextually to the promise of the Land.[4] In contrast to the biblical writer, in none of the recollections of the Land promise does the author of the *Testament* identify the patriarchs by name.[5] Consequently, it is never quite clear whether the claim to the Land is being made in the name of the first patriarchs or the more immediate fathers of the exodus generation.[6] The vagueness may well be deliberate, for in the second recollective pattern— memory of a "covenant and oath"—the two sets of fathers are in fact joined.

The intriguing nondeuteronomic phrase "covenant and oath" appears without clarification five times in the *Testament*. Used as an historical introduction in the opening frame, it reappears in the intercessory prayer of the ten tribes at the beginning of the Babylonian exile, in Joshua's description of Moses' intercessory role, and finally, at the end of the work in Moses' own assurance that the nation would never be driven from the Land to be completely destroyed. Like its counterpart, recollection of the fathers, it is contextually associated, except for one occasion involving an emended text, with assurance of the promise of the Land. The "covenant and oath" reassure that Joshua will bring the people to the land "promised to their fathers" (1:9). It is the basis in the historical revelation upon which an appeal is made that God not forget his promise to the patriarchs that "their seed would never fail from the land" (3:9).[7] And in the closing frame (11:17; 12:13) reference to the covenant and oath comes as a reassuring response to Joshua's concern that with the death of Moses, the intercessor, the Israelites would be driven from the Land and destroyed.

There are only two biblical referents for such a covenant and oath. One is, as might be expected, the covenant and oath entered into by the Israelites before their entrance into the Land (Deut. 29:9-14).[8] Inasmuch as the *Testament of Moses* is constructed around Deuteronomy, it would be natural to assume that the terminology has been drawn from that text. However, insofar as the oath is specifically described in the *Testament* as one "which You [God] swore...by Yourself" (3:9), the phrasing more recalls the scene of the *Aqedah*.[9]

> "By Myself I swear," the Lord declares: "because you have done this and have not withheld your son, your favored one, I will bestow My blessing upon you and make your descendants as numerous as the stars of the heaven and the sands on the seashore; and your descendants shall seize the gates of their foes. And all the nations of the earth shall bless themselves by your descendants, because you have obeyed My command." (Gen. 22:16-18)

The association between covenant and oath and the *Aqedah* also appears in the rabbinic liturgical literature of the *Zichronot* prayers of Rosh Ha-Shanah, dated in the Amoraitic if not Tannaitic period.[10] Exploring the possibility that the tradition has an even earlier history—that the author of the *Testament* deliberately exploits a connection between the covenantal promises and the merits of Abraham at the scene of the *Aqedah*—one may examine some of the verbal echoes connecting various biblical passages and the appearance of those same echoes in the *Testament*.

There are many references in the Pentateuch to God having sworn to give the Land to the seed of Abraham, Isaac, and Jacob,[11] but only in Moses' intercession at the time of the Golden Calf (Exod. 32:13) is reference made to God having sworn an oath "by Himself," as set forth at the *Aqedah* scene.[12] In the *Aqedah* context, the oath stresses the promise of progeny, and yet mentions the Land aspect of the covenant only indirectly: "Thy seed shall possess the gates of its enemies" (Gen. 22:17). However, when Moses at Sinai reminds God of the oath, the Land promise is stated fully:

> Remember Your servants, Abraham, Isaac, and Israel, how You swore to them by Your Self and said to them: I will make your offspring as numerous as the stars of heaven, and I will give to your offspring this whole land of which I spoke, to possess forever. (Exod. 32:13)

The implicit connection between the *Aqedah* and Moses' intercession at Sinai in the biblical narratives provides the key to understanding the *Testament of Moses* and its otherwise puzzling structure. The single occasion on which the content of the oath is stated in the *Testament* is in the context of an intercession created by the author. Narrowing the focus of the appeal solely to the Land promise and expanding the historical scope of the *Aqedah* as a source of merit to a later period, this intercession, occasioned by the exile to Babylonia, recalls in both its structure and content the Exodus passage cited above:

> God of Abraham God of Isaac, and God of Jacob, remember your covenant which you made with them, and the oath which you swore to them by yourself, that their seed would never fail from the land which you have given them. (3:9) [13]

The *Testament* thus presents an early form of the aggadic tradition which treats the *Aqedah* as a source of intercessory merit for future generations. But whereas the association between the *Aqedah* and intercession is explicit in later legend and lore, [14] in the *Testament*, as in the biblical narrative, it is only implied by the use of certain crucial terminology. Abraham's willingness to sacrifice his son at God's command is nowhere directly mentioned in the *Testament*. Indeed, although much is made in the work of Moses' intercessory powers, there is also no direct reference to the intercession at Sinai. Instead, by employing the phrase "covenant and oath" and thereby associating the covenant with an oath involving the Land promise which God swore by himself (3:9), the author of the *Testament* triggers memory of the relevant biblical passages. Thus the writer calls attention to a causal connection between martyrdom and promise in the life of the first patriarch and between intercessory appeal and recollection of that promise in the life of the nation. Moreover, by projecting that connection into the context of the Babylonian exile, he transforms it from a single historical event into an ongoing force reflecting a relationship that persists long after the exodus and Sinai. [15]

The phrase "covenant and oath" ultimately provides a unity otherwise missing in the *Testament*, linking the outer frames with the revelations and the eschatology. However, "covenant and oath" does not appear in the second half of the revelation, which covers the period from the time of the return from Babylonia to the eschaton. Instead, we find a counterpart to the *Aqedah*, the story of Taxo and his sons, which connects the end of Israel's history to its beginnings. It is a comparable narrative to the *Aqedah*, enacted for "the sake of heaven," [16] and serves as the final intercessory deed which activates the end-time of Israel's history.

THE NAME AND CHARACTER OF THE LAND

Before turning to the treatment of covenant and Land in that final act, however, the place of the other aspects of biblical Land theology in the *Tes-*

tament of Moses must be considered. Unlike the Deuteronomist, the author of the *Testament* is not interested in stressing the conditional nature of the covenant. To the contrary, the primary purpose of the work is to demonstrate that, regardless of historical circumstance, the covenant through which the Israelites acquired the Land from God is permanent and eternal. Thus the author ascribes to the Land no special qualities derived from divine ownership which, if only by implication, might suggest insecurity of right and tenure. Nor, for that matter, does he once refer to the Land by the common biblical nomenclature of "land of Canaan." Instead, throughout the work he pointedly assumes Israelite ownership of the Land. Grounding right of ownership in the promise to their forefathers (1:8; 2:1; 11:12), he repeatedly refers to "their" (the Israelite) Land—from the moment of entry[17] through the exile[18] and return[19] to descriptions of the corruption and punishment that precede and follow Herod's reign (5:6; 6:5, 8).[20] The *Testament* writer is also not concerned with the territorial extent of the Promised Land. Its geographic dimensions are never mentioned in recollections of the promise. In the historical review the author speaks in general terms of "the land," except for his descriptions of the Babylonian siege (3:2) and the Hasmonean era (5:6), where his focus reflects a Jerusalem-centered Judea.[21]

THE LAND AND THE LAW

Given its emphasis on the eternality of God's commitment to the "covenant and oath," the *Testament of Moses* does not reflect the scope of the biblical interest in the connection between adherence to the Law and retention of the Land. One finds numerous references to the covenant but no mention of specific *halachot*, and, in comparison with *Jubilees*, relatively little stress on the Law per se. In fact, the only section of Deuteronomy 31 which is not in some fashion incorporated either into the frame chapters or into the survey of biblical history is the description of Moses' command to have the Torah Law read every seven years when the Israelites would come to the Temple to commemorate Succot (Deut. 31:9-13). The emphasis in the *Testament* is on the Torah book as an eschatological revelation, not as Law. Thus, instead of instructing the Levites to preserve the Torah in the ark (Deut. 31:26), here Moses instructs Joshua on how to preserve the revelation ("this writing") until the end time, "so that later you will remember how to preserve the books which I shall entrust to you" (1:16-18). Nonetheless, in the presentation of his own theological perspective, the author of the *Testament* does set forth the general position that those who adhere to the commandments are rewarded and those who violate them are punished (12:10-11).[22] And in the description of Israel's history after the conquest and settlement, temporary loss of the Land appears as a national punishment.

Following the pattern of Deuteronomy, albeit without its rich descriptive detail, the sin is idolatry, specifically described as offering "their sons to foreign gods" and setting up "idols in the Temple that they may worship them" (2:8).[23] The punishment which immediately follows is invasion of the Land by a king "from the east" who will burn "their city (*lit.*, colony) with the holy Temple of the Lord," and exile the people to his own country (3:1-3).[24] Thus far, the cycle appears to follow the traditional pattern of Deuteronomy 4 and 28-30. At this point, however, the *Testament of Moses* moves in a significantly different direction. The two tribes, it is predicted, will reproach their previously exiled brethren (the ten tribes) for their fate.[25] In response, all the tribes will turn to God with an intercessory plea which parallels Moses' petition on behalf of the Israelites at Sinai (Exod. 32:13).[26] This prayer is the first of a pair which effect turning points in the cycle.[27] Here the exiled remember Moses' prophecies,[28] acknowledge that their exile is a consequence of their violation of the commandments, and appeal to God to remember his "covenant and the oath" to preserve eternally the seed of the patriarchs in the covenanted Land.

The substance of the petition is drawn from Exodus, but the sequence of events which follow are structured around Deuteronomy 31. The witnessing ceremony the tribes recollect is that of Deut. 31:28, and the change brought about by the prayer is no more than that predicted in Deut. 31:20-21 of the Israelite's recognition of a causal relationship between their disobedience and their situation of exile.[29] Affirmation of that relationship is as close as the *Testament* comes to a description of repentance. It is followed neither by a confession of sins nor by any indication of a return to fidelity.[30] As a preface to redemption, therefore, the scene remains incomplete. The author immediately moves on to describe a second intercession scene seventy-seven years later.

In that scene, a second prayer is offered in exile by an unnamed figure, usually identified with Daniel.[31] Functioning as an intercessor, the offerer of this prayer recalls the covenantal relationship that originated with the "fathers," and appeals to God's compassion to end the exile.

> Lord of all king on the lofty throne, you who rules the world, who has willed that this people be for you a chosen people, yea, who has willed to be called their God according to the covenant which you made with their fathers, yet they, with their wives and children, have gone into a foreign land,

surrounded by the gates of strangers where there is great majesty. Have regard for them and have compassion for them, O heavenly Lord. (4:2-4)

It is this plea, according to the *Testament*, that effects the return to the Land (4:5-6).

It has been suggested that the prayer was modelled on the intercessory prayer of Dan. 9:4-19.[32] Both open with a statement of the covenantal relationship, and both appeal to God's compassion. But those similarities aside, there are major differences in structure and content between the two prayers. The deuteronomic pattern of the Daniel prayer is that reflected in Deuteronomy 4 and 28-30: punishment (that is, exile) follows sin and repentance precedes restoration to the Land, be it implied, as in Deuteronomy 4, or explicitly stated, as in Deuteronomy 28-30. In contrast, the second prayer, like the first in the *Testament*, evidences the more limited pattern of Deuteronomy 31-32.[33] Substantively the difference involves the emphasis put on repentance and confession of sins as a preface to the appeal for restoration. A significant portion of the Daniel prayer is devoted to just such a confession (Dan. 9:5-14). In the *Testament* prayer there is no confession of sins and no repentant statement. The plea for compassion is based on God's relationship to the world and to Israel, not on Israel's repentant condition. It opens by addressing God as the "Lord of all," a God "who rules the world," and goes on to state that the "chosen people," with whose forefathers this God had covenanted, is now in the dejected state of being held captive in a foreign land. The statement implies, even if it does not state, that Israel's lowly condition reflects poorly upon the ruler of the world who "has willed to be called their God." The attraction of Deuteronomy 32 for the author of the *Testament* is its unusual closure for the cycle. God's vindication of Israel is attributed to the provocation of the arrogant gentiles who defame God's omnipotence by believing that their victories stem from their own hand (32:27-33). As in the *Testament*, divine intervention is related to concern with the perceptions of the nations. Consequently, the absence of engagement between God and a repentant people offers an opportunity to demonstrate the power of intercession as a replacement for repentance.[34]

Much as the substance of the intercessory plea by the ten tribes parallels Moses' intercession at Sinai as described in Exod. 32:13, the substance of the second, the plea that activates the return to the Land, most closely parallels the second account of that Sinai intercession when it is recollected in Deut. 9:26-29.[35] Appeal is made there to God's promises to the forefathers (9:27), to his election of Israel (9:29) and, albeit in an historical as opposed to cosmic context, to his great power (9:29). Moreover, the crux of the argument implied in the *Testament*—that the dejected state of God's chosen in exile reflects poorly on the Chooser—is explicitly stated in Deuteronomy 9: the failure of the Israelites to obtain the Land promised to their forefathers will be attributed (by the Egyptians) to lack of power or ability on the part of their God.[36]

That the author of the *Testament* might specifically have Deuteronomy 9 in mind as an example of intercession replacing repentance might be argued as well from the doubling of the intercessions in both texts. In the deuteronomic recollection of Moses' intercession at Sinai, the exchange between God and Moses is interrupted such that Moses' response to God's anger comes after the description of his descent to the camp of the Israelites and after a general rehearsal of various examples of their rebelliousness.[37] The break in the dialogue on the mountain results in a doubling of the accounts of Moses' fasting and praying, the first presented in reaction to the sight of the molten calf (Deut. 9:18-19) and the second coming after the destruction of the calf and a rehearsal of subsequent apostasies (Deut. 9:21-29). It is in the second exchange that we find Moses' belated response to the dialogue that began before his descent. The two accounts are in fact one, broken up only by reason of the recollective nature of the biblical narrative. Nonetheless, the consequent doubling provides a precedent and a structural model for a pair of intercessory prayers such as we find in the *Testament of Moses*.[38]

Repentance on the part of the apostates is not a factor in either the intercessory prayer of Deuteronomy 9 or in the *Testament*. In both cases the intercessor presumes the unworthiness of those on behalf of whom prayer is offered. In the biblical narrative, however, intercession is used solely to assuage divine anger, to inhibit rather than to invite divine action. If the author of the *Testament* had limited intercessory prayer to an attempt on the part of the united tribes to stay an imminent exile, he would have remained within this tradition.[39] But such is not the case. Instead, in an attempt to rewrite deuteronomic eschatology such that it would encompass post-exilic history, the *Testament* places both the tribal prayer and the one that follows it into a structure that does not so much supplement Deuteronomy 9 and 32 as offer an alternative to them. Using a *Doppelschema* to create a chronological framework, the author combines an intercession (modelled on Deuteronomy 9) with a cyclical paradigm (modelled on Deuteronomy 32) to design an historical cycle which produces a significant interpretive resolution. It accounts for the fact that the return to the Land was not accompanied by the kind of spiritual renewal prophesied in the traditional paradigms of Deuteronomy 4 and 28-30. In this new cycle, repentance is no longer a factor. It does not even follow, let alone precede, the return of the exiles to the Promised Land.

With this posture the *Testament* takes a far more radical step than *Jubilees*. Both works approach the eschatology of Deuteronomy from a post-exilic perspective. Both acknowledge that the return to the Land was not accompanied by the kind of spiritual renewal prophesied in the traditional paradigm.[40] And both employ a *Doppelschema* in order to set post-exilic history into the biblical framework. But much as he manipulates biblical texts and structures, the author of *Jubilees* does not alter the traditional pattern as it pertains to pre-exilic Israelite history, namely, sin, exile, the repentance, and return from exile. His problem is solely with the post-exilic period, with the delayed eschaton, not with the paradigm itself. He solves that problem by creating a failed intercession which emphasizes the necessity of full repentance before the onset of the final end-time within the second cycle of his *Doppelschema*. For the author of the *Testament of Moses*, the problem goes beyond accounting for the place of post-exilic history in a salvationist scheme of history. Ultimately, in stark contrast to *Jubilees*, the problem rests with the entire concept of spiritual return as a paradigmatic stage within that history.

The absence of the notion of a repentant nation in the *Testament* may reflect historical realism on the part of this author, much as delay of a full repentance stage suggests in *Jubilees*, a sense that the repentant nature of the generation immediately preceding the return from exile was no greater than that of the generations which succeeded it. But I would suggest that the total absence of a repentance stage in the historical cycle more reflects the author's effort to maintain a tension between divine and human control in the working out of Israel's destiny. In the dialogues which open and close the work, he makes a point of stressing the extent of God's total foreknowledge and control of all history "from the beginning of the creation of the world even to the end of the age" (1:13; 12:4-5). The election of Israel, her future punishment at the hand of the gentile nations, as well as the appointment of Moses as intercessor were all foreknown and predetermined "from the beginning of the world" (1:13-14; 12:6). Thus, God's omnipotence over history and his predestination of Israel's future within history are paradoxically combined with the reward/punishment motif so dominant in Deuteronomy.[41] The author of the *Testament* handles this paradox by creating a distinction (in a most nondeuteronomic way) between "historical" and "eschatological" time. Repentance is a factor only within the latter. At the end of days there will be a *"diem paenitentiae,"*[42] but it is a metaphysical rather than an historical phenomenon. Instead of preceding and initiating the eschaton, it will be an antecedent, a consequence, of the move out of history and into the end-time. Intriguingly, this lack of confidence in Israel's capacity for self-reformation through historical experience is the very position rejected in *Jubilees*, where the troublesome post-exilic period is made into a kind of pre-eschaton, a "between-time" in which Israel, living in the Land, is to seek a deeper level of repentance which will in fact bring the final end as promised.

The exclusion of repentance from the historical cycle, that is, from the predetermined "before time," in the *Testament* at once acknowledges Israel's incapacity to reform itself through the historical experience of exile and avoids the pitfalls of an antinomian position. It creates a place within the theological system for the extended pre-eschatological period in the Land after the return. By substituting intercessory prayer for repentance as the initiating force for the return stage in this historical cycle, the author essentially deprives the troublesome post-exilic period, the return to the Land without the accompanying spiritual changes prophesied in Deuteronomy, of eschatological significance. This is not to say that the claim to possession of the Land is negated. As previously noted, the author makes a point of affirming that claim. Rather, the return is so theologically underplayed that one suspects that the review of biblical history primarily serves as the background for the eschatological cycle which immediately follows.

THE LAND AND ESCHATOLOGY

The second cycle begins with the Maccabees and the Antiochan persecution and ends with the reign of Herod's sons.[43] Theologically, this cycle completes the unfinished business of its predecessor and brings Jewish history to the eschaton which the author believes is imminent in his own day. Containing, like several of those described in Deuteronomy, a doubling of the sequential stages of sin and punishment,[44] it duplicates the pattern of the first cycle in the *Testament*.

The intercession here is notably different from that found in other intercessory narratives, such as those of Moses, Daniel, and Judah Maccabee,[45] as well as from the two examples presented in the first cycle of the *Testament of Moses*, namely the appeals of the tribes in chapter three and the Daniel-like figure in chapter four. The narrative of Taxo is a story of intercession without prayer or liturgical recourse to the deity. There is no repentance, not even a statement comparable to the earlier acknowledgment of the fulfillment of Moses' prophetic warnings. Instead, required by unnamed oppressors to violate the commandments, an historically unidentified character named Taxo proposes to his seven sons that they join him in fasting and withdrawing to a cave where they will die with the assurance that their deaths will be avenged by God (9:6-7).[46] Immediately following the narrative of Taxo comes an apocalyptic poem describing the eschaton in which the guardian angel of Israel and God himself wreak vengeance on the oppressor nations.[47] The poem and the revelation close with the exaltation of Israel and the destruction of her enemies.

There is no overt Land theology in this second cycle. The setting does not involve exile, and no recollection of the patriarchal Land promise is included. Settlement in and possession of the Land is simply assumed.[48] In the description of Israel's various sins, one finds a stress on pollution of the sanctuary and cult, but nothing of pollution of the Land. Moreover, although the sins described include transgressions which directly threaten retention of the Land in biblical literature, no connection is made here between these violations and the conditional nature of the hold on the Land.[49]

The Taxo narrative not only is devoid of any reference to the connection between obedience and Land, it also denies the basic deuteronomic assumption of an inherent connection between violation of the covenant and the misfortunes which befall Israel in the unfolding of her history. In direct opposition to that assumption, Taxo tells his sons that their "fathers" and "ancestors" had never violated the covenant,[50] and that the oppression Israel suffers in his own generation is ill deserved in relationship to the sins of other peoples and nations.[51] Indeed, the suffering goes beyond "all bounds of mercy" and is worse than the destruction and exile that befell the First Jewish Commonwealth (9:2).[52]

Such a claim to purity and sinlessness not only stands in stark contrast to the position of the author of *Jubilees*, who rests his doubled redemption scheme on a total repentance that includes "their sins and the sins of their fathers," but also is strange and unfitting in the context of traditional intercessions in biblical and post-biblical literature.[53] However, if one views Taxo's martyrdom and the argument that the suffering of Israel is undeserved in the general context of the *Aqedah* recalled by the references to God's "covenant and oath" in the frame and the first part of the revelation, the entire martyr story takes on a new perspective. The father urging his sons to martyrdom, the assertions of purity, and the confidence of divine response all point to an intercessory typology based on the *Aqedah*. Taxo's willingness to martyr his sons has its parallel in Abraham's comparable willingness. Similarly, the purity of Taxo and his sons reflected in the sinlessness of Israel is paralleled by the purity of Abraham and Isaac.

Interestingly, the narrative of Taxo is framed as intention"rather than as accomplished fact, thus making the parallel with the *Aqedah* even stronger. In both cases martyrdom activates divine intervention in the destiny of Israel. In the prehistory of the patriarchal period the intervention is a promissory consequence of, not a motivating force for, the martyrdom. In the end-time of Israel's history, however, divine intervention is foreknown, indeed, forecast by Taxo: "For if we do this, and do die, our blood will be avenged before the Lord" (9:7). An important transformation has taken place. No longer is the *Aqedah* the basis for an appeal on behalf of sinful patriarchal progeny, as it was when the Israelite nation first appeared on the historical stage at Sinai. Rather, at the end of Israel's history martyrdom becomes what it was in the patriarchal beginning: an activating force for the divine promise.

Insofar as the eschatological poem which follows focuses almost entirely on God's vindication of Israel, it would appear in the broadest sense to be an elaboration on Deut. 32:36-43.[54] This eschaton contains no reference to the Land. Israel will be raised to the "heaven of the stars," from whence she will view God's avenging destruction of her enemies on earth (10:9-10). The scholarly debate over the extent to which the extramundane abode should be understood literally or metaphorically[55] does not clarify the relationship between Land theology and eschatology in the *Testament*. If Israel's place in the end-time is literally in the "heaven of the stars," has the Land covenant, repeatedly referred to in the *Testament*, been abrogated? And if the description is a metaphorical one, what is the temporal future of Israel within such a metaphor?

The answers to such questions lie in the very aspect of the work which contemporary scholars have neglected, in the relationship between the *Testament* and the sacred text which it is recasting. It is no accident that for his eschaton the author again chose Deuteronomy 31-32 as the base structure. In that particular paradigm for Israel's future, the Land theme is notably underplayed. There no exile from the Land in the punishment stage and no return to the Land in the restoration—a perfect model for an eschaton that is to take place within the historical circumstances of the post-Herodian era when Israel is, and in fact for some period of time has been, settled in the Land. The single reference to the Land in the cycle of Deuteronomy 31-32 appears at the very end of the poem when God assures that He "will cleanse (atone for) the land of His people" (Deut. 32:43). Modelling the structure but not the substance of that ending, the author of the *Testament* places his eschatological reference to the Land promise not in the poem, but in Moses' response to Joshua's anxiety over Israel's future at the end of the *Testament*:

> It is not possible for the nations to drive them out or extinguish them completely. For God who has foreseen all things in the world will go forth, and

his covenant which was established, and by the oath which.... [MS ends] (12:12-13)

The closure is a crucial one which, like the chapters it is rewriting, ends as the biblical story of Israel begins, with God's commitment to the future of Israel in the Land.

Although Deuteronomy serves as the structural frame of reference for the *Testament*, the controlling metaphor in this rewriting is not the vision of Deuteronomy but rather the "covenant and oath" as set forth at the scene of the *Aqedah*. In the biblical description of the oath in that scene (Gen. 22:13),[56] the Land aspect of the covenantal promise is notably limited. The content of the oath expands to a full statement of the covenantal promises only later, when the *Aqedah* serves an intercessory function within Israelite history (Exod. 32:13).[57] By shifting the context of the covenant from an historical context back to the metaphysical stage of the patriarchs, namely to the scene of the *Aqedah*, the martyrdom of Taxo and his sons reverses the process. Again the covenant is primarily understood in terms of the promise of a future to the progeny of the martyrs, and again God's action on behalf of Israel is direct rather than mediated by the merits of the fathers. The Land promise is not lost. Rather, its primary place in the covenant has been superseded by the immediate issue at hand: the survival of the people of Israel, the promised seed of the patriarchs. The model for such a supersession is itself the *Aqedah* scene where, in response to contextual circumstance, the covenant is expressed most forcefully in terms of the promise of progeny.

The dialogue between Moses and Joshua immediately following the eschatological poem in the closing chapters of the *Testament* confirms this shift in perspective. In that dialogue Joshua expresses his anxiety about a future without Moses, the intercessor who is capable of "reminding the Lord of the ancestral covenant and the resolute oath" (11:17-19). Moses' response is to assure Joshua that neither his intercessions nor "the piety of this people" ultimately govern the destiny of Israel (12:8). That control rests only with God, who has foreseen everything from the beginning of Creation to the end of time and has assured Israel's future through his covenant.

The perspective at the end of the *Testament* is extra-historical. It asserts surety in fulfillment of the covenant and oath outside of an historical frame of reference. The immediate context for Moses' words is the conquest of the Land under the leadership of Joshua, yet the perspective is governed not by that context, but by the author's own theology and eschatology. "The end of the age" (12:4) returns to the beginning from which it was foreknown. The covenantal promises will be kept in spite of what experience seems to indicate, be it from the perspective of Abraham and Isaac ascending Mount Moriah or of Israel in the post-exilic period with fulfillment of the promises so little in evidence.

The structure of the *Testament of Moses* evidences a purposeful design. Within the parameters of historical time Israel will be rewarded and/or punished for its sins. The innocent and pure will be martyred and their martyrdom will have meritorious value. But ultimately, God's covenant and oath stand outside the parameters of experienced time. In and of themselves the divine covenant and oath, not intercession or covenantal nomism, make it "not possible for the nations to drive [the Israelites] out or extinguish them completely" (12:12).

CHAPTER 5

The Historical Covenant of *Pseudo-Philo*

U nlike the first two works, *Pseudo-Philo* covers not only the pentateuchal narratives, but those of Joshua, Judges and sections of 1 Samuel as well. However, the account is notably uneven. Only nineteen of the sixty-five chapters in the work focus on the Pentateuch, and there is a distinct difference between the styles adopted for presentation of the pentateuchal narratives and the early prophetic material. Like a chronicler, *Pseudo-Philo* presents a rapid and highly selective review of the period from Adam to the conquest of the Land, and into this review he inserts a few narratives not found in Hebrew Scriptures. In contrast, his rewriting of the early prophetic material, particularly of Judges, is extensive.

It has been suggested that the author of *Pseudo-Philo* had read *Jubilees*, and that his uneven presentation of the biblical narratives reflects an intent to supplement and extend the earlier work.[1] Indeed, certain aspects of *Pseudo-Philo*'s treatment of covenant theology suggest familiarity with *Jubilees*. In several passages created to describe the election of Israel, *Pseudo-Philo* uses a plant metaphor that in a positive voice complements the metaphoric "uprooting" used in *Jubilees* to describe Israel's rejection.[2] In addition, although he does not develop the Noah narratives to the same degree, *Pseudo-Philo*, like the author of *Jubilees*, introduces the patriarchal covenant in a prepatriarchal setting, uses Noah as a point of reference in relating Israel's history, and frequently describes Israel's election from a cosmic perspective.[3] Moreover, as we shall see, the two authors share certain perspectives on biblical Land theology that bespeak a common post-exilic point of view. However, the similarities at best confirm familiarity or reflect a common tradition, for significant differences in the theological agenda of the two writers argue against the notion that *Pseudo-Philo* was composed as a supplement to the earlier text.

The author of *Jubilees* is primarily interested in the covenantal relationship between God and Israel, in Israel's fidelity to that relationship, and in the extent to which eschatological fulfillment of the covenantal promises in the post-exilic period ultimately depends upon total repentance. In contrast, *Pseudo-Philo* is mainly concerned with God's involvement *within* the history of Israel and in divine, rather than Israelite, fidelity to the covenantal promises.[4] The author rewrites biblical narratives such that they demonstrate a divine plan and divine control at the individual as well as the national levels. Obedience is rewarded and disobedience is punished, but never is the ultimate fulfillment of the divine promises threatened. In contrast to Israel's erratic commitment to the covenant, God's fidelity consistently stands firm. The difference between such a theology and the eschatological perspective of the author of *Jubilees* not only discourages the notion of a supplemental relationship between the two works, but also, given the significance of theological premises, suggests a major difference in their respective treatments of the biblical concept of covenanted Land.

In spite of dramatic stylistic differences between the pentateuchal summary and the more elaborate presentation of Joshua and Judges, a certain thematic consistency governs *Pseudo-Philo*. In both sections one finds the dual emphasis upon a divinely-directed history and the surety of the fulfillment of God's promises in spite of Israel's infidelities. Moreover, the treatment of the various aspects of Land theology in the two sections is consistent. Indeed, when one approaches the uneven structure of the work as an internal matter, it becomes clear that one principle governing the treatment of the Land concept in the pentateuchal material is that the earlier section is developed to provide an appropriate and consistent background for the later narratives of Israel in the Land during and after the conquest. This principle is evident in *Pseudo-Philo*'s treatment of all aspects of biblical Land theology—the patriarchal Land promise, the descriptions of the Land, and the relationship between the Land and Law.

PATRIARCHAL HISTORY

In *Pseudo-Philo* the accounts of the patriarchal covenants are focused almost exclusively upon Abraham; covenantal encounters with the other forefathers are described more generally as promises "made to the fathers."[5] The Abraham material appears in a variety of forms: created narratives of a predictive character without biblical parallels; rewritten biblical narratives; and inserts, usually recollective and/or transitional in nature, into biblical contexts.[6]

The first reference to the election of Abraham comes in an interruption of the genealogies with which *Pseudo-Philo* begins his treatments of the

Genesis stories. At the time of the delivery of her son Serug, Melcah, wife of Reu, predicts the future birth and election of Abraham:

> From him there will be born in the fourth generation one who will set his dwelling on high and will be called perfect and blameless; and he will be the father of nations, and his covenant will not be broken, and his seed will be multiplied forever. (4:11)

No mention is made here of the Land; the promissory aspect of the covenant involves only assurance of multiple seed. Moreover, the promise of progeny is not Israel-centered. Abraham will be the "father of nations," a designation appropriate to the cosmic genealogical context in which the created passage is set. The treatment bears a certain similarity to that in *Jubilees* (2:19-20), where the covenant also first appears in a retrojected cosmic setting with no reference to the promise of the Land. However, whereas the stress in *Jubilees* is on the election of Israel and its relationship with God, in this *Pseudo-Philo* passage the covenantal focus is on the promise of multiple seed. The contrast involves more than a subtle distinction. It points to a very real difference in the two authors' understanding of the covenant, and, as we shall see, illuminates the nature of their respective departures from the Land-centered presentation of the covenant in the Genesis text.

The Land theme first appears in *Pseudo-Philo* in a miracle story set in another unbiblical predictive context. Imprisoned together with eleven other men protesting against the building of the tower at Babel, Abraham refuses to join in their escape plan. Instead, confident of divine assistance, he remains in the prison and, when placed for execution in a fiery furnace, is miraculously saved by an earthquake. The covenant scene follows in the form of a divine forecast in which God shares his thoughts and plans for Abraham's future with the reader.[7]

> And before all these I will choose my servant Abram. and I will bring him out from their land and will bring him into the land upon which my eye has looked from of old.... For there I will have my servant Abram dwell and will establish my covenant with him and will bless his seed and be lord for him as God forever. (7:4)

The passage parallels Gen. 12:1-2, but by presenting the scene through the omniscient lens of God's intent rather than through narration of the actual encounter, *Pseudo-Philo* is able to develop a particular interpretation of the Land covenant. Albeit the special character attributed to the Land, the focus for the first covenant-making no longer rests on the Land. The issue of Abraham's faithfulness is introduced in relationship to the building of the Tower of Babel (chapters 6 and 7) rather than in the context of his willingness to leave his native land[8] and family in direct response to a mysterious divine command. Moreover, here the content of covenant is particularly associated with election: the blessing of and assurance of relationship with Abraham's future seed. From this perspective, the Land is introduced as the locale for the election, rather than as itself a primary component of the covenant.[9]

The change does not involve a denial of the promise of Land. To the contrary, here as well as in subsequent additions to the biblical story Pseudo-Philo affirms the Land promise. However, his presentation does involve a shift of emphasis. Pseudo-Philo is primarily concerned with the promise of peoplehood and numbers, and the Land is significant insofar as it is necessary to the fulfillment of that promise. Pseudo-Philo always presents the promise of Land in association with that of seed. Thus, whereas the Land component of the triadal covenant occasionally stands alone in the biblical narrative, in Pseudo-Philo that status is given over to the promise of multiple progeny (18:5).[10]

The emphasis on seed is again evident in the single account of covenant-making with Abraham. Telescoping the promises given at Shechem (Gen. 12:7), after the separation from Lot (Gen. 13:15), and upon the prediction of Isaac's birth (Gen. 17:5, 7-8, 15) into a single encounter, Pseudo-Philo sets the scene of Abraham residing in Canaan immediately after separating from his nephew:

> And God appeared to Abram, saying: "To your seed I will give this land, and your name will be called Abraham, and Sarai, your wife, will be called Sarah. And I will give to you from her an everlasting seed and I will establish my covenant with you." (8:3)

Essentially the scenario is that of Gen. 17:4-16, with its change of the patriarchal name, formal statement of the covenantal relationship, and affirmation that the promised seed will in fact come from Sarai, now to be called Sarah.

However, a number of significant changes have taken place. The biblical passage is structured such that the promises of peoplehood and of Land are treated as dual components of the covenant. Each is stated separately and preceded by a formal statement of the covenantal relationship. In contrast, the structure of Pseudo-Philo's covenantal scene clearly highlights the promise of progeny: the Land will be given to Abraham's seed, that seed will be everlasting, and the covenant will be established with Abraham. Here, as in all subsequent references to the Land promise in the passages he creates, the author presents that promise in terms of Gen. 12:7, as a promise to Abraham's seed.[11] The selection of this particular verse is strik-ing for the more usual pattern in Genesis is the promise of land to the pa-triarchs alone, or to them and their descendants.[12]

Even more significantly, in his single direct presentation of the patriar-chal covenant, *Pseudo-Philo* has God promise Abraham an "everlasting seed" from Sarah. The presentation is striking, for nowhere in the biblical descriptions of patriarchal covenant-making is the promise of seed de-scribed as eternal.[13] Only possession of the Land and the covenant itself are "everlasting." Indeed, the biblical text *Pseudo-Philo* has chosen as the base for his covenant-making scene, contains just such descriptions: the covenant is forever ברית עולם and the Land an eternal possession אחזת עולם (Gen. 17:7-8). By applying the adjective "everlasting" solely to the promise of seed, *Pseudo-Philo* destroys the parallel language that equates Land and covenant in the biblical passage, elevates the promise of progeny, and denigrates the status of the Land promise as a focal point for the covenant.[14] Finally, in contrast to the biblical "land you sojourn in...all the land of Canaan" (Gen. 17:8), the land promised to the "everlasting seed" in *Pseudo-Philo* is one lacking territorial description. Neither here nor elsewhere in the work are geographic specifications provided as in the vari-ous biblical promissory narratives.

In addition to creating narratives which predict the patriarchal cove-nant, *Pseudo-Philo* also develops narrative structures to recollect that cove-nant. In Hebrew Scriptures, recollections of the promises to the forefathers function as a bridge between the patriarchal period and the exodus. In these transition passages no mention is made of the promise of progeny. To the contrary, the promissory references are, as previously described, notably Land-focused, thereby extending the bridge between the patriarchs and the exodus to the acquisition of the Land.[15] *Pseudo-Philo* does not even summa-rily include such narratives. Instead, he develops his own transition within a birth narrative which has Amram, Moses' father-to-be, protesting against a plan of the elders to counter the Egyptian slaughter of male children by refraining from cohabitation with their wives.[16]

> It will sooner happen that this age will be ended forever or the world will sink into the immeasurable deep or the heart of the abyss will touch the stars than that the race of the sons of Israel will be ended. And there will be fulfilled the covenant that God established with Abraham when he said, "Indeed your sons will dwell in a land not their own and will be brought into bondage and afflicted four hundred years."...Now therefore I will go and take my wife, and I will produce sons so that we may be made many on the earth. For God will not abide in his anger, nor will he forget his people

forever, nor will he cast forth the race of Israel in vain upon the earth; nor did he establish a covenant with our fathers in vain; and even when we did not exist, God spoke about these matters. (9:3-4)

Like the narratives created around Abraham,[17] Amram's speech views the election of Israel from a cosmic perspective. More important for our purposes, both contextually and substantively, the covenant as recollected here is associated primarily with the matter of fertility. The reference to being "cast forth in vain upon the earth" implies recognition of a Land aspect to God's covenantal relationship with Israel. However, that recognition not only is indirect, but again is set in causal relationship to fertility—in a situation of exile the promise of peoplehood cannot be fully achieved—rather than as a covenantal promise in its own right.

In addition to creating this recollection, *Pseudo-Philo* rewrites two pentateuchal passages which already contain recollections of the covenant. Both of these passages involve Moses' confrontations with God over Israelite infidelity and threats to the people's future as a result of those infidelities.[18] In the first instance, the dialogue over worship of the Golden Calf, God recollects the covenant by asking Moses:

Are the promises that I promised to your fathers when I said to them "To your seed I will give the land in which you dwell"—are they at an end? (12:4)

Thus, a citation of Gen. 12:7 supplants the biblical recollection where Moses reminds God of God's oath to Abraham, Isaac, and Jacob to "make your offspring as numerous as the stars of the heaven," and "to give to your offspring this whole land of which I spoke, to possess forever" (Exod. 32:13). The appeal of Gen. 12:7 as a replacement cannot be attributed simply to its conciseness. I would suggest, rather, that the author deliberately uses a recollective pattern that avoids the biblical language of a promise of a "whole" Land which the seed are "to possess forever."

In the second instance, the narrative of the rebellion at Kadesh Barnea, the biblical text recollects the Land promise to the patriarchs in a dramatic description of God's refusal to permit the wilderness generation to enter the Land:

Nevertheless, as I live and as the Lord's Presence fills the whole world, none of the men who have seen My Presence and the signs that I have performed in Egypt and in the wilderness, and who have tried Me these many times and have disobeyed Me, shall see the land that I promised on oath to their fathers; none of those who spurn Me shall see it. (Num. 14:21-23)[19]

Pseudo-Philo's description of the punishment contains none of this Promised Land language. Instead, God tells Moses how he will "afflict their bodies with fire in the wilderness" and their souls will be "shut up in the chambers of darkness" (15:5). Recollection of the patriarchs is then placed in a strikingly unbiblical addendum to the speech: God would report back to the fathers on how he had fulfilled his word to redeem their seed from Egypt, while the Israelites had been so inconstant that he now would "do to them as they wished." The Land promise has no place in such a rewriting, for no longer does the recollection involve the land referred to in the Numbers narrative. Instead, citing Gen. 15:13 to recall God's promise to redeem the patriarchal seed—"Your seed will stay a while in a land not its own, and I will judge the nation whom it will serve"—*Pseudo-Philo* substitutes the promise of redemption from Egypt for the Land promise (15:5). The alteration, like much of the rewriting, is theologically motivated. The biblical text explicitly raises the question of God reneging on a promise to bring the wilderness generation into the Land. The rewritten version removes that question by changing the promise to redeeming Abraham's descendants from Egypt, a promise that in fact had been kept.

In addition to creating new recollective scenes and rewriting biblical ones, *Pseudo-Philo* also inserts simple phrases or clauses recollecting the promises to the patriarchs into new contexts. Avoiding the Land-focused contexts in which such recollective phrases appear in multiple pentateuchal passages, the author judiciously places his recollections of the patriarchal promises into contexts which involve numbers and peoplehood.[20] One such insertion is made into the narrative of the Israelite crossing of the Red Sea. *Pseudo-Philo* has the Israelites bitterly ask Moses: "Are these the covenants which He made with our fathers saying: 'To your seed will I give the land wherein you dwell?'" (10:2). Not only does the biblical narrative contain no reference to the patriarchal covenant (the frightened Israelites simply express their desire to return to Egypt), but the insertion of the Gen. 12:7 citation in the context of the Red Sea scenario is barely appropriate. Awkward as it is, that citation places recollection of the patriarchal promise of Land in the context of a perceived threat to the survival of the patriarchal seed, thereby reenforcing not only the connection between Land and people, but also the association of covenant with progeny and peoplehood.

Another elaboration, added to the description of the Yom Kippur legislation, makes an explicit connection between covenant and population. God will "declare the number of those who are to die and who are to be born." A "fast of mercy...for your own souls," is to be kept "so that the promises made to your fathers may be fulfilled" (13:6).[21] The addition serves no purpose other than to strengthen understanding of the promises as specifically involving population growth. That understanding is reenforced by another recollection, this time of a promise "declared to your fathers in a foreign land" and inserted into the description of the first census (14:1). Again allowing the reader access to God's mind and intent, *Pseudo-Philo* justifies the census as evidence of the constancy of the divine promise:

> Write down their number until I fulfill all that I have spoken to their fathers and until I set them firmly in their own land;[22] for not a single word from what I have spoken to their fathers will I renege on, from those that I said to them: "Your seed will be like the stars of heaven in multitude." By number they will enter the land, and in a short time they will become without number. (14:2)

Composed as a midrash on Num. 1:1-3, the elaboration creatively intensifies the focus on peoplehood as the essential aspect of the patriarchal covenant. Landedness is there, but again only as the condition under which the assurance of great numbers will be met. Outside the Land, the people can and should be counted; once established inside the Land, their numbers will be uncountable in fulfillment of the promise of multiplication of the seed.

Thus *Pseudo-Philo*'s insertions of phrases/clauses recollecting the patriarchal promise follow the same pattern as his created narratives and his rewriting of promissory biblical passages. By context, by citation of Gen. 12:7, and/or by creative changes to the narrative, he uses his recollective inserts to emphasize the promise of great numbers and treat the territorial aspect of the covenant as a means through which the multiplying of the people will be expedited. Complementing this, he omits biblical recollections which, by nature of their contexts, place strong emphasis on the Land aspect of the promise.

The second part of the work is more developed and the narratives therein infinitely more complex. Nonetheless, the author's goal with recollections of the patriarchal promises is the same as in the earlier section: to focus the narrative such that elected peoplehood constitutes the essential core of the covenant. And the structures employed in pursuit of that goal remain similar to those in the pentateuchal section: new narratives are created, and biblical recollections with a strong territorial perspective are rewritten, replaced or ignored.

Conquest and apportionment of the Land is the central motif of the biblical book of Joshua. Multiple references are made to God giving the Land directly to the conquering Israelites, and recollections of the Land promise to the fathers are placed at seminal points in the biblical narrative—at

Joshua's assumption of leadership (Josh. 1:6), upon entrance into the Land (Josh. 5:6), and at the completion of the conquest (Josh. 21:41).[23] In *Pseudo-Philo*'s rewriting of these narratives the Land promise is significantly underplayed. None of the many references to God giving the Land to the conquering Israelites are included,[24] and each of the recollections of the Land promise to the patriarchs is either diluted or deleted. Instead of assuring Joshua that he would apportion "the land that I swore to their fathers to give them" (Josh. 1:6), God simply recalls how he had told Moses that "the kings of the Amorites" would be delivered into Joshua's hands (20:2). In the address to the nation created for Joshua which immediately follows the rewritten charge, *Pseudo-Philo* includes a reference to "words" spoken to the fathers, but the promissory reference is to preservation of the people, not acquisition of the Land.

> But if you do not heed his voice and you become like your fathers, your affairs will be spoiled and you yourselves will be crushed and your name will perish from the earth. And where will the words be that God spoke to your fathers? (20:4)

The point is made explicit in what immediately follows, an analysis of the reaction of the nations should the Israelites not heed the warning and be destroyed. Otherwise contextually awkward, the insertion of concern over the nations believing God to have failed triggers a recollection of a similar speculation in the biblical descriptions of Moses' intercessions at Sinai (Deut. 9:28) and Kadesh Barnea (Num. 14:16), both occasions when the Israelites were threatened with destruction.

The biblical recollection of the Land promise on the occasion of the circumcision of the Israelites when they first enter the Land (Josh. 5:6) is completely deleted. Keeping the account of the punishment of the wilderness generation intact as an explanation for the disappearance of Joshua's peer generation (20:1), *Pseudo-Philo* mentions neither the entrance into the Land nor the ceremony of circumcision that accompanies the occasion. Even more significant is the absence of any attention to the subject which comprises the heart of the biblical book (Josh. 9-21), the actual conquest and apportionment of the Land.[25] In four verses the narrative moves from a description of Joshua's appointment to a national celebration of victory set at Gilgal.[26]

> All the house of Israel sang together in a loud voice saying: "Behold our Lord has fulfilled what he said to our fathers: 'To your seed I will give the land in which you may dwell, a land flowing with milk and honey.' And behold he led us into the land of our enemies and delivered them broken in

spirit before us, and he is the God who sent word to our fathers in the secret dwelling places of the souls, saying, 'Behold the Lord has done everything that he has said to us.' And truly now we know that God has established every word of his Law that he spoke to us on Horeb.'" (21:9)

The celebratory song contains a recollection of the patriarchal promise and a clear Land dimension. But it has none of the force of the celebration of conquest which it replaces:

> The Lord gave to Israel the whole country which He had sworn to their fathers that He would give them; they took possession of it and settled in it. The Lord gave them rest on all sides, just as He had promised to their fathers on oath. Not one man of all their enemies withstood them; the Lord delivered all their enemies into their hands. Not one of the good things which the Lord had promised to the House of Israel was lacking. Everything was fulfilled. (Josh. 21:41-43)

The focus in the biblical version is singular: the Land. In contrast, *Pseudo-Philo*'s citation of Gen. 12:7 again interposes the dual perspective that connects fulfillment of the Land promise with that of elected peoplehood.

A similar, but more obvious shift of focus to the peoplehood promise is effected in the rewriting of the testament scene at the end of Joshua's life. In the biblical version of the testament Joshua reviews how God had guided Israel throughout its history, from Abraham's move from Mesopotamia to Canaan, through the exodus, the defeat of the Amorites, and the frustration of Balaam in the wilderness, to the defeat of the Canaanite nations, and charges the people to choose fidelity to the God who had so redeemed them (Josh. 24:2-24). Using the structural outline of a look backward, *Pseudo-Philo* changes the theme of the historical review from recollection of a series of redemptive acts culminating in acquisition of the Land to a description of the wondrous development of a great people out of the seed of Abraham. Beginning with a recollection of his own narrative of the patriarch's origins in Mesopotamia, he recalls the promise of Gen. 12:7 (23:5a), devotes more than half of the total review to the miraculous seed that would flow from the "closed up" Sarah (5b-8),[27] and moves rapidly to a celebration of the giving of the Law at Sinai,[28] giving sparse attention to the exodus, with its close links to the Land promise (Exod. 3:8, 17; 6:2-8; Deut. 4:37-8). He does close the review with entrance into the Land and a citation from the parallel passage in Joshua (24:13), but within the selection of recalled "wonders" acquisition of the Land loses the climactic quality it has in the biblical narrative. No longer is physical movement—from Mesopotamia to Canaan, from Canaan to Egypt, from Egypt to the wilderness, and ultimately victorious return to Canaan—the governing motif of Israel's history. Instead, that motif becomes the history of the promise to create a people, from the original assurance of seed from the unfertile matriarch to the birth of a people, from the solidification of that people into a single unit at Sinai to their entrance as an elected people into the Land.

The resulting shift of emphasis is reinforced in the charge created for the closing of Joshua's testament. Again he links the Land to the peoplehood theme, with the greater stress on the latter. If the Israelites listen to their fathers, their Land "will be renowned over all the earth," their seed will be "special among all the peoples." They will be planted "like a desirable vine" and tended "like a loveable flock," and, ultimately, they and their seed will be given eternal life such that in the end of time their fathers will know that "I have not chosen you in vain (23:12-13)."

The biblical book of Judges contains just one recollection of the covenant, one which expresses the covenantal relationship solely in terms of the promise of Land (Judg. 2:1-2).[29] *Pseudo-Philo* deletes that recollection, even rewriting the context in which the recollection appears, and develops new recollections and references to the election of Israel, which he inserts into his narratives of the various judges. Four of the recollections are placed in newly created scenes which center on the theme of an eternally elected people. In the Kenaz narrative the theme is placed in a dream vision which the priest Eliezar related on his deathbed to his son Phinehas (28:4).[30] In the Deborah sequence it is stated in the initial confrontation between the judge and the people (30:7).[31] In the Jephthah narrative the theme appears in a prayer offered by the people on the urging of the new leader (39:7), and in the Samuel story it is placed in the mouth of the Israelites despairing in their quest for a new leader (49:6).[32] Only the Jephthah recollection contains a reference to the Land, which again is causally linked to the promise of peoplehood:

> Look, Lord, upon the people that you have chosen, and may you not destroy the vine that your right hand has planted, in order that this nation, which you have had from the beginning, and always preferred and for which you made dwelling places and brought into the land you promised, may be for you as an inheritance. (39:7)

On two other occasions *Pseudo-Philo* inserts recollection of the covenant into passages he rewrites rather than creates. In a manner not unlike that employed in his rewriting of Joshua's final testament, he transforms Deborah's victory song into an elaborate recollection of the history of wonders performed by God on behalf of Israel. Again the emphasis is on election, the promise of seed, and preservation of the people; again minimal attention is paid to the exodus, which associates redemption with the promise and acquisition of the Land. Deborah begins with the election of the nation through Abraham (32:1), elaborately describes the offering and saving of Isaac at the *Aqedah*, the births of twins to the barren Rebecca and the twelve sons to Jacob (32:2-6), passes over the exodus with a few words—"and he brought them out of there"—and moves to an extensive description of wondrous alterations of nature at Sinai (32:7-8) subsequently paralleled by the delay of the sunset in the war against the Amorites and the defeat of Sisera's army by the stars.[33] The review is presented as evidence of God's faithfulness to "ancient and recent promises"; heaven and earth (the witnesses of the covenant in Deuteronomy) as well as the angels of the heavenly host are urged to report back to the fathers "in their chambers of souls" that God had not forgotten his promise of "many wonders will I do for your sons" (32:13).[34]

A comparable replacement occurs in the rewriting of Gideon's challenge to the angel who calls him to leadership. In the biblical narrative Gideon bitterly asks: "Why has all this befallen us? Where are all His wondrous deeds about which our fathers told us saying, 'Truly the Lord brought us up from Egypt?'" (Judg. 6:13). In *Pseudo-Philo*'s rewriting, oratorical celebration of the exodus again is replaced, this time with the fact of election alone serving as "the wonders that our fathers described to us" (35:2).

Pseudo-Philo's apparent lack of interest in the exodus, with his clear avoidance of the type of panegyric that theme receives in biblical literature, is an extension of his overall treatment of the patriarchal promises. The rewriting is primarily motivated by the author's theological posture regarding the surety of the covenant and divine constancy. Given that posture, nothing can be promised to the patriarchs that in fact is not delivered on the historical stage. Concomitantly, no experience in Israel's history—be it within the biblical period or beyond—can call into question that which God has already promised. Interwoven, the two standards account both for the author's version of the patriarchal covenant and for his selectivity in rewriting Israel's subsequent history. Viewed from such a perspective, *Pseudo-Philo*'s treatment of the biblical covenant and Land is internally consistent. The Land promise is always directed to the patriarchal seed, not to the patriarch alone or to him and his seed, for in fact no patriarch gained possession of the Land.

The covenant assures eternal peoplehood, not everlasting possession of the Land, for in historical fact, once achieved Israelite possession was not eternal. Within Israel's history possession was lost, and the fact of that loss—the Babylonian exile—negates any statement of the patriarchal covenant that would include divine assurance of everlasting possession. As for the exodus, it cannot be viewed as a singular expression of the patriarchal covenant as it is presented in the biblical narratives (that is, as the bridge between the promise of Land to the fathers and the acquisition thereof by their progeny), for in fact the experience of redemption and entry into the Land is not singular. If all of Israel's history reflects the constancy of God's promises, then the redemption from Babylonian exile and the return to the Land in 538 must also have a place within the framework of the patriarchal covenant. Consequently, not unlike the Chronicler,[35] *Pseudo-Philo* plays down the exodus motif in his rewriting. The exodus has significance, but only as an act of redemption in fulfillment of a particular finite promise which does not specifically involve the covenant.[36] Insofar as redemption and Land acquisition are covenantal, they do not involve singular, finite events in time. In this rewriting they become phenomenological, ongoing conditions which, assured by God's fidelity and constancy, are repeatedly played out in Israel's history.

THE NAME AND CHARACTER OF THE LAND

Pseudo-Philo's treatment of the descriptions of the Land is closely related to his handling of the recollections of the covenant. Nothing is promised which is not in fact fulfilled, either in subsequent narratives or in post-biblical history up to the writer's own day. Not only does the author omit all references to "eternal possession of the Land," he also deletes or rewrites any scriptural passage that contains geographic or territorial descriptions of the Land, be it in his summary presentation of covenant-making (8:3) or in any of his later recollections of it. His description of the Sinai scene avoids both the reference to the "whole" Land in Exod. 32:13 as well as the geographical specifications of Moses' recollections of Sinai in Deut. 1:6-7. And whereas a description of the geographic dimensions of the Land precedes recollection of the patriarchal promise in the biblical narrative of Moses' last days (Deut. 34:1-4), *Pseudo-Philo*'s version of that scene avoids both the geographic dimensions and the recollection of the promise to the patriarchs: "Then the Lord showed him the land and all that is in it and said, 'This is the land that I will give to my people'" (19:10). Similarly, the geographic description which the biblical writer uses to introduce the conquest under Joshua (Josh. 1:3), as well as several references to "the whole land" in the description of the conquest (Josh. 2:24; 9:24 21:41), are all absent.

Pseudo-Philo does, however, attribute a special metaphysical quality to the Land. It is a place upon which God had "looked from of old,"[37] one from which He had deliberately withheld the "springs of [his] wrath" at the time of the Flood (7:4).[38] It is "flowing with milk and honey" (15:4; 21:9), a "holy land"[39] watered by a place in the heavens specifically designated for that purpose (19:10).[40] Nonetheless, certain significant aspects of the biblical treatment are lacking in *Pseudo-Philo's* descriptions. He never ascribes personality or moral action to the Land in the manner of Lev. 18:28 and Num. 13:32. And though he describes God as "giving" Israel the Land, he never explicitly states that the Land belongs to God.

The most striking aspect of *Pseudo-Philo's* Land descriptions is the absence of the mixed biblical message regarding ownership. As noted earlier, in the Torah books the Land belongs at times to God, at times to Israel, and on many occasions, to the nations which Israel is to dispossess. In contrast, *Pseudo-Philo* is markedly consistent with attribution of ownership. Using the phrase "land of Canaan" on only two occasions and then only by way of citation (8:1; 23:5), he also deletes the many biblical attributives that associate the Land with the indigenous population.[41] Moreover, throughout his text he reconstructs narratives such that Israelite ownership of the Promised Land is casually assumed. Abraham's departure from Mesopotamia is a leave-taking from "their," not his own, land (7:4). In his brief summary of the Law, honoring parents is tied to many days "in *your* land" (11:9); the prohibition against coveting is supported by the warning "lest others should covet *your* land" (11:13). And in his description of the ritual sacrifices to offered in the case of leprosy, the levitical "in the land of Canaan" (Lev. 14:34) is replaced by "in *your* land" (13:3). (All emphases mine.)

This pattern—deletion of references to a land of the Canaanites and insertion of deliberately casual language of possession on the part of the Israelites—is sustained in his rewriting of the Joshua/Judges narratives.[42] In confronting the two and a half tribes who had constructed an altar by the side of the Jordan, *Pseudo-Philo* has Joshua and elders say: "What are these deeds that are done among you, when we have not even yet settled in *our* Land? Are not these the words that Moses spoke to you in the wilderness, saying, 'Beware that on entering *your* land you grow corrupt'" (22:2).[43] Joshua summons "all Israel in *their* land" to hear his testament and renew the covenant (23:1). Under the oppression of Sisera, the Israelites complain that they have been humiliated "so that we cannot dwell in *our* own land" (30:4).[44]

Particularly telling is *Pseudo-Philo's* account of the encounter between Jephthah and Getal, the king of Ammon (39:8-9).[45] The conflict is, as in Judges, over the "land of the Amorites (Judg. 11:21; Ps.-Philo 39:9). But whereas the biblical book has Ammon charging the Israelites with having taken his land, here it is Jephtah who lays the charge of stealing Israelite cities against Ammon. Moreover, whereas the author of Judges acknowledges conflicting theological claims—the God of Israel, not Chemosh, god of Ammon, "dispossessed the Amorites"—justifies the conquest on historical grounds (Judg. 11:23-4), in his reworking of the dialogue *Pseudo-Philo* presents the argument in universal theological terms that deny any basis whatsoever to the Ammonite:

> Truly I have learned that God has brought you forward that I may destroy you unless you cease from the iniquity by which you wish to harm Israel. And so I will come to you. For they are not gods, as you say they are, who have given you the inheritance that you possess; but because you have been deceived by following after stones, fire will come after you for vengeance. (39:9)

The Land belongs to the Israelites because God gave it to them in conquest. The theme is not a new one; indeed, it is repeatedly expressed in Joshua. The innovation comes in what is omitted: the idea that this Land in particular belongs to God and the concept that its earlier inhabitants had had a right of ownership (by virtue of occupation) which they had forfeited. By deleting both of these, *Pseudo-Philo* not only removes the inherent tension between the various ascriptions of ownership in biblical literature, but offsets any future, post-biblical assertion that physical occupation in and of itself would suggest right of possession.

The rewriting is significant because it has immediate repercussions for the biblical concept of a conditional covenant, of an inherent connection between adherence to the Law and retention of the Land. To a significant extent, this conditional covenant rests upon the notion that God owns the Land and that if the Israelites violate the Law given at Sinai, they will be dispossessed as the previous occupants had been. It is not surprising, therefore, to find that *Pseudo-Philo* retains notably little of the biblical link between Land and Law, be it expressed in terms of specific legislation or in the broader terms of a conditional covenant that makes retention of the Land contingent on fidelity to the Law.

THE LAND AND THE LAW

Lacking interest in specific legislation, *Pseudo-Philo* limits his summary of pentateuchal law to an interpretive exposition of the Ten Commandments, followed by brief references to sacrifices, leprosy, legislated holidays, and to tithing.[46] Within this limited presentation the great anticipation of Landedness and the intimate association of Land and Law which permeate biblical legislation are nowhere to be found. There are no enumerations of specific commandments to be kept "when you come to the Land," no concern with defilement and pollution, and no specific violations to be avoided lest the Land be lost. Detached from its levitical Land base, tithing is instituted in the context of the census so as to recall the wonders done on behalf of the small number of Israelites redeemed from Egypt (14:4), and major festivals are described with no mention either of their connection to the Land or to pilgrimage.[47]

References to the Land are few and notably casual. Certain sacrifices are to offered "if there be leprosy in your land" (13:3), and coveting is forbidden lest "others should covet your land" (11:13). The choice of these particular commandments out of all the Land-based legislation in the Pentateuch is not a haphazard selection. Each involves a certain manipulation of biblical texts, and each provides an opportunity for using the phrase "your Land" in place of biblical phrasing that the author wishes to avoid. In the levitical prescription of the sacrifices to be brought in the case of leprosy, there is no mention of the Land; rather, the context is the "camp" (Lev. 14:3). However, in Lev. 14:34, which prescribes the rituals for dealing with a leprous house, one finds the words "the land of Canaan…the land you possess." Similarly, the biblical prohibition against coveting (Exod. 20:14) contains no reference to the Land. However, in Exod. 34:24 the command for the triennial pilgrimage is supported by "I will drive out nations from your path and enlarge your territory; no one will covet your land when you go up to appear before the Lord your God." I would suggest that in both instances *Pseudo-Philo* has used similarity of context to replace biblical phrasing he finds unsuitable. In the case of leprosy, he substitutes "your land" for the unacceptable "land of Canaan." With the prohibition against coveting, he shifts "your land" to a new context which involves coveting, but which does not contain the equally unacceptable biblical connection between enlargement of territory (full acquisition of the Land as geographically described in the biblical version of the Land promise) and obedience to the commandment of pilgrimage.[48]

Pseudo-Philo's aversion to linking acquisition of the Land to fulfillment of commandments is consistent with his overall treatment of biblical Land theology. In his versions of patriarchal covenant as well of that conveyed at Sinai the geographic dimensions and the scope of Israel's tenure rights are both omitted. Committed to demonstrating how God remains faithful to his word—"God has established every word of his Law that he spoke tous on Horeb (21:9)—*Pseudo-Philo* presents the conquest in the time of Joshua as a fulfillment of the promise to the patriarchs as well as to the Sinai generation." By identifying success in conquest with God's fulfillment of both, he limits the Law/Land connection to acquisition of the Land and breaks the biblical connection between subsequent Israelite fidelity to the Law and retention of the Land.

Nonetheless, he does not totally ignore the conditional aspect of the covenant of Sinai. Interested only in depriving exile from the Land of covenantal theological significance, *Pseudo-Philo* does in fact create a connection between adherence to the command to honor parents and prosperity.

> Love your father and your mother, and you shall honor them, and then your light will rise. And I will command the heaven, and it will give forth its rain, and the earth will give back fruit more quickly. And you will live many days and dwell in your land, and you will not be without sons, for your seed will not be lacking in people to dwell in it. (11:9)

The language here is considerably softer and the connection less direct than its biblical counterpart, which specifies "that you may long endure on the land which the Lord your God is giving you" (Exod. 20:12). By deleting the contingency or conditional language of the biblical למען ("in order that") and by presenting "dwelling in the land" as only one of a series of consequences which, not insignificantly, conclude with the reward of great numbers, *Pseudo-Philo* successfully deletes the immediate link between obedience and retention of the Land as presented in the biblical version of the command.[49]

The consequences of obedience which *Pseudo-Philo* enumerates are ones which appear in biblical *tochachot*. But in the biblical structure there is also a strong negative component emphasizing loss of the Land which complements (and frequently overpowers) the positive reward aspect. In contrast, *Pseudo-Philo* avoids the threatening tone of a *tochacha*, substituting in its place a general promise of fertility for adherence to the commandments, a prediction of how the commandments in fact will not be kept, and an assurance that, nonetheless, God will ultimately remain faithful to his promises.

> If they walk in my ways, I will not abandon them but will have mercy on them always and bless their seed; and the earth will quickly yield its fruit, and there will be rains for their advantage, and it will not be barren. But I know for sure that they will make their ways corrupt and I will abandon them, and they will forget the covenants that I have established with their fathers; but nevertheless I will not forget them forever. For they will know in the last days that on account of their own sins their seed was abandoned,[50] because I am faithful in my ways. (13:10)

The passage is particularly indicative of the way in which *Pseudo-Philo* selects and adapts biblical material for his own purposes. The reward promised for fidelity to the covenant here is markedly similar to the one described in Lev. 26:3-5, 9-10:

> If you follow My laws and faithfully observe My commandments, I will grant your rains in their season, so that the earth shall yield its produce and the trees of the field their fruit. Your threshing shall overtake the vintage, and your vintage shall overtake the sowing; you shall eat your fill of bread and dwell securely in your land (3-5)....I will look with favor upon you, and make you fertile and multiply you; and I will maintain My covenant with you. You shall eat old grain long stored, and you shall have to clear out the old to make room for the new. (9-10)

Significantly, the middle section of the Leviticus passage (26:6-8), which stresses the Land, is not used in the rewriting.[51] It is the last section of the levitical passage (26:10-11) which has no Land focus—"I will establish My abode in your midst, and I will not spurn you. I will be ever present in your midst: I will be your God and you shall be My people"—that appears in negative form in *Pseudo-Philo*'s description of abandonment.

A major structural change has taken place. The author has shifted from the conditional voice of "if" to the absolute voice of divine foreknowledge—"I know for sure." Consequently, in spite of the Leviticus 26 base, the passage no longer bears the structure or tone of a *tochacha*. Moreover, the structure of the passage parallels that of Deut. 31:18, a description of a series of acts and consequences followed by a disavowing conjunction, "yet/nevertheless."[52] But whereas the closure to the prediction in the Deuteronomy passage reaffirms God's hidden countenance—"Yet I will keep My countenance hidden on that day because of all the evil they have done in turning to other gods"—in this summary of the Law, God states exactly the opposite: "But nevertheless I will not forget them forever" (13:10). The same type of formulation appears in the one-scene summary of Moses' farewell speeches. The prophet predicts rather than threatens that God, not the Israelites, "will depart from your land." Consequently, their enemies will rule over them, "but not forever, because He will remember the covenant that he established with your fathers" (19:2).[53] The pattern is consistent: threats are phrased as predictions, exile from the Land is never mentioned,[54] and God's fidelity to the covenant is always assured.

Pseudo-Philo grounds this assurance, the central motif in his covenant theology, in a reconstruction of the intercession scene on Sinai. Having substituted the promise of "eternal seed" for the eternal grant of the Land in the patriarchal covenant, he replaces the divine threat of imminent destruction at Sinai with a long-term prediction: When the Israelites enter the Land, they will do even greater iniquities. Yet God will "make peace with them," and the Temple ("a house...for me") will be built. But when the Israelites yet again sin, the Temple will be destroyed and "the race of men will be to me like a drop from a pitcher and will be reckoned like spittle" (12:4). Given the substance of the divine prediction, Moses' response, a plea equating abandonment of Israel with abandonment of the entire world, elicits an assurance of mercy that clearly applies to Israel's future history. *Pseudo-Philo* repeats the scenario in his narrative of the end of Moses' life. This time the predictive form has a biblical base: God's description of Israel's future in Deut. 31:16-18. But whereas the biblical text contains only the divine prediction, *Pseudo-Philo* reconstructs it as another intercessory dialogue. Recalling his anger at Horeb, God repeats the prediction made at Sinai: the Temple where the Israelites will serve him for 740 years will be turned over to their enemies who will destroy it (19:7). Again Moses pleads for mercy: "correct them for a time, but not in anger" (19:9). This time, however, he receives not only an affirmative response, but also a sign. "Like the bow" at the time of Noah, Moses' staff will serve as God's reminder "all the days" so that whenever the Israelites sin, God's anger will be limited. They will be spared in accordance with the divine mercy which Moses' appeals have activated (19:11).

The dialogical structure aside, *Pseudo-Philo*'s rewriting follows the general outlines of Deut. 31:16-18, where prediction replaces warning and abandonment by God stands in place of exile from the Land. Clearly, this biblical text provides the pattern for the notably consistent treatment of a variety of key passages in *Pseudo-Philo*: the intercession scene on Sinai (12:4, 8-10), his summary of the Law (13:10), and the condensation of Moses' final addresses (19:2). In each instance prediction replaces biblical warning and abandonment by God replaces the threat of loss of the Land. Each of these passages also contains an assurance of God's mercy and fidelity to the covenant, a theme also drawn, but far more creatively, from Deuteronomy 31. Moses' staff is substituted for the witness poem referred to in Deut. 31:21 and presented as an assurance of God's "return" and ultimate vindication of Israel. However, the motivation for that vindication, the haughty assumptions of Israel's enemies gloating over her fall, bears no relationship to the covenant. So *Pseudo-Philo* instead uses the staff as "a witness between Me and My people" (19:11) that, like Moses' intercessory activity, will activate divine mercy. The reconstruction involves a major shift in covenantal perspective. Whereas the poem stands as God's witness against Israel in Deuteronomy (31:21), the staff in *Pseudo-Philo* stands as a "witness" for all time against God's anger whenever Israel sins. Unlike the poem, which is to remind the Israelites of their covenantal responsibilities, the staff serves solely to ensure God's fidelity to the covenant. Such a theo-

logical posture totally undermines the biblical notion of conditional covenant. In this covenant theology there not only is no theologically significant place for the Land, but also no role for a repentant Israel.[55] The result
is not unlike that set forth in the last cycle of the *Testament of Moses*. Both
works stress intercession instead of national repentance, and each offers an
innovative intercessory substitute after Moses's death. But whereas the
substitute in the *Testament*, Taxo's martyrdom as a reenactment of the
Aqedah, functions only in an eschatological framework, in *Pseudo-Philo*, the
staff, activator of God's mercy, is the governing factor in all of Israel's history.

The primacy of God's covenanted mercy is the principle that *Pseudo-
Philo* wishes to demonstrate in presenting the beginning of the national history in the Land. Having developed the new covenantal paradigm in his
summary of pentateuchal narratives, he applies it, almost as an exegetical
tool, to the rewriting of Joshua and Judges. In his reworking of the book of
Joshua, the deletion of the threat of disinheritance is most glaring. Implied
in the charge to Joshua (Josh. 1:6-7)[56] and in the dual stances on Mounts
Ebal and Gerizim (Josh. 8:30ff.) at the beginning of the biblical book, the
threat is explicitly stated in Joshua's final testament to the people: "you will
perish from this good land which the Lord your God has given you" (Josh.
23:12-13, 15-16). None of this concern is retained in *Pseudo-Philo*'s rewriting. No reference is made to the Land in the charge to Joshua (20:2), in
the description of the renewal of the covenant no mention is made of the
stand on Gerizim, mountain of the curse (21:10), and Joshua's final testament contains only enumeration of the blessings that will ensue from obedience (23:12-13). Moreover, while acquisition of the Land is presented as
fulfillment of the promises to the fathers (21:9), in the rewards promised
for future obedience continued tenure of the Land is not mentioned. Instead, the focus is on God's care of the people in time and eternal life at
the end of time (23:12-13).[57] The omission of the threat of loss of the Land
cannot be attributed to an accident of summary, for even in a created addition to the narrative, Joshua's address to the nation on his accession to
leadership, destruction of the people, not loss of the Land, is the threatened consequence of infidelity (20:4).[58]

Concomitant with his deletion of the threat of exile, in his exposition
Pseudo-Philo creates opportunities to demonstrate the ongoing functioning
of the divine mercy which had been activated by Moses' intercessions. In
one instance he has Joshua recall, after the model of Moses, how he had
appealed to God's mercy "to sustain your people" when Achan stole from
the forbidden booty (21:4). In another he turns a narrative on its head in
order to provide occasion for an appeal to divine mercy. In the biblical

story of the altar constructed by Reuben, Gad, and half of Manasseh, the two and a half tribes successfully convince the representatives of the people that the altar was never intended for sacrifices (Josh. 22:26ff.). No sin is committed, and no appeal to mercy is called for. In *Pseudo-Philo's* version, however, the two and a half tribes do intend to offer sacrifices upon their altar, the very building of which is compared to the construction of the Golden Calf. The plea for "mercy on the covenant with the sons of your servants" (22:6-7) which follows implicitly recollects the parent appeal at Sinai.

Such inversions are not necessary with the book of Judges, for it is replete with tales of Israel's violation of the covenant, the consequent punishment at the hands of the various Canaanite nations, and appeals to God's mercy. However, the biblical work begins with a summary overview (chapter 2) that is theologically unacceptable to *Pseudo-Philo*. In order to test Israel's faithfulness, God had purposely left the work of conquest incomplete during Joshua's lifetime (Judg. 2:22-23). The Israelites repeatedly fail that test. They remain faithful during the lifetimes of the various leaders God sends out of pity for their moanings, but their fidelity is short-lived, for after each judge they revert to their old infidelities (Judg. 2:11-19). Consequently, God determines not to "drive out before them any of the nations that Joshua left when he died," that is, not to complete the Israelite conquest of the Land (Judg. 2:21). The stories of the various judges that follow then fill in the details of this preview. Contextually the biblical summary serves as a bridge between the narratives of Joshua and Judges. At the same time, it elaborates on the resolution of the contradiction between presumption of a full conquest (Josh. 21:41) and the final testament which acknowledges a "remnant" of the nations remaining in the Land (Josh. 23:12-13).

None of this material appears in *Pseudo-Philo*. Having focused the covenant primarily on peoplehood and having omitted all references to "whole Land" as well as to specific borders in his descriptions of the promise and the subsequent conquest, *Pseudo-Philo* has no contradiction to resolve. In his narrative the Israelites simply proclaim at Gilgal that "the Lord has done everything that he has said to us" (21:9), and in *Pseudo-Philo's* version of the leader's final testament, Joshua reveals God's confirmation of that fulfillment (23:11). The problem of the biblical Joshua thus avoided, *Pseudo-Philo* proceeds to delete the theologically troublesome preview of Judges 2 and to weave his own theology into the narratives of various judges. The cyclical pattern is retained in these rewritten stories: the Israelites sin, are punished, repent, are sent a new leader, and after his/her death, sin again. But instead of the details of a broken covenant and a

failed or incomplete conquest, *Pseudo-Philo's* narratives consistently minimize repentance and emphasize how God's mercy sustains the covenantal
relationship in spite of Israel's behavior.

In the biblical text divine mercy ("pity") is mentioned once in the preview summary of Judges (2:18) and nowhere again in the individual narratives that follow. In contrast, in the rewriting there are a number of
scenarios in which the judge and/or the people reflect upon the functioning
of divine mercy in their history. After Phinehas reveals his father's description of Israel's sinfulness, Kenaz and the people note that their sins would
warrant destruction, but "according to the abundance of his mercy" God
"will spare us" (28:5).[59]

The theme is further developed in the redeveloped Deborah narratives.
Upon assuming leadership the prophetess chastises the people for their inability to sustain fidelity to the covenant and announces that "the Lord
will take pity on you today" specifically because of his commitment to the
covenant with their fathers (30:7).[60] Accordingly, God's call to the stars to
do battle against Sisera's armies includes, "For even if my people have
sinned, nevertheless I will have mercy upon them" (31:2). And finally, Deborah's hymn particularly emphasizes the role of divine mercy in the victory. She acknowledges the working of that mercy "even if man delays in
praising God" (32:13), calls upon the angels of the heavenly host to tell the
fathers "in their chamber of souls" that God has not forgotten the least of
his promises (32:13), and names the stars as future witnesses to join the
sun and moon as a delegation in times of stress to remind the "Most High,"
much as Moses' staff in 19:11, to send "the saving power of his covenant"
(32:14).

And the same theme of divine mercy is inserted into the Gideon and
Jephthah narratives. The angel who calls Gideon assures him that God
"will have mercy, as no one else has mercy, on the race of Israel, though
not on account of you but on account of those who have fallen asleep"
(35:3).[61] In response to Jephthah's initial unwillingness to assume leadership, the Israelites argue that "the God of our fathers" had repeatedly delivered them from their enemies in spite of their sins. And Jephthah himself
notes that God, unlike a mortal man, "has the time and place where He as
God may restrain himself out of his long-suffering" (39:5).[62] Immediately
upon accepting the role he calls upon the Israelites to repent and have
trust, for "even if our sins be overabundant, still his mercy will fill the
earth" (39:6).[63]

Thematically the mercy motif is developed from the single reference to
pity (i.e., mercy) in Judges, the general statement of 2:18, "For the Lord
would be moved to pity by their moanings because of those who oppressed

and crushed them." Technically, each of the cases described above involves an addition to the biblical narrative, either freely created or, as in a few instances, developed in a midrashic exegetical style.[64] Substantively, they add a totally new dimension and tone to the narratives of Judges, for they turn the biblical motif on its head: instead of demonstrating the cumulative incidences that led to the divine decision to discontinue driving the remaining nations out of the Land (Judg. 2:21-22), the reconstructed narratives explicitly confirm that the covenantal promises made by God will not be undone even as a consequence of Israel's infidelities. Sometimes the confirmation is placed in the mouth of the judge (27:7; 30:7; 32:13-14; 39:5-6), other times in the mouths of the Israelites or their elders (28:5; 30:4), and at times it comes directly from God or an angel (31:2; 35:3).

At one level, the cycle of sin, punishment, repentance, and temporary redemption repeatedly played out in Judges remains, but the central motif has changed. The Israelites are no longer primarily concerned with sovereignty and political control over the Land. With one exception,[65] the focus of their interest rests on survival as a covenanted people.[66] Whereas abandonment by God is understood in Judges in terms of the connection between obedience and the Land promise, that is, as the withholding of divine assistance in the completion of the conquest, in *Pseudo-Philo* the expressed concern is always destruction of the elected people. At another level, however, the cycle can be viewed as relatively meaningless, for God's eternal mercy functions quite independently of the cries of the Israelites.[67] It is not necessarily activated by the plight or even by the repentant prayers of the people. Rather, Israel is saved over and over by God's recollection of the covenantal promises he had made to the "fathers." At best, human prayer can appeal to that recollection, but it has no access to the souls of "the fathers" (33:5), for the intercessory capacity of the "fathers" rests solely on God's recollection of their merit and his covenantal relationship with them (35:3).[68]

The theological structure is again reminiscent of the one developed in the *Testament of Moses*. In both works redemption involves God's recollection of unconditional promises to the fathers rather than repentance; in both works that recollection is tied to Moses' intercession at Sinai.[69] However, whereas the author of the *Testament* is primarily interested in developing the connection between that intercession and the *Aqedah* as the source of divine beneficence for Israel in the time of the eschaton, the present writer is far more concerned with the historical process than with its end.[70] The elaborate theological system he develops is essentially applied only to national history. The fate of particular individuals in life, as well as after death, is determined purely by divine justice. The theology is double-tiered.

The normative principle of divine justice that the author envisages is a relatively simplistic system of reward and punishment—God rewards good and punishes evil. The significance of the covenant lies specifically in the fact that it breaks through the workings of this divine justice, activates divine mercy, and consequently, permits the covenanted community of Israel to continue in spite of its sins and infidelities. But the covenant functions only at the national level. It does not apply to individuals, even in national leadership roles; nor, for that matter, does it seem to have much eschatological relevance.

THE LAND AND ESCHATOLOGY

Scattered throughout the work are references to an end of "this age" and the beginning of a new era initiated by a divine visitation in which each individual will be judged "according to his works and according to the fruits of his own devices" (3:10).[71] There is no political dimension in this description of the judgment: the individual souls of the living and the resurrected are divided simply into the "wicked" and the "just."[72] The former are annihilated, the latter rewarded by eternal life with "the fathers" in the "immortal dwelling place that is not subject to time" (19:12). Little detail is provided about the nature of the age after the final judgment. There will be "another earth" and "another heaven" in which death will have no place (3:10). The heavenly lights will last longer (19:13), but even greater light will be provided by the twelve precious stones hidden by Kenaz (26:13). The new earth "will not be without progeny or sterile for those inhabiting it" (3:10).

Although the nation is the primary object of concern throughout the work, its fate in the end-time is never clarified. Moreover, the only reference to the Land in *Pseudo-Philo*'s eschatology appears in an enigmatic passage in which God tells Moses he will not enter the Land in "this age," but from afar he can view the Land and the place where the people will serve God for 740 years (19:7).[73] Moses is then taken on a tour of heaven and subsequently told that after the final judgment he and his fathers will dwell in the "place of sanctification I showed you" (19:13), a reference to the Temple and, perhaps, to the Land as well.

Pseudo-Philo's eschatological perspective is underdeveloped and unsystematic. In contrast, the nature and working of the covenant in Israel's history (his primary interest, and, not coincidentally, also the primary interest of the biblical narrative with its comparably underdeveloped eschatology) is notably systematic and consistent. His rewriting of scriptural narratives carries its own internal logic. Treating the biblical storyline as handmaiden to theology, he reconstructs the narratives such that they consistently demonstrate the constancy and surety of God's fidelity to the covenant. Such a theology permits no shifts in the divine will. Nothing is promised or predicted that in fact does not occur, and no contradictions exist either within the text or between the text and later historical circumstances known to the author.

In contrast, biblical Land theology not only presents multiple examples of textual inconsistencies, but also stands in direct contradiction to the historical experience of Israel. The patriarchal covenants describe a land promised to the fathers and to their offspring. In fact, only that offspring actually comes into possession of the Land, and even then, not until the generation after the exodus. The biblical descriptions of the Land do no better service for *Pseudo-Philo*'s principle of theological consistency. Ownership of the Land is attributed to different parties, and in biblical as well as later history the territory of Israel rarely encompasses specified geographic borders or the "whole land" of Hebrew Scriptures. Moreover, the patriarchal Land promise which speaks of "eternal possession" is contradicted by the Law at Sinai which makes retention of the Land contingent on obedience and is also belied by historical experience. Not only is Israelite tenure intermittent as early as the period of the Judges, there is also a history of exile from and return to the Land.

The covenant theology which *Pseudo-Philo* develops in place of the biblical structure responds to all these inconsistencies. The promise of the patriarchal covenant, as well as later recollections thereof, is altered such that the primary focus is on peoplehood, not Land. Its territorial boundaries never specified, the promise of Land is limited to the descendants of the patriarchs ("to your seed I will give this land"), and in fact that particular promise is totally fulfilled by the conquest of the Land under Joshua. It is the promise of seed and peoplehood that is played out in history, and that is eternally secured by God's recollection of the covenant.

At no time in Israel's history is the redesigned covenant compromised. When Israel sins, she is punished, but always God's mercy comes into play such that the covenant is assured. The call of the first patriarch from Mesopotamia to Canaan, the exodus of his descendants from Egypt, the stories of desert wandering and the Land conquest are not the seminal events in this version of covenanted history. In their place stand the miracle births of the later patriarchs, the covenanting of their progeny as a nation at Sinai, and, most significantly, the continual evidence of the workings of God's mercy in sustaining the nation in spite of its infidelities once it is in the Land.

The emphasis on the constant workings of God's wonders on behalf of the covenanted but wayward Israelites is most strongly paralleled in the biblical book of Judges. Indeed, *Pseudo-Philo*'s extensive treatment of that book and the substantive textual consistency that permeates his entire work suggest that he used Judges as his base, and, working backwards, developed his summary of the earlier material on the basis of his reconstruction of the later. The individual narratives in the biblical book of Judges place far greater emphasis on the survival of the people than on the acquisition or retention of the Land.[74] It contains no recollection of the patriarchal Land covenant, no mention of Land dimensions or notion of the Land as an "eternal possession," and no concept of exile from the Land as a punishment for infidelity to the covenant. These are the very themes that are missing throughout *Pseudo-Philo*'s rewritten narrative, be it in the summary form of the pentateuchal materials or his more extensive treatment of Joshua and Judges. While their absence well might be attributable to the selection of Judges as a narrative base, that choice itself reveals a particular historical perspective, one in which oppression rather than the threat of exile calls forth a reinterpretation of the biblical story. Such a perspective suggests that the work was written before captivity and exile became vital issues for first century Judeans, that is, before the destruction of Jerusalem in 70. Indeed, *Pseudo-Philo* betrays notably little interest in the phenomenon of exile, be it the historical one of 586 or the one he envisages on the horizon.[75] For him the imminent threat is loss of faith, not loss of the Land. Hence, shifting the thrust of the covenant so as to emphasize the assurance of numbers and peoplehood, he rewrites the biblical narrative in such a way as to reveal and confirm the steadfastness of God within Israel's history.

CHAPTER 6

Land and Covenant in Josephus' *Jewish Antiquities*

U nlike the authors of the pseudepigraphic works, Josephus presents his *Jewish Antiquities* as a recounting of "the precise details of our Scripture records" (I.17) and as "a translation of our sacred books" (*Ap.* I.54). The assurance is more revealing of the author, his audience, and his agenda than of the work it describes.[1] Immersed in hellenistic literary culture, Josephus composed the multivolumed *Antiquities*, a history of the Jews from the creation to the period immediately preceding the war with Rome, to enlighten Roman readers regarding the ancient and honorable nature of the Jewish past.[2] Neither the historical nor the apologetic character of the work was conducive to the faithful treatment of the biblical source set forth by its author;[3] to the contrary, a hellenistic flavor permeates the rewriting. Coupled with that flavor is the influence of more personal forces, not least of which is the fact that the author, writing under Roman patronage, was a Jew for whom the destruction of the Temple and loss of national sovereignty were of weighty significance.

PATRIARCHAL HISTORY

The most striking aspect of Josephus' narrative of the patriarchs is the absence of formal covenant-making scenes together with the Land promise which accompanies them in the scriptural source. The usual equivalent of the Hebrew ברית in the Septuagint, *diatheke*, a term associated with disposition of property in Targumic and Talmudic literature,[4] is never used in the portion of *Jewish Antiquities* that parallels scriptural narratives.[5] Moreover, the classical biblical concept of God relating to a particular people through a particular Land also does not appear. Instead, minimizing both the covenantal encounter and the Land aspects of the patriarchal experience of that covenant, Josephus describes a series of divine predictions regarding the future seed the patriarchs will bear and the providential care they and their seed will receive.

The motif of divine assistance/providential care first appears in the description of Abraham's initial departure from Mesopotamia. Like the author of *Jubilees*, Josephus places the initiative for the move with Abraham. "At the will and with the aid of God" (I.157), the patriarch decides to emigrate because of the hostility of the Mesopotamian peoples toward his new theological ideas. The decision to settle specifically in the land of Canaan is presented as God-directed. However, in stark contrast to the dramatic biblical command (Gen. 12:1) that prefaces the Land promise of Gen. 12:7, Josephus presents the directive not only as a parenthetical aside, but, even more significantly, as one without any covenantal significance: "At the age of seventy-five, he left Chaldaea, God having bidden him to remove to Canaan, and there he settled, and left the country to his descendants" (I.154).

The promise of the Land at Shechem, a culmination point in the biblical story of the first covenantal encounter, as well as the restatement of the promises upon Abraham's return from Egypt, are omitted. The patriarch's movements into and out of the Land are treated as casual migrations; he settles in Canaan, goes to Egypt for a while, and upon his return, divides the Land with Lot, "taking for himself the lowland that the other left him" (I.170). Without anything comparable to the Land-focused covenantal scene of Gen. 13:14-17, the narrative moves right on to the war between the Sodomites and the Assyrians.

Within the context of Abraham's role in that war, Josephus introduces the first of several revelatory predictions that replace biblical covenant-making in *Antiquities*. Commending the patriarch for refusing the offer of spoils from the Sodomite king, God reveals that "a son would be born to him whose posterity would be so great as to be comparable in number to the stars" (I.183). Abraham's immediate response is to offer a sacrifice to express his gratitude. Thereupon, a "voice divine" predicts the future enslavement of his posterity in Egypt after which "they would overcome their foes, vanquish the Canaanites in battle, and take possession of their land and cities" (I.185).

The presentation contrasts starkly with the covenant-making encounter of its biblical counterpart. Only the prediction of future numbers is in direct speech. The announcement of the future conquest is presented, like the rest of the scene, in the indirect voice of the historian-narrator.[6] Josephus further detracts from the significance of the predicted conquest by placing it outside the context of the patriarch's expression of gratitude—after, rather than before, the sacrificial offering. The Genesis text for the same scene presents the sacrifice as a divinely-commanded response to Abraham's request for a sign that his seed will in fact possess the Land as God has just indicated (Gen. 15:7). The sacrifice confirms the promise, occasions a divine explanation for why its fulfillment will be delayed until the fourth generation, and is followed by a formal statement of the covenant explicitly expressed in terms of possession of the Land from the "river of Egypt" to the Euphrates (Gen. 15:18-21). In Josephus there is no formal covenant-making, no Land promise, and hence no explanation for its delayed fulfillment.[7] What is the third affirmation of a covenantal relationship and a third promise of the Land in Genesis becomes instead a divine prediction of numerous descendants cast in language that, at best, celebrates the military prowess of Abraham's abundant future seed.

The same pattern of indirect narration and prediction rather than direct covenantal promise is evident in the treatment of the other two covenant scenes between God and Abraham that Josephus retains: the occasion of the prediction of Isaac's birth and the close of the *Aqedah* scene. The historian rewrites the first scene as a divine revelation predicting "great nations and kings" from the son by Sarah, who "would win possession, by war, of all Canaan from Sidon to Egypt" (I.191). Again prediction replaces promise, and again the conquest is presented as a reflection of the power of future progeny, rather than as a sign of the covenant. The charge regarding circumcision is retained, but its function is significantly altered. No longer a mark of the covenant (Gen. 17:10), its stated purpose is to keep Abraham's posterity "from mixing with others" (I.192).

Embellished by a long statement of faith spoken directly by the silent biblical Abraham (I.228-231), the account of the *Aqedah* is similarly reconstructed. Elaborating on the predictions of prosperity, power, and great numbers, the narrative foretells that Isaac (notably, not God) will bequeath a "great dominion" to his offspring and Abraham's descendants will swell "into a multitude of nations." The future conquest of Canaan again is mentioned, but, as before, the revelation involves a prediction (with divine assistance implied) of military success—"they would subdue Canaan by their arms and be envied of all men" (I.235)— not a promise of a covenantal inheritance.

Just as the Genesis narrative of the promises to Abraham sets a pattern for the promises to the subsequent patriarchs, so Josephus sets his own pattern in his presentation of the Abraham story. Covenantal encounters are presented as predictions of future destiny rather than as promises supported by divine oaths. Encounter scenes that have a strong Land focus in the biblical narrative are either deleted, displaced, diluted, and/or reinterpreted such that they stress future greatness in numbers rather than the promise of the Land. Insofar as acquisition of the Land is included, it is predicted only for the future seed, not for the patriarch alone or for him and his descendants. And the acquisition is predicated on providential assistance, not promissory grant or gift.

Since the Land is the controlling theme both contextually and substantively in the biblical description of Isaac's involvement with the covenant (Gen. 26:1-22), Josephus deals with this narrative much as he dealt with the encounters associated with Abraham's migrations (Gen. 12:7; 13:14-17). He omits the encounter and reduces the narrative to a description of internal migration. Isaac's contemplation of migration to Egypt elicits no assurance that God will give "all these lands to you and to your offspring, fulfilling the oath that I swore to your father" and no statement of the triad of covenantal promises. The historian simply tells the reader that the patriarch had "resolved to go into Egypt...but at God's bidding removed to Gerara" (I.259). The narrative of successful digging of the well at Rehoboth that follows the covenant-making is retained, but instead of reflecting the biblical confirmation of patriarchal faith in the Land promise as in Gen. 26:22, the choice of name is explained simply by its etymological root, "a name which denotes 'spacious'" (I.262).

In his rewriting of the narrative of Isaac's transfer of the covenantal blessings to Jacob, Josephus effects an intriguing substitution of context. Noting only that Isaac consented to Jacob's marriage "in compliance with his wife's wishes" (I.278), the historian-narrator omits the biblical transmission of blessings when Jacob departs to Haran (Gen. 28:3-4) and uses Isaac's earlier blessing of Jacob disguised as Esau, a biblical scene which has neither a land component nor covenantal significance, as an opportunity to present his version of the divine promises bestowed on the patriarchs. Setting this blessing in direct voice, Josephus has the patriarch acknowledge both a relationship between God and the patriarchal line as well as a promise, but that promise has nothing to do with covenanted Land.

> Lord of all the ages and Creator of universal being, forasmuch as thou didst bestow upon my father great store of good things, and to me hast vouchsafed all that I possess, and to my descendants hast promised thy gracious aid and to grant them ever greater blessings; now therefore confirm these promises...graciously protect this my son and preserve him from every touch of ill; grant him a blissful life and the possession of all good things that thou hast power to bestow; and make him a terror to his foes, to his friends a treasure and a delight. (I.272-73)

The same theme and comparable language are used in Josephus' version of the dialogues between God and Jacob. God's relationship to the earlier patriarchs and future relationship to Jacob and his descendants is alternately described as a source of "succor" and "providential care," as an "escort," "protector and helper," and "guide," and even as a matter of destiny (I.280, 282; II.8, 172, 194). Additionally, the dialogues are structured such that they, like Abraham's encounters, relate particularly to the issue of future numbers. Retaining God as direct speaker in his version of the first encounter at Bethel, Josephus shifts the focus such that the divine speech addresses Jacob's anxiety over his forthcoming marriage rather than the new migrant's anxiety over a future return to the Land. Thus, where the Genesis narrative has God reassuring Jacob of fulfillment of the Land promise, Josephus has God assuring that providential care will bring future seed from consummation of "this marriage upon which thine heart is set" (I.282).

A form of the Land promise does appear in the rewritten revelation. However, it is linked to a patriarchal heritage of divine assistance—God's recollection of how he had "led Abraham hither from Mesopotamia" and had "brought" Isaac "to prosperity"—rather than to a covenantal tradition that speaks of a grant of "eternal possession" of the Land.[8] The promise to Jacob at best assures that his descendants will be granted "dominion over this land," a far cry from the "land upon which you are lying I will give to you and to your offspring" (Gen. 28:14). Moreover, the biblical concept of full possession of the Land is further diminished by the additional note that the seed of those descendants "shall fill all that the sun beholds of earth and sea" (I.282). Exegetically, the addition may well be derived, as was the development of the promise in *Jubilees* (32:18-19), from the lack of specificity in Gen. 28:14. But whereas the author of the latter work used the biblical verse to escalate the territorial promise to cosmic proportions, Josephus uses it to shift the focus of the revelation away from territoriality and toward the assurance of great numbers.

A stress on peoplehood also appears in Josephus' rewriting of Jacob's later encounter with the angel when he is assured "that his race would never be extinguished" (I.332). The rewriting is significant because the wrestling scene is the only one of the two biblical name-changing scenes for Jacob (Gen. 32:29; 35:10) retained in *Antiquities*. The second Bethel encounter—God's confirmation of the change predicted by the angel and restatement of the covenant with specific emphasis on transfer of the Land promise to the third patriarch (Gen. 35:12)—is reduced to a notation that Jacob "offered sacrifice at Bethel, where he had seen the dream when journeying of yore to Mesopotamia" (I.342).

Josephus comes closest to employing traditional covenantal language in his expansion of the reassurance given to Jacob before he goes to join

Joseph in Egypt. Describing the third patriarch as fearful that his sons would become so prosperous in Egypt "that their descendants would never more return to Canaan to take possession of it, as God had promised" (II.171),[9] the historian has God, after recalling the history of his providential care over the patriarch, assure him:

> And now am I come to be thy guide upon this journey, and to foreshew to thee that thou wilt end thy days in Joseph's arms, to announce a long era of dominion and glory for thy posterity, and that I will establish them in the land which I have promised. (II.175)

This sequence of God guiding Jacob to Egypt, an era of dominion, and finally establishment in the land of Canaan introduces the possibility that the "era of dominion" is a reference to Joseph and his progeny in Egypt. The likelihood of such is reenforced by the biblical text for the same scene, which is limited to God reassuring Jacob, "Fear not to go down into Egypt; for I will make you *there* into a great nation" (Gen. 46:3) (emphasis mine).

This limitation aside, we do seem to have here a promise of Land. But without a previous covenantal base to refer to, that promise must be understood in terms of the pledge of assistance in conquest made to Jacob at Bethel. More significantly, Josephus again chooses to insert the promissory language into a rewriting of a Genesis passage which does not involve the Land covenant while deleting it from his version of the Bethel encounter where, in the biblical text, the covenanted Land concept is explicitly stated.

The motivation behind such exchanges of position is to place the predictions that substitute for covenantal promises in contexts which, in contrast to the biblical narratives of patriarchal covenant-making, do not focus on the Land or suggest that Land acquisition is the pivot for the prediction. Thus, Josephus places the predictions of subsequent conquest in Isaac's blessing of Jacob disguised as Esau and in a scene prefacing the third patriarch's anticipation of reunion with his lost son, rather than in the biblical contexts of paternal reassurance and restatement of the divine promise on the occasions of Jacob's movements from and back to the Land.

Given the nature of his rewriting of the patriarchal narratives, it is understandable that the historian demonstrates no more fidelity to biblical Land theology when he comes to the transitional recollections connecting the patriarchs to the post-patriarchal generation. Jacob dies in Egypt without recalling the promises at Bethel to Joseph and without conveying his surety that God would bring the favored son "back to the land of your fathers." Similarly, when Joseph comes to his deathbed, he does not recall God's oath to the patriarchs regarding the Land promise.[10] Instead,

Josephus describes the dying Jacob offering prayers that his sons "might attain to felicity" and foretelling "in prophetic words how each of their descendants was destined to find a habitation in Canaan" (II.194), a destiny that the narrator has in no way distinguished from that of any other people or place. A subsequent notation that when the Hebrews later "migrated from Egypt" they conveyed Joseph's bones to Canaan "in accordance with the oath which Joseph had laid upon them" (II.200) provides no enrichment of the foretold destined settlement.

In his treatment of the connections between the patriarchs and the exodus/wilderness generations Josephus maintains the approach he developed in the patriarchal narratives. Omitting, replacing, or rewriting the biblical Land-focused recollections, he develops his own special themes: prediction of the future, God as caretaker and ally, and assurances of great population growth. In some instances this involves creating new transitional passages; in others it is a matter of reworking biblical ones.

The first transitional recollection is a created one set within a revelatory dream in which God reassures Amram of his son's future by reviewing the providential care God had given to Abraham:

> He had their piety in remembrance and would ever give them its due recompense, even as He had already granted their forefathers to grow from a few souls into so great a multitude. He recalled how Abraham, departing alone from Mesopotamia on his journey to Canaan, had in every way been blessed, and above all how his wife, once barren, had thereafter, thanks to His will, been rendered fertile; how he had begotten sons and had bequeathed to Ishmael and his descendants the land of Arabia, and to his children by Katura Troglodytis, to Isaac, Canaan. (II.212-13)[11]

The passage is quite revealing. Not only is the gift or reward for piety specifically set in terms of fertility and numbers, but the bequest of the Land is totally removed from a covenantal context. Canaan is not in any way different from Arabia or Troglodytis. Moreover, Abraham, not God, is the grantor of the territorial inheritances to his various children. The reference to Katura's children goes back to an earlier section in *Antiquities* where Josephus states that "all these sons and grandsons Abraham contrived to send out to found colonies" (I.239).[12] The mention of colonies is not incidental. Colonies and the spread of Jews into diaspora living are an aspect of Josephus' notion of the future revealed to the patriarchs and, as we shall see, colonial dispersion plays a significant role in his eschatology.

Other than the above-cited dream of Amram, Josephus creates only one additional link between the Hebrews enslaved in Egypt and the patriarchal past. Following the text of Exod. 3:6, he puts this speech in the mouth of the divine voice speaking from the burning bush. The biblical text stresses God's identity as the God of the patriarchs who now responds to the cry of affliction and promises to bring the descendants of the patriarchs out of Egypt into a Land flowing with milk and honey. Omitting the language of promise, Josephus establishes a far more casual connection between the patriarchs and the future acquisition of the Land by their descendants. Focused entirely on Moses, the rewritten divine speech combines predictions of the leader's future glory and honor with the assurance that through the strength of his leadership and wisdom, the Hebrews would come to inhabit the Land "wherein Abraham dwelt, the forefather of your race" (II.269). Moses becomes what Abraham was in the patriarchal stories, the sagacious leader who, with God as companion and ally, will direct the fate of the Jews.

God's role is further developed in a speech without biblical parallel that Moses addresses to the Hebrews at Sinai:

> For it is not Moses, son of Amram and Jochebed, but He who constrained the Nile to flow for your sake a blood-red stream...; He who opened for you a path through the sea; He who caused meat to descend from heaven; He thanks to whom Adam partook of the produce of land and sea, Noah escaped from the deluge, Abraham our forefather passed from wandering to settle in the land of Canaan; He who caused Isaac to be born of aged parents, Jacob to be graced by the virtues of twelve sons, Joseph to become lord of the Egyptians' might, He it is who favors you with these commandments, using me for interpreter. (III.86-87)

The theme of God working in history is quite biblical. There is, however, a major shift in Josephus' creation. The historical review and admonition in Scriptures that offers a parallel to this created one centers on God's oath to the patriarchs regarding the promise of the Land. The Israelites are not to attribute acquisition and possession of the Land to their own prowess or goodness, but rather to God who gives them the Land "in order to fulfill the oath" he made to Abraham, Isaac, and Jacob (Deut. 8:16-18; 9:5-6). By shifting the context of the admonition from the conquest to Sinai and the focus from the Israelites to Moses, Josephus once again avoids the uniqueness of the biblical concept of a covenanted Land specifically given to the Israelites by God.

The common scriptural pattern of recollecting the covenant with the fathers in terms of God's oath—"the Land that I swore to your fathers"—is not found in Josephus' rewriting.[13] Indeed, it would seem that he deliberately elects to develop biblical passages that do not incorporate that recollective phrase. Moreover, when he develops his ally theme in contexts that retain the language of promise, he describes the promise in terms of alliance: "to tender actual aid" (III.306), "seconding their ardour and championing their cause" (III.309), "to deliver to them" (IV.168), "assured of God's cooperation" (IV.315), "given us to win this land" (V.94), "the benefactions of God" (V.115).[14] Nowhere in these passages is there a reference to God giving[15] the Land to the Israelites, yet in at least four instances that "giving" is a major theme in the biblical passages Josephus is paraphrasing.[16]

In only one passage where the ally theme is connected with promise does Josephus come close to the idea that the Land was intended to be an eternal possession. When the two and a half tribes are ready to return to the other side of the Jordan, Josephus has Joshua say to them:

> Seeing that God, the Father and Lord of the Hebrew race, has given us to win this land and, being won, has promised to preserve it to us forever, and seeing that, when at His behest we besought your assistance, ye offered your ready services for all.... To the worship of Him pay ye heed, and of that polity which He Himself has instituted through Moses, observe ye every precept, in the assurance that while ye remain faithful to these, God also will show Himself your gracious ally, but if ye turn aside to imitate other nations, He will turn away from your race. (V.94,98)

The alliance language ("given us to win," "will show Himself your gracious ally") is here combined with a promise to "preserve" the Land "to us forever." Josephus is paraphrasing and embellishing, not citing, a biblical text[17] and has, until now, consistently avoided any notion of a gift of eternal or covenanted Land. Consequently, the assurance of preservation "forever" must be understood in terms of continued alliance, and, within the overall context of the passage, as a promise conditional on fidelity to the Law—an aspect of classical Land theology which Josephus does retain.

To a significant extent Josephus' problem with covenanted Land theology—be it in the patriarchal narratives or in later recollections—has its roots in a desire, natural to an historian, to universalize and normalize God's relationship with Israel. For Josephus, the tie between God and Israel is one of special concern, but it is only one example of God's providential care for the world. Moreover, it is a reflection of God's justice, not a special love expressed through the promise of the Land. Thus, in place of a covenanted Land promise, Josephus builds a case for divine "alliance."[18] Israel's possession of the Land ceases to be a matter of promises sworn to the forefathers. Normalized, it depends rather on morality and obedience, or ultimately, even on the fortuitous swing of God's rod.[19]

THE NAME AND CHARACTER OF THE LAND

The most striking aspect of Josephus' treatment of biblical descriptions of the Land is that so much is omitted. Josephus retains nothing of the experiential descriptions because the intimate tie between the patriarchs and the Land portrayed in Genesis is unfavorable to his reconstruction of the encounters between the patriarchs and God. He deletes the divine language as well as the touring/seeing experiences that would promote such intimacy. His patriarchs move about in the Land, but their internal migrations never prompt descriptions that indicate any form of bonding.

Josephus also gives minimal attention to description of the geographic boundaries of the Land. This deletion is surprising for an historian. But in the Pentateuch the boundary descriptions either are incorporated within covenanted Land promises to the patriarchs or appear as part of warnings of delayed fulfillment of the Land promise. Josephus deletes both of these contexts. Within his patriarchal narratives there is no promise of covenanted Land that would call for specification of borders. At most, and then on only one occasion, the prediction that replaces promissory gift speaks of "all Canaan from Sidon to Egypt" (I.192). With specific borders no longer delineated in his prediction narratives of the patriarchs, Josephus, like the author of *Pseudo-Philo*, is able to avoid the issue of incomplete conquest as an expression of unfulfilled promise.

Josephus is most comfortable with the biblical usage of "land of Canaan." He distinguishes between Canaan and Palestine: Canaan he identifies, for the benefit of his Roman readers, as the country "now called Judaea," settled by "Chananeus, the fourth son of Ham" who "named it after himself Chananaea" (I.134). Palestine is defined as the coastal territory from Gaza to Egypt, the land of the Philistines, which in its Greek form preserves the name of its first settler, Phylistinus, one of the eight sons of Mersaeus, another son of Ham (I.136).[20] The edifying pattern is repeated in the pentateuchal narratives that follow: Abraham leaves Chaldea "for the land then called Canaan, but now Judaea, where he settled, he and his numerous descendants" (I.160), and eventually he migrates "to Gerara in Palestine" (I.207). In order to avoid the Philistines, Moses "did not conduct his people by the direct route to Palestine, but chose to accomplish a long arduous march through the desert in order to invade Canaan" (II.323). Comfortable with the changes wrought by historical conquest, Josephus employs proper terms and possessive pronouns that reflect those changes. As long as "Canaan" is under the control of the Canaanites, it is "their" land (I.185);[21] after it is conquered, it takes on the proper name of

Judea and the referent for possessive pronouns changes accordingly (I. 129; III. 245; V.255; X.40, 109).[22]

There is no sense in *Antiquities* that the Land has a particular relationship with the deity or that it possesses any special or mystical qualities of its own. In contrast to the biblical notion that the Land cannot tolerate moral pollution even when occupied by Canaanites, Josephus' account maintains the ordinary character of the Land. He deletes the reference to "the iniquity of the Amorites" (Gen. 15:16)—which implies a moral criterion for occupation, if not possession, of the Land—from the prediction of four hundred years among "evil neighbors in Egypt" in the first of his three divine revelations to Abraham (I.185). Moreover, whether he is referring specifically to Canaan or to land or earth in general, he consistently uses the most general word, *ge*, for land. In fact, in two passages, I.282 and IV.115, he uses *ge* in both senses, once in reference to the land of Canaan and immediately thereafter as "the earth."

As for descriptive language in praise of the Land and its fertility, Josephus avoids the poetic biblical phrase "flowing with milk and honey" as well as the contrast with Egypt in Deut. 11:12 that attributes the Land's water source directly to the deity. Instead, at best characterizing the Land as a whole as "favored" or "fortunate" (II.269; III.300), he describes the range of its terrain (his appreciation of Jerusalem and Jericho notwithstanding) rather analytically.

> For the nature of the land of Canaan is such that one may see plains, of great area, fully fitted for bearing crops, and which compared with another district might be deemed altogether blest, yet when set beside the regions of the people of Jericho and Jerusalem would appear as naught. Aye, though the territory of these folk happens to be quite diminutive and for the most part mountainous, yet for its extraordinary productiveness of crops and beauty it yields to no other. (V.77)

The absence of any metaphysical attributes in this, the most enthusiastic of Josephus' descriptions of the Land, cannot be attributed to a compromise out of deference to his Roman audience.[23] To the contrary, on at least one other occasion (II.292), the historian makes the very connection between the forces of nature and God that he withholds from his descriptions of Canaan. Thus, the omission in the case of Canaan all the more suggests the extent to which the historian wishes to distance his presentation from the biblical concept of a Land owned by God.

THE LAND AND THE LAW

Although he intended to compose a full treatise on the laws, Josephus devotes a significant portion of Books III and IV in *Antiquities* to an elaboration of the "code of laws." On two occasions he makes specific reference to Land-linked legislation. The first, placed after the revelation at Sinai, involves a narrator-based distinction between the laws "already in operation" during Moses' lifetime and those "he devised beforehand, to the end that they should practise them after the conquest of Canaan" (III.280). Within the first category, the Ten Commandments, the various sacrificial offerings, and the purity and leprosy laws are connected to the Land only through descriptions of offerings to be made at the Temple. The second grouping includes sabbatical and jubilee laws. In this instance the historian avoids the biblical link between Law and Land by omitting the personification of the Land and the reference to God's ownership that appear in the source text of Leviticus 25 (III.281-286).

A more extensive exposition of the laws, presented at the end of Moses' career, is prefaced by "whensoever, having conquered the land of Canaan..." (IV.199),[24] Josephus' telling version of the biblical "when you come to the Land...." Directly spoken by Moses, this narration includes not only Land-linked commandments but also, in summary form, a significant portion of pentateuchal law.[25] Again the omissions are striking, for just as the historian had ignored the scriptural concept of pollution of the Land in his exposition of levitical material, so he now deletes all references to defilement of the Land (IV.173, 202, 265) from non-levitical legislation grounded in that same concern.[26]

Equally telling is the omission of any reference to the "oath God swore to our fathers" (Deut. 26:3) in Josephus' version of the prayer of thanksgiving to be offered in the tithes ceremony (IV.242).[27] Not casual, the deletion is grounded in the author's rejection of the concept of a patriarchal Land promise, a rejection that is expressed rather subtly in an unscriptural elaboration that places affirmation of that promise in the mouths of political rebels. Describing the precipitant effort to undertake the conquest after Kadesh Barnea as a rebellion against the leadership of Moses, Josephus has the rebels (speaking in a direct voice combined with indirect narrative) attribute their effort to the belief that all being "of the stock of Abraham," they would "show themselves sensible, if, scorning the arrogance of Moses and in reliance upon God, they were to determine to win this land which He had promised them" (IV.4-5).

As previously noted, this same rejection of patriarchal Land promise accounts for the absence of any notion of incomplete conquest. In spite of repeated references to the biblical command to destroy (in *Antiquities*, "anni-hilate") the Canaanites, Josephus never makes the biblical connection be-tween failure to adhere to that command and the failure to conquer "all" the Land as promised. Instead, he attributes the cities left unconquered un-der Joshua to "the strength of the sites on which they stood and of the so-lidity of the walls with which the inhabitants had crowned the natural advantages of their towns" (V.71), and describes the limited continuation of the conflict in the period immediately after the leader's death as the re-sult of "luxury" that "unnerved" the Israelites "for fatigues," making them "ill-disposed" for warfare (V.134).

He creates a natural transition from Joshua to Judges by replacing the incomplete conquest theme of Judg. 2:1-3, 20-23 with a less metaphysical explanation, albeit spoken by a divine oracle: "Under the mastery of luxury and voluptuousness" and caring "little of the order of their constitution and no longer hearken[ing] diligently to its laws," the Israelites had spared the Canaanites who now would seize the occasion to "treat them with great ruthlessness" (V.133). This motif then is used throughout his rewriting of Judges to account for the shifting fortunes of the Israelites (V.180, 185, 198, 255). The consequences of violation of God's command is never stated as involving a withholding of promised borders. Rather, expressed in natural terms, the weakness of the vice-ridden Israelites provides opportu-nity for Canaanite oppression.

In a similar vein, Josephus builds his distaste for a concept of uniquely sacred Land into his storyline. Recounting the episode of the altar built by the two and a half tribes who had settled on the eastern bank of the Jor-dan, he completely ignores the biblical version that focuses the issue of fi-delity on the requirement to offer sacrifices in "the land of the Lord's own holding" (Josh. 22:19).[28] Josephus makes no distinction between territories on the two sides of the Jordan. Instead, he develops the matter of "strange gods" and going over "to the vice of the Canaanites" around the themes of kinship and sedition (V.107).[29] Even more telling, he puts into the priest's mouth the totally unscriptural, "Think not that by crossing the river ye have also passed beyond God's power: nay, everywhere ye are within His domain, and escape from His authority and His vengeance is impossible" (V.109).

Much as he rejects the biblical notion of incomplete conquest associated with the patriarchal Land promise, so he denies the biblical connection be-tween Land fertility and fidelity to the Law. This form of the linkage be-tween Land and Law is not so much omitted as rendered nonspecific in *Antiquities*. Establishing the connection in two speeches set into the mouth of Moses, Josephus makes no special claims for Canaan. Just as the Israelites "will enjoy a fruitful earth,[30] a sea unvext by tempest, a breed of children born in nature's way" if they follow God's commandments (III.88), so the Pharaoh of Egypt will avoid the expression of divine wrath in nature if he adheres to God's will:

> For to them that rouse the divine ire dread calamities arise from all around them; to them neither earth nor air is friendly, to them no progeny is born after nature's laws, but all things are hostile and at enmity. (II.292)

He does maintain a connection between adherence to the laws, maintenance of national sovereignty, and retention of the Land. However, that connection involves neither a covenantal past nor a notion of particular sanctity adhering to the Land. It is rather a matter of a commitment to virtue expressed in adherence to the laws and the stability of established national institutions. The relationship is clearly stated in positive terms in an unbiblical prayer inserted into the leader's presentation of the laws.

> This land which God hath given[31] to you that are contemptuous of fatigue, and whose souls are schooled to valor, may He grant you to occupy it in peace, once ye have conquered it; may neither foreigner invade it for its injury, nor civil strife o'ermaster you, whereby ye shall be led to actions contrary to those of your own fathers and destroy the institutions which they established; and may ye continue to observe laws which God has approved as good and now delivers to you. (IV.294-95)

The prayer is devoid of a covenantal context. The connection between adherence to the Law and peaceful life in the Land is more implied than explicitly stated, and the focus on the Land is quickly dissipated by the theme which follows—God is an ally for those who are martially prepared (IV.297-98). Still, the description of peace and security expresses something of the blessings assured by obedience in the biblical Land theology. However, the unbiblical reference to "civil strife," a notable characteristic of Judea in the first century of the common era, suggests that in creating the prayer Josephus has in mind something more than a restatement of biblical blessings.

That "something" becomes more evident in the historian's rewriting of Moses' final discourses. He develops two major addresses, one a variant of Deuteronomy 4, the other, a summary version of Deut. 28:49-68. Comprised of three sections—an exhortation to keep the laws, a recollection of past errors, and a warning about the future—the first address follows the structure, but not the substance, of its biblical base text. Opening with an unscriptural elegy of the rewards of virtue and obedience to the laws

(IV.180-183),[32] Moses quickly turns to the subject of rebelliousness against "what your rulers require you to do" (IV.187), which then becomes the theme for both the recollection and the warning:

> It is just in this thing that the path of safety lies, and to prevent you from breaking out into any violence against those set over you, by reason of that wealth which will come to you in abundance when ye have crossed the Jordan and conquered Canaan. For should ye be carried away by it into a contempt and disdain for virtue, ye will lose even that favor which ye have found of God; and having made Him your enemy ye will forfeit that land, which ye are to win, beaten in arms and deprived of it by future generations with the grossest ignominy, and dispersed throughout the habitable world, ye will fill every land and sea with your servitude. And when ye undergo these trials, all unavailing will be repentance and recollection of these laws which ye have failed to keep. (IV.189-91)

The passage is intriguing. In his patriarchal narratives Josephus defines God's promise in terms of great numbers to the posterity of Abraham, Isaac, and Jacob. Indeed, in his version of the promise to Jacob at Bethel, the development of a diaspora is a blessed consequence of those numbers; and as we shall see, a great diaspora is part of the blessing for Israel placed in the mouth of Balaam. Yet here Josephus presents another picture of dispersion—not as the product of prosperity and overflowing numbers, but rather as the punishment for disobedience.

The historian is no longer avoiding the biblical connection between Land and Law. Indeed, he appears to be developing that connection in order to explain the history of the Jews. The development, however, requires a major reconstruction of the biblical source text, as does much of Josephus' rewriting. In Deuteronomy 4 the subject of the recollection is the Golden Calf, and the specific sin warned against is the making of a comparable image once "you have begotten children and children's children and are established in the land" (Deut. 4:25). Should the admonition not be heeded, the predicted punishment is dispersion and a great reduction in numbers. But ultimately, if the people repent, the merciful God will not let His people perish "and will not forget the covenant He made on oath with (their) fathers" (Deut. 4:27, 31).

Josephus makes dramatic changes at every stage of the paradigmatic passage. Shifting the focus of the recollection of past inclinations to disobedience, he presents that drama as a rejection of Moses' leadership rather than as a rejection of God. Consequently, the comparable future violation of divine law becomes "violence against those set over you," not the biblical sin of idolatry. The punishment for the sin no longer entails loss of the

Land *and* a major reduction in numbers, but loss of the Land alone. And although repentance may follow, in Josephus' version of the paradigm it will be "unavailing." His rewriting of the earlier pentateuchal narratives has laid a solid foundation for all these changes. There is no violation of covenant, for there is no covenant to violate. For Josephus the issue is civil/political—a lack of virtue in not accepting the leaders God selects— not theological. The punishment for that lack of virtue involves no negation of a divine promise, for the assurance of great numbers, not eternal possession of the Land, was the prediction revealed to the forefathers. Lastly, given the absence of any divine "oath" to the contrary, repentance can be "unavailing" and the paradigm can close without restoration to the Land.

A totally different schema, however, appears in the speech Josephus presents as Moses' final oration (IV.312-14). Constructed as a narrator-voiced summary of the gloomy predictions in the last part of Deuteronomy 28 with direct speech by Moses only at the end, the description refers neither to rebellion nor to dispersion. The sin is transgressing "His rites"; the consequence is enemy invasion, razing of cities, destruction of the Temple, and enslavement. Thus far, albeit its summary form and the specific reference to the Temple, the scheme is close to the one presented in the biblical source. But whereas that text specifies uprooting from the Land and, by way of recollection, goes on to double the first two stages before closing with repentance and restoration as the final stages, Josephus takes a different tact. Rejecting, as before, repentance as a moving force, he has Moses now include a God-initiated restoration stage ("God who created you will restore those cities to your citizens and the Temple too").[33] However, unlike the biblical model, restoration does not mark a closure, for Moses finishes with "yet will they be lost not once, but often" (IV.314).

Clearly, both addresses are intended as previews of Israel's future history. The "sin" of rebellion "against those set over you" parallels Josephus' own speech (as well as that of Agrippa) in *The Jewish War* (II.356ff; V.376-419). The consequent dispersion without promise of return reflects the author's own attitude toward any attempt to undo the Roman conquest of Judea. These themes and the direct voice in which the first address is presented all point to the first century and the failed war against Rome.

The structure and substance of the second address indicate that it is intended as a full historical overview, spanning the invasion of 586 through the post-exilic restoration down to Josephus' own day. Yet, the absence of any reference to exile in the description has led at least one scholar to suggest that the prediction in fact refers only to the destruction of 70.[34] That interpretation does not take into account, however, the extent to which

Josephus rejects both the concept of covenanted Land as well as the biblical perception of Landedness as the most significant aspect of Israel's historical destiny. Moreover, it does not respond to the clue provided by the awkward combination of indirect and direct speech in the address. As previously noted, Josephus employs the latter to highlight a point of significance. Developing the prediction from his own time perspective, he presents the less significant distant past as the narrator's exposition (IV.313) and the more recent, and therefore more significant, events as Moses' own words (IV.314).

Josephus' reconstruction of the Deuteronomy speeches does not represent a new version of the Land covenant. Nor for that matter does it reflect an effort, comparable to the pseudepigraphic reworkings of the deuteronomic addresses, to fit Israel's post-biblical experience within the conceptual boundaries of biblical covenant theology. Instead, adjusting and revising the biblical text as necessary, Josephus, the historian, rewrites the narrative to reflect his own political, historical perspective. No secular historian, Josephus cannot explain 586, let alone the Roman destruction, without some reference to divine punishment. So he restructures the biblical passages to make them predict or prophesy a punishment which in fact has already been played out on the historical stage. Interweaving prophecy and history, in *Antiquities* Josephus makes history out of biblical theology, much as he makes theology out of history in *The Jewish War*.[35]

This technique is not limited to the Pentateuch. In his account of the monarchy Josephus elaborates on passages dealing with exile and dispersion such that they point either to the Babylonian exile or the destruction of the Second Temple. In his rendition of the dream of Solomon after the dedication of the First Temple, Josephus has God warn Solomon that if he does not keep faith with God, he will be cut off "root and branch"; the Temple will be sacked and burned, and, plagued by war, the people ultimately will be driven out of the Land to become "aliens in a strange land" (VIII.127-28). All of this he builds onto the simple verse "Then I will sweep Israel off the land which I gave them" (1 Kings 9:7). The verse ceases to be a warning; under Josephus' pen it has been transformed into a prediction of (and, in hindsight, an explanation of) the disaster of 586.

He does the same thing with the relationship between Josiah and the prophetess Huldah after the discovery of the Torah scroll. In the biblical text Josiah simply sends a priest to Huldah who prophesies, "Thus said the Lord: I am going to bring disaster upon this place and its inhabitants, in accordance with all the words of the scroll which the king of Judah has read" (2 Kings 22:16). Josephus, on the other hand, makes the scene explicitly predictive of 586, describing Josiah's fear of being "driven away" and "cast out of their own country into a foreign land," a fear that Huldah confirms in equally specific language—again explaining the Babylonian exile from prophetic hindsight (X.59-60).

In another interpretative addition to Kings, Josephus uses the technique to explain the destruction of 70. As this cannot be done so easily by insertion of detail into the text, he has to resort to a more creative rewriting. In 2 Chron. 15:2-6 there is a short account of a meeting between the prophet Azariah and King Asa after the latter's great victory over Gerar. In that narrative Azariah simply tells Asa that Israel had strayed from God, but since Israel had returned to God, the present victory was her reward. In order to use the text for his own purposes, Josephus turns the whole scene into a warning for the future. God had granted the victory because the people "had shown themselves righteous and pure, and had always acted in accordance with the will of God." But if they changed (and the implication clearly is that they will), the time would come "when no true prophet will be found among your people nor any priest to give righteous judgment, but your cities shall be laid waste and the nation scattered over all the earth to lead the life of aliens and wanderers" (VIII.296).

Given Josephus' attitude toward the post-exilic Daniel, whom, as we shall see, he counts as a "true prophet," he would not invoke such a prediction for the period immediately after the destruction of 586.[36] Thus, describing events which he has witnessed, Josephus is again retrojecting history into biblical prophecy. His talent in rewriting prophetic material in this way is only outdone by his bravado in describing himself as "skilled in divining the meaning of ambiguous utterances of the Deity" (*War* III.352).

THE LAND AND ESCHATOLOGY

His interest in biblical prophecy almost limited to prophecy as history already played out, Josephus pays notably little attention in his rewriting to the descriptions of redemption and return that complement the themes of exile and dispersion in prophetic literature. Given the Land-centered, covenantal orientation of the classical biblical prophets, Josephus uses the Midianite prophet Balaam and Daniel to serve as spokesmen for his own eschatology. The stature of these particular prophets in Josephus' eyes is related to the universalistic approach he tries to assume as an historian, that is, they prophesied about other nations in addition to Israel (IV.125; X.266-68, 276).

For stated reasons of political propriety, Josephus limits his exposition of Daniel to predictions of events already past. Describing the rise and fall of the Babylonian and Persian empires, he notes that the Roman power "will have dominion forever through its iron nature" (X.209). When he comes to the stone in Nebuchadnezzar's dream, he openly shies away from its dangerous political implications:

> I have not thought it proper to relate this since I am expected to write of what is past and done, and not of what is to be....If...any one wishes to learn about the hidden things to come, let him...read the book of Daniel. (X.210)

The hesitancy is justified, for, as he subtly indicates in other contexts, Josephus believes that the power of Rome is in fact temporary. In *The War* (V.367) he states that the rod of empire now rests over Italy, implying that it can and will move on; in *Against Apion* he quietly notes that great imperial powers have been reduced to servitude "through the vicissitudes of fortune," leaving unstated a similar probability for Rome (*Ap.* II.127); and in his account of Balaam's prophecies he hints at a future calamity (IV.125).[37]

In contrast, Josephus is most explicit about the future of the Jews. Totally out of scriptural context, he has the Midianite priest, Balaam, assure the indestructibility of the Jewish people, who, guided forever by divine providence, will excel through "virtue and a passion for pursuits most noble and pure of crime" (IV.114). As for the Land "to which He Himself hath sent you, you shall surely occupy [it]; it shall be subject forever to your children, and with their fame shall all earth and sea be filled" (IV.115). Suddenly, in the mouth of the Midianite priest whom Josephus clearly regards as the instigator of the sin of Baal Peor (IV.129), we find the promise that Josephus had deleted from its patriarchal context as well as from its place within the Sinai legislation. Moreover, he has Balaam combine that Land promise with an expansion of the promise of a diaspora rooted in overflowing numbers made to Jacob at Bethel:

> Ye shall suffice for the world to furnish every land with inhabitants sprung from your race. Marvel ye, the blessed army, that from a single sire ye have grown so great? Nay, those numbers now are small and shall be contained by the land of Canaan; but the habitable world, be sure, lies before you as an eternal habitation and your multitudes shall find abode on islands and continents, more numerous even than the stars in heaven. (IV.115-116)[38]

In order to understand this transformation of the biblical Land promise into a prophecy that includes a blessed diaspora described with language associated with the biblical covenant, one must look back at the threads interweaving the various aspects of biblical Land theology. Through the literary device of recollection, the patriarchal Land covenant is directly tied to the giving of the Law. And while the actual occupation of the Land is dependent upon obedience to the Law, the Land promise remains eternally covenanted and eternally viable, in that repentance and return to God effect restoration to the Land. Subsequently, in prophetic literature this return or restoration is tied to the messianic prophecies regarding the House of David.

In each case Josephus weakens, if he does not break, the thread. The promise to the patriarchs does not involve covenanted Land as an eternal possession. Disobedience of the laws leads to expulsion or dispersion without a covenant-rooted assurance of return. And there is no connection with, or even mention of, a Messiah out of the House of David. The biblical words attributed to Balaam—"A star rises from Jacob" (Num. 24:17)— which early in Jewish tradition came to be interpreted as a reference to King David, are strikingly missing in Josephus' rewriting of the prophecy. Indeed, throughout *Antiquities* Josephus makes a point of eliminating any attribution of an eternal or messianic character to a Davidic line.[39] He deletes the unconditional divine promise to David that his "throne shall be established forever" from his rendering of 2 Sam. 7:16 (VII.93) and describes Samuel voicing an explicitly conditional assurance to David that "the kingship would *long* continue to be his" (VI.165, emphasis mine). Similarly, the promise of an eternal Davidic line in 1 Kings 8:25 becomes a promise of "numberless successors" (VIII.113). As for the more conditional promise to maintain Solomon's line forever if the people act righteously (1 Kings 9:5), Josephus adds the unscriptural threat to "cut him off root and branch," not suffering "any of their line to survive" should they not act righteously (VIII.127).

Rejecting Davidic messianism, he develops Balaam's prophetic voice to replace biblical eschatology with his own vision of future blessings: a glorious people whose eternal existence is assured by divine providence, a people who have a motherland but whose population is so great that they overflow into every island and continent. It is not a portrait true to the classical biblical end of days, and perhaps for that reason Josephus chose to put it into the mouth of Balaam rather than into that of a classical prophet. It is, however, a portrait of an hellenistic (and hence its gentile spokesperson) world: a motherland as a point of reference with an extensive eternal diaspora which might be characterized as colonial in character.[40]

Although religion and politics are interwoven in the ancient world and in Josephus' ideology as well, the ultimate issues for the historian are political, not theological ones. His rejection of messianic eschatology, indeed, the treatment of biblical land theology throughout *Antiquities*, is a reflection of that priority. He deletes the theology of covenanted Land because he does not want the Land to be the focal point of the biblical narrative as it is for Davidic messianism, with its revolutionary implications in his own day. Fearing and despising the messianism of the Zealots, he structures his account of the origins and beliefs of the Jews in such a way as to remove the theological basis for that messianism. At the same time, he lays the foundation for his own version of the end-time by adding, even in the patriarchal setting, promises of a great population that would produce a Jewish diaspora.

His antipathy to nationalistic messianism, nonetheless, is not so great as to commit him to landlessness. Even to the possible displeasure of his Roman readers, he retains the Land in his prophecies of the future, albeit not as a core feature. For Josephus, Judaism is a religion of law, of virtue, of obedience to divine statutes. To those who adhere to the laws, God grants not the classical messianic kingdom, but "a renewed existence and in the revolution (of the ages) the gift of a better life" (*Ap.* II.218). Within such a system of values, the true martyr is not one who dies for the Land, but one who sacrifices himself for the sake of the Law. The most meritorious are those who "care more for the observance of their laws and for their religion than for their own lives and their country's fate" (*Ap.* I.212).

CHAPTER 7

Land and the Rewritten Covenant

A ll four authors who rewrite biblical Land theology reconstruct the narrative such that the Land no longer functions as the key signature of covenantal history. The crisis that provokes their reconstructions is neither temporal distance from the biblical world nor exile and physical distance from the Land. To the contrary, in this instance, it is precisely proximity to the biblical era and experience of life in the Land that necessitate a reassessment of priorities within the covenant. Viewing the biblical text as immediately relevant to their existent situations and yet finding no place for a post-exilic perspective within its theology of Land and covenant, the authors of these texts develop new narratives that deemphasize the theological significance of the Land.

Within that broad commonality each of the writers approaches Scriptures with a particular orientation that influences both the selection and substantive treatment of text. The rewritings tend to be either eschatological or historical. In the two eschatologically-oriented texts, *Jubilees* and the *Testament of Moses*, the restructured theology of covenant is developed in the context of an explicit or implicit reworking of Moses' final addresses; the rewritten narrative is specifically linked to the author's perception of his own period as an imminent end-time. Not necessarily seeking an appropriate grounding for post-biblical eschatology, *Pseudo-Philo* and Josephus' *Jewish Antiquities*, the two historically-oriented rewritings, employ a wide range of narratives and develop the story of Israel as a demonstration of a particular governing principle.

Whatever its general orientation, each treatment is notably systematic. Within each new system the various aspects of biblical Land theology are reconstructed and woven into an alternative system which, when uncovered, reveals the particular post-exilic agenda of its author. In each instance the concept of covenant is modified or reformulated such that some assurance other than the Land promise assumes the pivotal position and becomes the central motif in the rewritten narrative. Concomitantly, each of the other aspects of biblical Land theology—the description of the Land, the link between Land and Law, and Land-focused eschatology—is redeveloped.

The most fluid and creative rewriting, the *Testament of Moses*, is the most traditional in its formulation of the patriarchal covenant. Developing a special structure for the end-time, the author is able to retain the promise of the Land "to the fathers" as the dynamic impetus for Israel's history. However, when the end approaches, not insignificantly, well after the return from Babylonian exile, the promise of the Land ceases to serve as the centrifugal force in God's relationship with Israel. In its place the author sets another patriarchal promise: God's oath to preserve and multiply Abraham's seed at the scene of the *Aqedah*. Much as the promise of Land in the original covenant is a recollected, recurring motif in Israelite history, so a contemporary *Aqedah* recollects its patriarchal foremodel, saves the Judean progeny of the first patriarch, and ushers in the end-time.

Motivated by a comparable eschatological interest, the author of *Jubilees* circumvents the limitations of the biblical system with a more radical reconstruction. The covenant, described solely in terms of the election of Israel as God's "first-born," originates as divine intent at Creation. Its first patriarch is Noah, and its eschatological fulfillment—a return to longevity—has a metahistorical rather than an historical reference point. The author is not so revolutionary as to totally break the traditional biblical nexus between theology and history. Within the broad context of his eternal, cosmic covenantal structure he retains the notion of covenanted history. However, insofar as history is but a reflection of the election from eternity, its internal dynamic permits obstruction, but never destruction, of the foreordained divine election.

Like the doubled covenant system of the *Testament of Moses*, the metahistorical framework for biblical history enables the author of *Jubilees* to maintain a significant level of fidelity with the biblical narratives of the patriarchal promissory encounters. However, consistently cast in the dual light of its predeluvian origins and future fulfillment, the rewritten patriarchal covenant now has the special relationship between God and Israel as its definitive feature. The Land promise, including the assurance of everlasting possession, is retained, but it neither functions as the pivot for the triad of promises (the biblical covenant), nor does it have a place in the forehistory of divine covenantal decree (the expanded covenant of *Jubilees*). Reduced in significance, the promise of Land is attached to the patriarchal covenant solely as an affirmation of God's commitment to effect restoration within history of the legitimate allocation of the earth's territory.

The tie between history and theology remains an intimate one for the authors who rewrite biblical narratives around a particular historical principle. For *Pseudo-Philo*, history is to demonstrate theological truths, the most fundamental of which is the surety of God's fidelity to his promises. For Josephus, the priority in the relationship is reversed: theology serves as the handmaiden for Israel's history which, by definition of his audience, if not of his own perspective, is normative. As developed in Genesis, the covenantal promises to the patriarchs satisfy neither principle. On the one hand, the assurance of eternal possession of the Land is contradicted by biblical history as well as by post-biblical events. On the other, the very concept of a divine promise of eternal possession of territory is not a basis for normative history. Functioning from such diametrically opposed positions, the response of both authors is to rewrite the patriarchal covenant with a highlight on the assurance, often expressed in the case of Josephus as a prediction, of great numbers rather than of Land.

The theological challenge of the name and description of the Land in the biblical narratives is totally circumvented in both of the eschatologically-oriented works. Context solves the problem in the *Testament*, where the historical narrative begins with Israel in possession of the Land. Israelite ownership of the Land is assumed, and specification of territorial boundaries is irrelevant. On the other hand, the author of *Jubilees*—"Little Genesis"—creates his own circumvention by setting the origins of Israel's involvement with the Land in prepatriarchal forehistory. Theologically sensitive to the implied relationship between nomenclature and rights of ownership, he makes a deliberate point of negating that connection with a prepatriarchal myth that shifts the narratives of the patriarchal Land promise into a restoration story. Having done so, unlike any of the other rewriters of biblical narrative, he is able to retain the term "Canaan/Land of the Canaanites" as well as closely paraphrase descriptions of the territorial dimensions of the Land in the biblical text. The creative resolution serves two major functions: it legitimates Israelite possession of the Land by breaking the connection between conquest and ownership, and at the same time minimizes the theological significance and drama of the later return from Babylonian exile by making return a recurrent, rather than singular, event in covenantal history.

The name and borders of the Land are more troublesome for the historical writers. Concerned with theological consistency, *Pseudo-Philo* assiduously avoids "Canaan/Land of the Canaanites" and is equally fastidious about the possessive pronouns he uses to describe the Land. The not-so-theologically inclined Josephus treats the name of the Land as a bit of historical data reflecting the fluctuations of time and conquest. But the delineation of the geographic boundaries of the Land in biblical promissory contexts is as problematic for him as it is for *Pseudo-Philo*. Consequently, albeit for different reasons related to the principle governing each rewriting, both authors omit territorial delineations from their narratives.

Except the future-focused *Testament*, all the rewritings retain some aspects of the biblical description of the attributes of the Land. But in none of them do such attributes include the moral ones that metaphysically empower the Land such that landedness becomes either the controlling motif in covenantal history or the trigger for the eschaton. The other forms of the biblical connection between Land and Law, however, are retained, but reinterpreted and/or modified accordingly to fit the needs of each individual system.

In *Jubilees* and the *Testament* the key issue is to develop the connection between Land and Law in a manner that allows, and thereby explains, the delay of the eschaton in the post-exilic era. Each does so through a covenantal system that maintains both the unconditional and conditional biblical conceptualizations of the covenant. The author of *Jubilees* retains the biblical tension between the two by developing a subtle discordance between the assurances of election and of Land. Unconditionality is implied, if not asserted, in the initial presentation of the covenant as God's election of Israel "forever and ever" set forth in the Creation story. In a comparable cosmic context the Land also is allocated to the line of Shem "to possess forever." But grounded in a cast of lots rather than in divine decree, at its prepatriarchal inception the Land allocation is not a component of the unconditional covenant. In *Jubilees* it acquires its covenantal significance only in the context of patriarchal history, which begins a process of progressive fulfillment and restoration of the cosmic order. On the historical stage the distinction between election and Land promise persists, for the former involves fulfillment and the latter, restoration. Israel is to follow the commandments in order to fulfill the foreordained destiny to be God's holy nation. The holy nation will surely dwell in the Land allotted to it, but that settlement is a matter of restoration, not of fulfillment.

The distinction is a significant one, for within his narrative the author of *Jubilees* makes a point of not connecting the conditional covenant with acquisition and/or retention of the promised Land. Indeed, he develops a number of techniques that reflect a conscious effort to break the connection: using the language and structure of the biblical link between Land and Law but making it a relationship between election of people and adherence to Law; omitting the biblical association between adherence to commandments and acquisition of the Land; and employing a deliberate vagueness such that warnings against violation of the Law are not clearly associated with the threat of loss of the Land. The purpose of all this is to deprive the return from exile of covenantal and, hence, eschatological significance. In order to accomplish that, the author of *Jubilees* underplays the significance of exile. The sole reference to the loss of the Land appears in the eschatological overview which prefaces the work (1:13-14). In the context of the redevelopment of the deuteronomic paradigm in that overview, the treatment of the Land/Law motif throughout the work becomes abundantly clear. Violation of the commandments does lead to exile, but the correlation is not a direct one, for the exilic condition is only a reflection of the desecration, the polluted nature, of God's elect people. In covenantal terms the real loss is one of sanctification, not of Land. Consequently, the ground is prepared for the argument behind his eschatology: the true signature of restoration is total spiritual regeneration, not return to the Land.

The *Testament of Moses* achieves the same goal by splitting covenantal history in two. The biblical link between adherence to the Law and retention of the Land (the conditional covenant) governs Israel's history from the entry into the Land until the time of the Maccabees. In the period that follows, however, a second cycle begins in which the link between Land and Law is no longer maintained. Sin is punished, but the hold on the Land is not threatened. A preface to the eschaton, this cycle stops short of historical resolution, for the oppression continues beyond punishment, intensifying to the point where ultimately suffering bears no relationship whatsoever to sin. Indeed, the oppressed openly proclaim not only their own purity and fidelity, but that of their ancestors as well. Culminating in a story of martyrdom, this suffering of innocents activates the eschaton in which the unconditional covenant, a metaphysical but unrevealed reality throughout Israel's history, becomes manifest. However, in contrast to its biblical counterpart, the *Testament*'s unconditional covenant does not emphasize everlasting possession of the Land, which would only serve to highlight the return to the Land without the expected redemption. Instead, recollecting the substance of the biblical promise at the scene of the *Aqedah*, this covenant pointedly focuses on God's unconditional assurance that Abraham's progeny will never be extinguished. The redevelopment is successful. At the close of the work Moses reveals that the two covenants are in fact interfaced by God's foreknowledge and control over history. The unstated, but clearly implied, correlate of that revelation is that the contradictions between the covenants are an illusion fostered by the revelatory limitations of historical phenomena. Thus undercutting historical experience as final evidence of theological truths, the *Testament* lays another solid foundation for belittling the eschatological significance of the troublesome return from Babylonian exile.

Pseudo-Philo's treatment of the biblical connection between Land and Law contrasts sharply with those of the eschatological writers. His desire to demonstrate that Israel's history provides sure evidence of God's ongoing fidelity to his promises permits neither the positing of a metahistorical realm which the historical process stumbles to fulfill and restore nor the discrediting of historical experience as a source of theological truth. Maintaining the full biblical interplay of theology and history, the primary function of his rewriting is to stand biblical history on its head. No longer is history a manifestation of the workings of the conditional covenant and the story of Israel's infidelity and its consequences. Instead, it is presented as evidence of the unconditional covenant, as the story of God's uninterrupted and, even more significant, ongoing commitment to his promises.

The difficulty that the biblical connection between Land and Law presents to this new context does not involve the essential nature of the covenant. That issue is resolved by the substitution of the assurance of great numbers for eternal possession of the Land as the key feature in both the patriarchal and Sinaitic covenants. Rather, regardless of priorities within the covenantal triad, threatened withholding of any divine promise denies the very surety that *Pseudo-Philo* wishes to affirm. Consequently, the rewriting is dual faceted. On the one hand, the author reconstructs and/or deletes the primary biblical indicators of the conditionality of the Sinai covenant—the threats of incomplete conquest and loss of the Land. He omits all references to specific territorial boundaries and assurances of eternal possession from the descriptions of the patriarchal covenant and writes the threat of exile out of the Sinai covenant. On the other hand, he subtly develops links between adherence to Law and growth in numbers that are constructed only in positive formulations. When the negative formulation is contextually unavoidable, he shifts the voice from the conditional to the predictive, substitutes God's temporary abandonment of the people for loss of the Land, and, most significantly, consistently closes the formulation with a statement of his central theme: the assurance that regardless of Israel's actions ("nonetheless"), out of his mercy God remains faithful to his promises.

Although Josephus shares *Pseudo-Philo*'s focus on the historical process as well as his emphasis on the promise of numbers over that of Land, the biblical connection between Land and Law poses a very different problem for him in his *Antiquities*. Indeed, in many ways significantly closer to the biblical version, Josephus' treatment of this component of Land theology is an inversion of *Pseudo-Philo*'s. Affirming a correlation between natural disaster and divine ire for all people, Egyptians as well as Israelites, the historian rejects only the particular metaphysical nature of the biblical interpretation of the conquest. He is prepared to acknowledge the incompleteness of the conquest, but connects it to violation of a reinterpreted, generalized concept of divine will that functions as an ultimate rather than immediate cause. Not at all reluctant to deal with the subject of exile, Josephus takes a similar approach with that issue and again retains the biblical association between loss of the Land and violation of the Law. Interpreting the violation—"sin"—as the absence of civic virtue (in particular, the disobedience of the powers that be and the cultivation of rebellion) and divine will as a kind of ordained natural order, he is able to establish a natural causal connection between the two.

The stance, of course, reflects Josephus' personal political perspective on the Jewish war against Rome. However, placed in the context of the reinterpretations of biblical Land theology by the pseudepigraphic writers, Josephus' treatment of the Land/Law component takes on its own theological dimension. In spite of his avoidance of the term and concept of covenant, the historian, like the theologically-inclined rewriters of biblical narrative, preserves the distinctiveness of one aspect of the triadal biblical promises. In his case, as in *Pseudo-Philo*, that aspect is the assurance of fertility and numbers. However, again reflecting the inverted relationship between the two historical systems, the promise that nourishes the theologian's faith in history provides the grounds for the historian's eschatology.

In one way or another each of the four writers attempts to write the eschatological dimension of biblical Land theology out of the rewritten narrative. For the authors of the *Testament* and *Jubilees*, living in the Land and anticipating the eschaton well after the return from Babylonian exile, the central biblical eschatological themes of ingathering of exiles and celebration of physical return to the Land are stumbling blocks to be overcome. For the two historically-oriented authors, who are occupied with other agendas, Land-focused biblical eschatology is in one case irrelevant, and in the other, counterproductive and destructive.

The two eschatologically motivated works reinterpret the deuteronomic paradigm such that it no longer associates the eschaton with return to the Land after exile. Both focus on the repentance stage of that paradigm; in both intercession serves as a medium for the reconstruction; and in neither is there an emphasis on the Land in the portrait of the end-time. These commonalties aside, the works not only differ in approach, but offer diametrically opposed resolutions.

The reconstruction in *Jubilees* is presented through a creative interpretive device that presents a new revelation in the guise of a reaffirmation of the paradigm of Deuteronomy 28-30. Casting his rewriting of Genesis as an angel-narrated complement to the biblical revelation received at Sinai, the author has Moses intercede in protest when the angel forecasts Israelite history along traditional deuteronomic lines. God responds directly, rejecting the intercessory plea and ostensibly reconfirming the historical forecast. In fact, the divine response involves a major alteration to the traditional paradigm: a highlighting and doubling of the repentance stage that negates the traditional Land focus and subtly but clearly accounts for why return to the Land did not initiate the eschaton.

In contrast, the *Testament of Moses* totally does away with repentance as a necessary phase in the eschatological process. Deuteronomy 32 offers a paradigmatic base for just such a deletion. But in that eschatological drama Israel has no initiating role—a dimension crucial to a first-century Judean anticipating an imminent end-time. So the author of the *Testament* develops a martyrdom story that, like a biblical intercession turned on its head, triggers divine avenging wrath and, now in parallel with Deuteronomy 32, brings on the eschaton. This reconstruction requires no suggestion of a new revelation. To the contrary, it is deliberately developed as a biblical revelation secreted within an intertextual relationship between two promissory passages.

Thus, by very different methods both authors succeed in their common goal of removing return to the Land from the eschatological process. Moreover, both develop a characterization of the idealized end—return to the longevity of the cosmic forehistory in *Jubilees* and exaltation of an avenged Israel in the *Testament*—that is integrated with the covenant theology developed in their respective works. Neither incorporates specific references to the Land in the portrait of the eschaton. Yet, that Israel is living in the Land at the "time of the end" is a clear though understated assumption in both works. The assumption and its understatement bespeak the historical situations and theological quandaries that sparked the rewriting of the biblical narratives.

Pseudo-Philo and Josephus are motivated by comparable tensions, but operate within a completely different dynamic. Interested in the historical process rather than its eschatological ending, the two writers, albeit for very different reasons, both ignore the eschatological potential of the last chapters of Deuteronomy. That potential stands in opposition to the surety of faith within history that *Pseudo-Philo* wishes the rewritten narrative to demonstrate. Consequently, he reformulates selections from the Deuteronomy chapters, substituting conditional reward for negative threat and

consistently inserting assurances of God's mercy over against the conditionality. Like those of *Jubilees* and the *Testament*, this reconstruction is
rooted in an intercessory motif. But whereas the author of *Jubilees* creates
his own intercessory dialogue in order to dramatically adjust the paradigm
of biblical eschatology, the author of *Pseudo-Philo*, like that of the *Testament*, develops his central theme from a reworking of biblical texts. In fact,
in spite of dramatic differences in their interests, there are marked similarities between *Pseudo-Philo* and the *Testament*. Both writers derive the theological principles that govern their reinterpretations from the biblical
narrative of the dialogue between Moses and God at the scene of the Gold-
en Calf. Both rework that narrative by intertextual exegesis. The *Testament*
writer plays it over against the *Aqedah* promise of Gen. 26:3; *Pseudo-Philo*
interweaves it with a creative reconstruction of Deut. 31:16-18 that employs a cosmic symbol (Moses' staff likened to the rainbow after the Flood),
but without the cosmic implications of *Jubilees*. Moreover, in both narratives the primary covenantal component is the assurance of numbers (peoplehood), an assurance that governs and/or overrides history. But here the
similarities end. In the rewriting of the *Testament* that assurance is expressed in the form of a divine avenging wrath that becomes manifest at
the end-time. In diametrical opposition, for *Pseudo-Philo* the assurance is
divine mercy, blatantly manifested throughout Israel's history and totally
unrelated to eschatology.

Josephus, on the other hand, develops the last chapters of Deuteronomy
strictly as historical prophecy, neither expressing an overriding theological
principle nor providing a textual base for eschatology. Unlike *Pseudo-Philo*,
Josephus does have an eschatological vision that is national and historical
in orientation. Deliberately avoiding the traditional biblical eschatological
themes of Land and messiah king, he sets that vision in the mouth of a
prophet whose gentile credentials furnish a necessary discretion and endow
the words with legitimacy. The rewritten prophecy is not unlike the rewriting of the promise to Jacob at Bethel in *Jubilees*. Both have universal over-
tones, but whereas the former has God assure great territorial expansion,
the Judean in exile offers only a discrete description of a mother country
overflowing into a diaspora of great numbers.

The difference between the two approaches has less to do with the distinction between their theological and historical orientations than with the
particular situations of the writers and the historical circumstances in
which each rewriting was undertaken. In the case of Josephus and *Antiquities*, the writer himself has provided the historical background which
brings clarity to his redevelopment of biblical Land theology. On the other
hand, the *Sitz im Leben* of the pseudepigraphic writers can only be derived

from their works. Admittedly, reinterpretation of covenantal Land theology is only one element in their multifaceted reworkings of biblical narrative. Yet given the prominence of the Land concept in the theology of Hebrew Scriptures, the systematic reconstruction of the ideas of Land and covenant in each of the rewritten narratives is telling of the concerns of the author and at least allusive to the kind of historical setting in which the work was composed.

Election and sanctification of Israel lie at the heart of the covenantal system developed in *Jubilees*. Although ultimately assured by divine decree from the time of Creation, the achievement of that sanctification through adherence to the commandments must take place within the historical process. Otherwise, the end-time, in which history and Israel return to the ideal conditions of the cosmic beginning time, is delayed. Without an historical context, such a system could be understood simply as a variation on the biblical one. However, if its author is placed in the Land some time after the return from exile, various aspects of the rewritten covenantal theology are particularly suggestive. The author lives in a era of expansion (hence the cosmic perspective) that promotes his own expectation of an imminent end-time (the eschatological preface). That expectation calls forth both an explanation for the delay (the reinterpretation of the covenant) as well as a call to purification and repentance directed toward the unduly complacent who view the expansion and prosperity as automatic signs of the end (hence, the new revelation reconstructing the deuteronomic paradigm.)

In the *Testament of Moses* the dynamic is reversed. Far from a chastisement of complacency, this rewriting is an affirmation of covenantal eschatology in the face of a loss of faith. The author/redactor retains the Land-centered theology of the biblical narrative for Israelite history until well after the return (perhaps a reflection of a Maccabean substratum). But in his own day (after Herod's sons), clearly perceived as an eschatological one (reflected in the Deuteronomy context and in the textual interplay on deuteronomic paradigms), there is an entirely different set of priorities, as reflected in the transition to a new covenantal system. In this setting the connection between adherence to commandments and prosperity, however defined, is no longer perceived as functioning (the statement of innocence). Israel suffers under far greater oppression than it had under the Babylonians when punishment was in fact deserved (clearly stated in the narrative). Moreover, there is no evidence of God's concern, no prophetic leadership to offer guidance (the concern with Moses' imminent death in the frame of the *Testament*). There is only great loss of lives (the concern with the promise of numbers) and the martyrdom of innocents that belies any expectation of the eschaton—hence the Taxo narrative that makes martyrdom the trigger for the end, affirming both God's justice and continued involvement, albeit hidden, in Israel's destiny.

Clearly living in a time of comparable oppression further intensified by erratic leadership, as reflected in the choice of Judges as its focal text, *Pseudo-Philo's* chief concerns are a perceived threat to national survival reflected in numerous loss of lives (the great emphasis on the promise of numbers and peoplehood in his reconstructed covenant) and, concomitantly, his people's loss of faith in the covenant itself (reflected in his consistent focus on God's covenantal care and fidelity to his promises). Although the reconstruction evokes a scenario not unlike that of the *Testament*, markedly different interpretive resolutions suggest certain dissimilarities in their historical settings. Whereas the situation of the *Testament* provokes an outraged declaration of self-righteousness and a call for vengeance, loss of national self-confidence, perhaps induced by a more oppressive life situation or one of longer duration, vitiates any such activation of energy in *Pseudo-Philo*. Instead, aware of the frailty of an overwhelmed nation (hence the deletion of exhortations to fidelity and the ready acknowledgment of Israel's record of national faithlessness), this writer offers a far more passive resolution: the assurance of God's enduring mercy. The other authors share *Pseudo-Philo's* surety that ultimately God foreknows, is concerned with, and/or influences Israel's destiny. But whereas the divine role is but one aspect in the covenantal drama in their rewritings, it is the overriding, if not exaggerated, motif in *Pseudo-Philo's* reconstruction. Yet unlike all of them, *Pseudo-Philo* offers no eschatological vision to serve as a bridge between the harsh realities of contemporary national experience and a surer future. The omission is so glaring that it can only be purposeful—evidence perhaps of an increased anticipation of the eschaton that the author desires to discourage, much as the *Testament* writer wished to encourage it.

None of the writers writes the Land out the covenant or biblical theology. Albeit not at the heart of his metahistorical covenant, the author of *Jubilees* retrojects the Land allocation into that metahistory, traces its restoration to rightful heir through Israel's early history, and assumes Israel's presence in the Land at the end-time. The same assumption is made by the *Testament* writer whose review/preview of Israel's history follows the Land centered biblical model until after the return from exile. And, ignoring even the possibility of exile from the Land, *Pseudo-Philo* elects the period of early conquest and troubled settlement as the context for his reconstruction of covenant theology. Even Josephus, whom we know would have cause for such a deletion, includes the Land in the divine predictions he substitutes for the covenant structure and dangerously alludes to the Land functioning as a vibrant mother country in some future time. Landedness is part of the theological and historical heritages of all the writers. However it is as troublesome to them as it will become to the later rabbinic tradition which, in the light of destruction and exile, placed people and Torah over Land in the heart of its own system.

The reconstructions of the four authors downgrade the position of Land in covenant theology, not because possession of the Land is insignificant, but because it is so signficant that it stands in the way of a contemporary reading of Scriptures. Indeed the same can be said of those who currently struggle with the theological significance of the modern return to the Land. To the extent that their Land theology is rooted in the biblical narrative, conflicting priorities continue to invite ventures into some form of the art of interpretation.

Notes

NOTES TO CHAPTER 1

1. "The Controversy with Rav Amital over the Land of Israel," *Nekuda* 52 (December 24, 1982) and 56 (March 28, 1983), cited in Ian Lustig, *For the Land and the Lord* (New York: Council on Foreign Relations, 1988): 128, 142.

2. On the history of the interpretation, see W. D. Davies, *The Territorial Dimension of Judaism* (Berkeley: University of California Press, 1982) and Lawrence Hoffman, ed., *The Land of Israel: Jewish Perspectives* (Notre Dame: University of Notre Dame Press, 1986). For the geo-political application of the biblical Land concept in the Hasmonean period, see Doron Mendels, *The Land of Israel as a Political Concept in Hasmonean Literature* (Tubingen: Mohr, 1987). For modern interpretations, see Eliezer Schweid, *The Land of Israel: National Home or Land of Destiny* (Cranbury, N.J.: Associated University Presses, 1985) and Aviezer Ravitsky, *Messianism, Zionism, and Jewish Religious Radicalism* (Tel Aviv: Am Oved, 1993) (Hebrew).

3. In contrast, the reinterpretation of Land theology within the Bible has been a subject of study. See particularly, Sarah Japhet, *The Ideology of the Book of Chronicles and Its Place in Biblical Thought* (Jerusalem: Bialik Institute, 1977) (Hebrew).

4. The issues I address with these texts are of interest to historians of Christianity for they potentially could be relevant to the absence of Land theology in early Christianity.

5. The exceptions which I cite frequently and to which I am heavily indebted are: Moshe Weinfeld, "Inheritance of the Land—Privilege versus Obligation: The Concept of the Promise of the Land in the Sources of the First and Second Temple Periods," in *Zion* 49 (1984): 115-37 (Hebrew), and by the same author, "Universalism and Particularism in the Period of Exile and Restoration," *Tarbiz* 33 (1963-64): 229-42 (Hebrew); I. Heinemann, "The Relationship Between the Jewish People and Their Land in Hellenistic-Jewish Literature," *Zion* 13-14 (1948-49): 1-9 (Hebrew). Doron Mendels' study, *The Land of Israel as a Political Concept in Hasmonean Literature*, deals with the Land concept, but his concern is with the political, not the theological, dimension.

6. Note particularly G. Strecker, ed., *Das Land Israel in biblischer Zeit* (Gottingen: Vandenhoeck and Rubrecht, 1983); Davies, *The Territorial Dimension of Judaism*; Michael Stone, "Reactions to Destruction of the Second Temple," in *JSJ* 12 (1981): 195-204; Schweid, *The Land of Israel: National Home or Land of Destiny*; W. Marquardt, *Die Juden und ihr Land* (Hamburg: Siebenster-Taschenbuch, 1975); R.

Rendtorff, *Israel und sein Land* (Munchen: Kaiser, 1975); Martin Buber, *Israel and Palestine: The History of an Idea* (London: East and West Library, 1952).

7. Geza Vermes, *Scripture and Tradition in Judaism: Haggadic Studies* (Leiden: Brill, 1961), 95, 124-26.

8. For example, see George W. E. Nickelsburg, "The Bible Rewritten and Expanded" in Michael Stone, ed., *Jewish Writings of the Second Temple Period* (Assen: Van Gorcum and Philadelphia: Fortress Press, 1984), 89-129.

In his essay "Palestinian Adaptations of Biblical Narratives and Prophecies," in Robert A. Kraft and George W. E. Nickelsburg, eds., *Early Judaism and Its Modern Interpreters* (Philadelphia: Fortress and Atlanta: Scholars Press, 1986), 239-47, Daniel Harrington seems to vacillate between the broader and narrower categorizations. The texts he selects for analysis reflect the narrower usage, but he suggests that the term might also be applied to works that are not closely tied to the structure of the biblical narrative, e.g., *Paralipomena of Jeremiah*, *Life of Adam and Eve/Apocalypse of Moses*, and *Ascension of Isaiah*.

9. This position is most succinctly argued in Philip Alexander's "Retelling the Old Testament," in D. A. Carson and H. G. N. Williamson, eds., *It Is Written: Scripture Citing Scripture* (Cambridge: Cambridge University Press, 1988), 99-121. Alexander's argument for a genre classification is based on an analysis of four works (116-18), three of which I use in this study. The fourth, *Genesis Apocryphon*, is of a fragmentary nature and offers little evidence of how its author interpreted biblical Land theology. The additional work that I include, *Testament of Moses*, is not mentioned in Alexander's essay, perhaps because of the subtleness of its intertextual approach. Devorah Dimant, in "Use and Interpretation of Mikra in the Apocrypha and Pseudepigrapha," in J. Moulder, ed., *Mikra* (Assen/Maastricht: Van Gorcum and Philadelphia: Fortress, 1988), 402, urges restriction of the term to narrative works. However, unlike Alexander, she includes 1 *Enoch* and does not present an argument for a genre classification. The number of works falling under the rubric, however defined, remains open, particularly in light of the awaited publication of additional rewritings, or fragments thereof, from Qumran.

10. Harrington, "Palestinian Adaptations," 239-40 and in direct contrast to Alexander's statement that "account of events" only "incidentally" serve "theological ends" ("Retelling," 116-17).

11. I note certain exegetical techniques that are employed in each text, but a systematic analysis is a study in its own right. Although not directed specifically to exegetical techniques employed to redevelop biblical narratives, Dimant's "Use and Interpretation" and Louis Feldman's "Use, Authority and Exegesis of Mikra in the Writings of Josephus" in J. Moulder, ed., *Mikra*, 379-419, 455-518 are good starting places.

12. Josephus, of course, wrote his *Antiquities* while living in Rome. But as he spent much of his life in Judea and wrote as a Judean, I follow Harrington ("Pales-

tinian Adaptations" in Kraft and Nickelsburg, eds., *Early Judaism*, 239-58) and treat *Antiquities* as a Palestinian work.

13. For the most recent work on the fragments of *Jubilees* found at Qumran, see James VanderKam, "The *Jubilees* Fragments from Qumran Cave 4," in Julio Trebolle Barrera and Luis Vegas Montaner, eds., *The Madrid Congress* (Leiden, New York, Koln: Brill, 1992), 2:635-648. On the dating, see A. S. van der Woude, "Fragmente des Buches Jubilaen aus Qumran Hohle 11 (11QJub)," in G. Jeremias, H. W. Kuhn, and H. Stegemann, eds., *Tradition und Glaube: Das fruhe Christentum in seiner Unwelt: Festgabe fur Karl George Kuhn* (Gottingen: Vanderhoeck and Rubrecht, 1971); James C. Vanderkam, *Textual and Historical Studies in the Book of Jubilees*, HSM 14 (Missoula, Mont.: Scholars Press, 1977); Philip R. Davies, "Calendrical Change and Qumran Origins: An Assessment of VanderKam's Theory," *CBQ* (1983): 80-89; and the essays by Nickelsburg ("The Bible Rewritten and Expanded") and Dimant ("Qumran Sectarian Literature") in Stone, ed., *Jewish Writings*.

14. Introduction to *Jubilees* in R. H. Charles, ed., *Apocrypha and Pseudepigrapha of the Old Testament* (Oxford: Clarendon, 1913), 2:1.

15. Gene L. Davenport, *The Eschatology of the Book of Jubilees* (Leiden: Brill, 1971).

16. For critiques of Davenport, see E. P. Sanders, *Paul and Palestinian Judaism* (Philadelphia: Fortress, 1977), 387; Nickelsburg, "The Bible Rewritten and Expanded," in Stone, ed., *Jewish Writings*, 102; and R. Pummer, "The Book of *Jubilees* and the Samaritans," *Eglise et Theologie* 10 (1979): 153.

17. O. S. Wintermute's introduction to *Jubilees* in James Charlesworth, ed., *OTP* (Garden City: Doubleday, 1985), 2:46-47.

18. James C. VanderKam, *Textual and Historical Studies in the Book of Jubilees*. The passages most frequently cited deal with Jacob's wars against the Amorites and Edomites in *Jub.* 34:2-9; 37-38 and with the eschatological drama in chap. 23. VanderKam identifies the first two as descriptions of the Maccabean wars and the last as referring to the subsequent controversy over Hellenization.

19. R. Pummer ("The Book of *Jubilees* and the Samaritans," 156) and O. S. Wintermute are in general agreement with VanderKam's dating. Jonathan Goldstein is critical of VanderKam's identifications and suggests instead the earlier date of 169-67 ("The Date of the Book of *Jubilees*," in *PAAJR* 50 (1983): 78-83). Albeit on the basis of different criticisms of VanderKam's work, Nickelsburg ("The Bible Rewritten and Expanded," in Stone, ed., *Jewish Writings*, 102-03) is close to agreement with Goldstein on the date (around 168 BCE).

20. Mendels, *The Land of Israel*, 57.

21. R. H. Charles, *The Assumption of Moses Translated From the Sixth Century Manuscript* (London: Black, 1897).

22. Jacob Licht, "Taxo, or the Apocalyptic Doctrine of Vengeance," *JJS* 12 (1961): 95-103.

23. George W. E. Nickelsburg, "An Antiochan Date for the Testament of Moses," in George W. E. Nickelsburg, ed., *Studies On the Testament of Moses*, SBLSCS 4 (Cambridge, Mass.: SBL, 1973), 71-77 and more hesitantly, John J. Collins, "The Date and Provenance of the *Testament of Moses*," in *ibid.*, 15-32.

24. J. Priest, "*Testament of Moses,*" in Charlesworth, ed., *OTP* 1:921, and "Some Reflections on the *Assumption of Moses*," in *Perspectives on Religious Studies* 4 (1977): 92-111; D. M. Rhoads, "The *Assumption of Moses* and Jewish History: 4 BC-AD," in Nickelsburg, ed., *Studies*, 53-58; and E. Brandenburger, *Himmelfahrt Moses*, JSHRZ 52 (Gutersloh: Mohn, 1976).

25. On the dating of *Pseudo-Philo*, see Frederick Murphy, *Pseudo-Philo: Rewriting the Bible* (New York: Oxford University Press, 1993), 6, and D. J. Harrington, "*Pseudo-Philo*, A New Translation and Introduction," in Charlesworth, ed., *OTP* 2:299.

26. On the relationship to *Jubilees* see M. R. James, *The Biblical Antiquities of Philo* (2d ed.) (New York: Ktav, 1971), 45-46; John Strugnell, "*Philo (Pseudo) or Liber Antiquitatum Biblicarum*" in *EJ* 13:408-09; and Louis Feldman's contrasting view in his "Prolegomenon" to James's work, liii. For a review of the theories concerning the purpose of the work, see the discussions in Feldman's "Prolegomenon" and D. J. Harrington, Charles Perrot, and P. M. Bogaert, eds., *Pseudo-Philon: Les Antiquites Bibliques*, vol. 2 (Paris: Cerf, 1976).

NOTES TO CHAPTER 2

1. On the significance of the Land in biblical literature, see Davies, *The Territorial Dimension in Judaism*; Abraham S. Halkin, "Zion in Biblical Literature," in Abraham S. Halkin, ed., *Zion in Jewish Literature* (New York: Herzl Press, 1961) 18-37; Harry Orlinsky, "The Biblical Concept of the Land of Israel: Cornerstone of the Covenant between God and Israel," in Lawrence A. Hoffman, ed., *The Land of Israel: Jewish Perspectives*, 27-64; and Weinfeld, "Inheritance of the Land—Privilege versus Obligation," 115-37.

2. Emphasis mine. The parallels are even more striking in Hebrew:

והקימותי את בריתי ביני ובין זרעך אחריך לדורותם לברית עולם להיות לך

לאלהים ולזרעך אתריך. ונתתי לך ולזרעך אחריך את ארץ מגריך את כל ארץ כנען לאחזת

עולם והייתי להם לאלהים.

3. Abraham and Sarah's new names are directly linked to the multitude of their seed, but the covenantal future of that seed is described in terms of the Land. The Land promise receives comparable attention when Jacob's name is changed to Israel (Gen. 35:9-12), and is the single focus of the covenant formulation in the change of *El Shaddai* to *YHWH* (Exod. 6:2-8). On the significance of name change

and the biblical concept of Land, see Orlinsky's comments in "The Biblical Concept of the Land of Israel," 36-38.

4. "May *El Shaddai* bless you, make you fertile and numerous, so that you become an assembly of peoples. May He grant the blessing of Abraham to you and your offspring, that you may possess the land where you are sojourning, which God gave to Abraham" (Gen. 28:3-4).

5. Orlinksy takes exception to my description of the covenantal promises to Abraham as a gift. He argues that נתן has the sense of "assign, deed, transfer, convey," and that it implies a reward rather than a gift in all the promissory contexts ("The Biblical Concept of the Land of Israel," 31ff. and 62, n. 19). Similarly, in distinguishing between covenants as treaties and as grants, Moshe Weinfeld describes the Abrahamic and Davidic covenants as grant rewards for deeds already done ("The Covenant of Grant in the Old Testament and in the Ancient Near East," in *JAOS* 90 [1970]: 184 ff.). On the other hand, Halkin perceives the same distinction that I describe above, and calls the selection of Abraham and his seed "an act of grace on the part of God rather than a reward of human achievement" ("Zion in Biblical Literature," 18).

6. "I will give all these lands to you and to your offspring, fulfilling the oath that I swore to your father Abraham...inasmuch as Abraham obeyed Me and kept My charge, My commandments, My laws, and My teachings." The dual basis here is intriguing given the mixed presentation of the issue of merit in the various promises to Abraham. Significantly, in this Isaac passage, as with Abraham, the mention of merit (v. 5) comes only after the covenantal commitment to Abraham has been stated (v. 3).

7. At the first encounter at Bethel the reference to the earlier patriarchs appears in God's self-identification as "the God of your father Abraham and the God of Isaac" immediately preceding the promise of the Land (28:13). In the second, the promise is conveyed directly in terms of "the land that I gave to Abraham and Isaac" (Gen. 35:12).

8. "I appeared to Abraham, Isaac, and Jacob....I also established My covenant with them, to give them the land of Canaan, the land in which they lived as sojourners" (Exod. 6:3-4).

"Set out from here, you and the people that you have brought up from the land of Egypt, to the land of which I swore to Abraham, Isaac, and Jacob, saying, 'To your offspring will I give it'" (Exod. 33:1).

9. Critiquing R. E. Clements's argument that the Abrahamic and Sinaitic covenants are fused in deuteronomic literature, W. D. Davies notes that "outside the Pentateuch the promise to Abraham as such is seldom referred to" (*The Gospel and the Land* [Berkeley: University of California, 1974], 104). In fact, even outside of Genesis the recollections refer either to all three patriarchs by name and/or more generally to "the fathers."

10. Lev. 26:42; Deut. 11:8-9, 30:20, and 31:20 refer only to the Land. Deut. 7:12-13 describes the covenant in terms of God's love, fertility, and the Land God "swore to your fathers to give you." And the admonition of Deut. 8:1 speaks of thriving and increasing and being able "to occupy the land which the Lord promised on oath to your fathers."

11. The description of the covenant in Deut. 8:18 involves Israel's wealth, but the specific context involves the wealth they will acquire in the Land.

12. Usually expressed by a form of נשבע. The exceptions are Exod. 6:8, which uses נשׂאתי את ידי to express God's oath; Lev. 26:42, which speaks of God remembering the covenant and the land; Lev. 26:45, which refers to the covenant with the redeemed Israelites at Sinai; and Deut. 4:37-38, which refers to the covenant in terms of God having chosen the offspring of the patriarchs.

13. ארץ ישׂראל appears in 1 Sam. 13:19. Orlinsky suggests that the limited use of the term in biblical literature (five times) may be due to concern over possible confusion between it and the northern kingdom ("The Biblical Concept of the Land of Israel," 64, n. 29).

14. ארץ מגוריהם אשׁר גרו בה. The experiential description is used here as a modifier for "Land of Canaan."

15. The promise to Isaac of "all these lands" is elaborated by reference to the oath to Abraham (Gen. 26:3). On Jacob's return from Mesopotamia, he is told that "the land that I gave to Abraham and Isaac I give to you and your offspring to come" (Gen. 35:12). Assuring his son that God will bring him back to "the land of your fathers," Jacob passes the promise on to Joseph (Gen. 48:4, 21) who, in turn, tells his children and grandchildren that God will bring them to the "land He promised on oath to Abraham, Isaac and Jacob" (Gen. 50:24).

16. Recollected by Moses in Deut. 1:7.

17. The descriptions in Deut. 11:24 and Josh. 1:2-4 combine experience and geographic delineation of borders with the latter passage also including recollection of promises to Moses.

18. See Davies, *The Gospel and the Land*, 27ff., for a discussion of the implications of the biblical use of the term "land of Canaan."

19. In "Inheritance of the Land" Weinfeld cites this passage in his argument that the uniqueness of the biblical concept of land being given to the nation by God lies specifically in the accompanying notion of associated obligations.

20. See Gen. 31:18 and 37:1, in addition to multiple references to Jacob and his sons residing in the "land of Canaan" in Genesis 42 and 44-48.

21. It first reappears in Gen. 50:5, where Joseph in direct speech requests burial "in the land of Canaan."

22. Most frequently used in Genesis, "land of Canaan" appears over twenty-five times in the narratives of the exodus through the conquest.

23. See Deut. 4:38; 9:5; 12:29; 19:1; 29:7; Josh. 23:5; Judg. 6:9.

24. The Deuteronomist in particular uses the third person possessive pronoun to convey the extent to which Israelite success is due to God rather than to their might or virtuous character. See passages cited in above note.

25. Exod. 23:10, 26, 33; 34:24; Lev. 19:9, 33; 22:24; 23:22; 25:7, 9, 45; Num. 10:9; Deut. 11:14; 15:11; 19:2-3, 10; 24:14.

26. Lev. 26:1, 5-6, 19-20, 33; Deut. 28:12, 24, 52.

27. Emphasis mine. See also Exod. 13:5, 11; Deut. 12:29; 19:1; Judg. 6:9, and the ownership theme in Jer. 12:14-15.

28. "But the land must not be sold beyond reclaim, for the land is Mine; you are but strangers resident with Me." Echoed in Phinehas' description of the land east of the Jordan as "the Lord's own holding" in Josh. 22:19.

29. Verses 3-5 in particular are so understood by Davies in *The Gospel and the Land*, 27.

30. For example, Deut. 2:10-12; 4:37-38; 9:4-5; 18:9-14; Josh. 1:11; 15; 18:3; 23:3, 5; 24:13.

31. The descriptive phrase "flowing with milk and honey" is first used when God describes the Land to Moses (Exod. 3:8, 17) and is repeated throughout the narrative from the exodus to the entrance into the Land in early Joshua (Exod. 13:5; 33:3; Lev. 20:24; Num. 13:27; 14:8; 16:13, 14; Deut. 6:3; 11:9; 26:9, 15; 27:3; 31:20; Josh. 5:6-7).

Num. 14:7, Exod. 3:8, and Deut. 8:7 refer to the spaciousness of the Land, whereas "the good land" is used repeatedly in deuteronomic literature: Deut. 1:35; 3:25; 4:21-22; 6:18; 8:10; 9:6; 11:17; Josh. 23:16 הארץ הטובה; Josh. 23:13, 15; 1 Kings 14:15 האדמה הטובה.

32. The Land is never explicitly described as "holy" in Hebrew Scriptures. Such a quality is, however, implied in the pentateuchal concern with defilement and the Land's inability to tolerate moral pollution, a characteristic derived from God's relationship to the Land and not necessarily connected to the covenant or the Israelites (Gen. 15:16; Lev. 18:27-28; Num. 35:33). In prophetic literature the concept of "holy place" is associated particularly with Jerusalem and the Temple where God dwells. See Weinfeld, "Inheritance of the Land," 127.

33. Here the Land is portrayed as the rejector of its own defilers; at other times, God is the actor. The relationship between the two is spelled out in Lev. 18:25: when the Land becomes defiled God calls it to account "for its iniquity" and, consequently, it "spews out its inhabitants."

34. For example, Isa. 1:7-8; 6:11-13; 7:23-25; 24:4-13; 49:14-21; Jer. 2:7; 3:19; 12:7-13; 16:18; 23:10; Ezek. 20:6; 36:8-15; Hos. 2:23-25; 4:2-3; Joel 4:18; Amos 9:13-15; Mic. 1:3-9.

35. On the issue of the worthiness in Genesis passages, see Weinfeld, "Inheritance of the Land," 117.

36. Intriguingly, the conditional association between lifestyle and full geographic delineation of borders may be foreshadowed in the covenantal scene of Gen. 15:13-21, which follows the same sequence. First Abraham is told that the land promised to his seed will not be fulfilled until greater iniquities justify dispossession of the Amorite occupants (i.e., a precondition to fulfillment of the promise). Then the territorial borders involved in, the promise are described.

37. Josh. 2:24; 3:10; 6:2; 8:1; 10:8; 21:41; 23:3, 5; 24:13; Judg. 6:9.

38. Positively formulated in Exod. 23:25-26; Lev. 26:3-10; Deut. 5:30; 6:3; 7:12-15; 28:11-12; 30:9-10. Negatively formulated in Lev. 26:14-32; Deut. 11:17; 28:20-24.

39. Lev. 25:2, 19; 26:34-35. Personification of the Land is more common in prophetic literature, e.g., Hos. 4:2-3; Isa. 24:4-7; 33:8ff; Jer. 23:10.

40. Exod. 23:25-26; Lev. 26:3-10; Deut. 7:12-15; 11:13-15; 28:11-12, 20-24; 30:9-10.

41. Positively formulated in Deut. 5:30; 6:3; 7:12-13; 11:13-15; 28:8-12; 30:9-10. Negatively formulated in Lev. 26:14-32; Deut. 11:16-17; 28:20-35, 38-42.

42. On the development of the theme of conditional retention of the Land and on the subtle differences between the threats of exile in priestly and deuteronomic writings, see Weinfeld, "Inheritance of the Land," 115-37, and by the same author, "The Covenant of Grant," 184ff.

43. Lev. 18:6-30; 19:29; and 20:2-22 enumerate a series of prohibited sexual acts and relationships violation of which cause the Land to "spew you out." Deut. 24:1-4 adds remarriage to a wife who has had a sexual relationship, but violation of the proscription is described there as "bringing sin on the Land," without the accompanying threat of being "spewed out."

44. Num. 35:29-34. The contamination of the earth by the shedding of innocent blood, first referred to in the Cain and Abel story of Gen. 4:11-12, becomes particularized in the Sinai covenant with specific reference to the promised land (Num. 35:33-34; Deut. 21:1, 6-9; and also 2 Sam. 1:21-22). Defilement of the Land by ill-treatment of a corpse is mentioned only in Deut. 21:22-23.

45. Loss of the Land as a consequence of its defilement is a major theme in Leviticus and in prophetic literature, e.g., Jer. 23:10-12; Ezek 7:22-23; 36:17-19. While pollution of the Land is referred to in Numbers and Deuteronomy, the threat of exile in Deuteronomy is particuarly associated with violation of the prohibition against idolatry.

46. Lev. 26:34-38. A comparable concern appears in prophetic literature. See Isa. 56:1-8; 58:13-14; Jer. 17:21-27; Ezek. 20:12ff.; Amos 8:5; Neh. 13:17-18.

47. In Num. 33:55-56 the threat of exile is directly related to failure to expel the Canaanite nations; in Deuteronomy (4:25-28; 6:14-15; 11:16-17; 28:63-64; 29:25-27; 30:17-18) the threat is specifically associated with worship of the Canaanite gods. In Josh. 23:12-13, 15-16 exile is the threatened punishment for intermarriage

and worship of Canaanite gods. On idolatry and exile see also 1 Kings 9:6-7; 14:15; on intermarriage see also Ezra 9:11-14.

In Deut. 25:15 justice in weights and measures is linked with endurance in the Land, but the connection between perversion of justice and exile receives its full development not in Deuteronomy but in prophetic writings. For example, see Isa. 5:12-13; Jer. 7:5-15; 21:12-14; 22:3-5; Amos 5:23-27; Mic. 3:1-12.

48. Positively expressed in Deut. 4:40; 5:16, 30; 6:1-2; 8:1; 11:7-9; 16:20; 25:15; 30:20; 31:12-13; 32:47. Negatively expressed in Deut. 4:25-26; 30:17-18. In each case some verbal form of האריך or חיה is used, sometimes with ארץ and modifying phrase (4:26; 5:30; 8:1; 16:20), sometimes אדמה with and without modifying phrase (4:40; 5:16; 11:9; 25:15; 30:20; 31:13; 32:47). In 6:2 the verb appears without specification of place. Nonetheless, the reference here, as in those with spacial specification, is to extended life in the Land (referring back to 5:30), not to life *per se*. For similar usage note Deut. 6:15 (the referent for which is 6:10); 4:1; 8:1, and Orlinsky's comments thereon in "The Biblical Concept of the Land," 61, n. 15. On the terminology of Deuteronomy and deuteronomic literature, see Weinfeld, *Deuteronomy and the Deuteronomic School*, Appendix A. In light of their significance to *Jubilees*, attention is directed particularly to the various terms used for uprooting the Israelites from the Land as well as the use of אדמה, with or without qualifying phrase, in place of ארץ, as in Deut. 4:40; 6:15; 11:9; 28:21, 63; Josh. 23:13, 15-16; 1 Kings 9:7; 13:34; 14:15; Jer. 12:14.

49. For example, Isa. 11:12-16; 32:15; 35:1-7; 41:18-20; 43:19-21; 49:7-23; 51:3; 55:12-13; Jer. 16:14-15; 23:5-8; 31:10-14; Ezek. 34:25-30; 36:8-9, 24f.; Hos. 2:24-25; 11:8-11; 14:6f.; Amos 9:11-15; 37:11-26; 47:1-12. The restoration theme may also include restoration of the line of David, e.g., Isa. 9:5-6; Jer. 23:5; 33:14-15; Hos. 3:5; Amos 9:11.

50. On the connection between the liberation from Egypt and the promise of the Land, see Exod. 3:6-8; 15:17.

51. כי תוליד בנים ובני בנים ונושנתם בארץ והשחתם ועשיתם פסל תמונת
כל ועשיתם הרע בעיני יהוה אלהיך להכעיסו.

52. The details of Israelite apostasy are alluded to by the elaborate presentation of the prohibition against idolatry immediately following the description of the covenantal scene at Horeb (Deut. 4:15-20) and by the reference to God's anger with Moses "on account" of the Israelites (v. 21).

53. "The Lord will scatter you among the peoples, and only a scant few of you shall be left among the nations to which the Lord will drive you. There you will serve man-made gods of wood and stone, that cannot see or hear or eat or smell."

54. "When all these things befall you—the blessing and the curse that I have set before you—and you take them to heart amidst the various nations to which the Lord your God has banished you" (Deut. 30:1).

55. Literally, "atone" (וכפר) (Deut 32:43).

56. The editors of the Jewish Publication Society translation (Philadelphia, 1967) note the Hebrew is uncertain and, in accord with the Ugaritic *dm't* ("tears"), suggest rendering the passage more consistently with the rest of the poem, "And wipe away His people's tears" (cf., Isa. 25:8).

57. The notion of atonement for the Land is most rare in biblical literature. There is a concept of defilement of the Land requiring expiation (e.g., Num. 35:33), but the idea of atonement for the Land is much more developed in postbiblical literature. Note especially the concept in *Jubilees* 6:22, where Noah atones for the earth with his sacrifice (Chapter 3 below.) On atonement for the Land, see Jacob Milgrom, "Atonement in the Old Testament," in *IDB*, Sup., 81.

58. Such is the assumption in most of the scholarly works cited herein. For example, note Orlinksy's use of comparative linguistics in his discussion of the nature of the land promise; the source-document analyses of Davies, Weinfeld, and Clements in their understandings of the place of land in covenant theology; the document-based historical interpretations of the various names for the Land in Davies and Orlinsky; and the comparative analysis of K. Baltzer's *The Covenant Formulary in the Old Testament, Jewish, and Early Christian Writings* (Philadelphia: Fortress, 1971).

NOTES TO CHAPTER 3

1. I have taken the term "composite genre" from O. S. Wintermute's introduction to *Jubilees* in Charlesworth, ed., *OTP* 2:36-37. With reservations about its vagueness, Wintermute adopts the term from M. Testuz, who noted the mixture of history, testament, apocalyptic, ritual law, and chronology in the work.

2. Exod. 4:22 ("the seed of Jacob" will be God's "first born son"); 6:7 ("I will take you to be My people and I will be your God"); 31:16 ("The Israelite people shall keep the sabbath, observing the sabbath throughout the ages as a covenant for all time").

3. Exod. 4:22 and 31:16 contain no reference to the Land, but the statement of the reciprocal covenantal relationship in Exod 6:7 is interwoven with a recollection and reaffirmation of the patriarchal Land promise (6:8). Nothing of this context appears in *Jubilees*.

4. VanderKam attributes the portrait of Noah to the author's desire to ascribe to him a priestly function as a model of righteousness for those concerned with eschatological judgment. See his "The Righteousness of Noah," in George W. E. Nickelsburg and John J. Collins, eds., *Ideal Figures in Ancient Judaism: Profiles and Paradigms*, SBLSCS (Chico, Calif.: Scholars Press, 1980), 12:13-33. John C. Endres ("Biblical Interpretation in the Book of Jubilees," CBQMS [Washington, D.C.: Catholic Biblical Association, 1987], 18:226f.) argues that the characterization of Noah is an aspect of the author's rejection of all "developmental notions" of Israel-

ite religion. By establishing the Noahite covenant as "the prototype for all others," the author demonstrates a continuity in the covenantal relationship from Noah through Sinai.

5. All the territorial allotments are to be permanent (8:24, 29), but the author makes a particular point of stressing the eternality of Shem's inheritance: "for his possession and for his sons for eternal generations" (8:12); "this portion was assigned by lot to Shem and to his sons to possess it forever for his generations forever" (8:17); "and he knew that a blessed portion and blessing had reached Shem and his sons for eternal generations" (8:21).

6. Aprachshad is assigned "all of the land of the region of Chaldea toward the east of the Euphrates, which is near the Red Sea, and all of the waters of the desert as far as the vicinity of the tongue of the sea which faces toward Egypt, all of the land of Lebanon and Senir and Amana as far as the vicinity of the Euphrates" (9:4).

7. The biblical narrative focuses on the development of nations descending from the sons of Noah and describes national settlements rather than specifying territorial assignments for each son and grandson (Gen. 10).

8. In *Jubilees* Canaan is cursed twice: once by Noah because of Ham, as in the biblical narrative of Gen. 9:21-27 (7:10-12), and a second time by his own father and brothers for his own violation of the oath to honor the assigned boundaries (9:14-15; 10:30-32).

9. The Land is described as belonging to God in Lev. 25:23; as "good and wide" in Exod. 3:8 and as "wide" in Gen. 34:21, Judg. 18:10, and 1 Chron. 4:40. The phrase "everything in it...very good" may reflect the common biblical description of the Land as "good" or "very good." The adjective "blessed" is associated with the Land only in the description of Joseph's portion in Moses' blessing of the tribes at the end of Deuteronomy (33:13).

10. *Genesis Apocryphon* (10:13) also has Noah atoning "for all the earth." The concept of atonement for the Land also appears in 1QS 8:6, 10; 9:4. In Deut. 32:43, the single reference to atonement for the Land in Hebrew Scriptures, the atonement is undertaken by God after the Israelites have been punished for their sins. On the pollution of the earth in the biblical flood story, see Tikvah Frymer Krensky, "The Atrahasis Epic and Its Significance for Our Understanding of Genesis 1-9," *BA* (1977): 147-55.

11. The Watchers' intercourse with women (7:21) is described as זנות, which is associated with pollution of the Land in Exod. 34:15. The "impurity" of the forbidden union has its parallel in the land-polluting sexual alliances enumerated in Lev. 18:26-28; the shedding of innocent blood by the Nephilim (7:22-25) is paralleled by the same prohibition in the Land context of Num. 35:33-34. See James C. VanderKam's notes to 7:21 in *The Book of Jubilees*, vol. 1 (Louvain: E. Peeters, 1989).

12. The instructions also include blessing their Creator, honoring parents, and loving neighbors (7:20), which are not land-based in Torah legislation.

13. Lev. 19:23; 23:10; 25:2.

14. VanderKam's "Do not eat the life with the meat" is to be preferred. The phrase is נפש כל בשר דמו as in Lev. 17:14 and involves consumption of the blood with the flesh, not "living flesh" as translated by Wintermute. The reference is to "life with the flesh" with life understood as the blood of the animal being consumed.

15. "And if any Israelite or any stranger who resides among them hunts down an animal or a bird that may be eaten, he shall pour out its blood and over it with earth" (Lev. 17:13). In *Jubilees* the situation of slaughter for sacrificial purposes is specified.

16. "But make sure that you do not partake of the blood; for the blood is the life, and you must not consume the life with the flesh" (Deut. 12:23).

17. "For the life of all flesh—its blood is its life. Therefore I say to the Israelite people: You shall not partake of the blood of any flesh, for the life of all flesh is its blood. Anyone who partakes of shall be cut off" (Lev. 17:14). The prohibition in *Jubilees* extends so far as to include not permitting someone to eat the blood with the flesh in your presence.

18. "You shall not pollute the land in which you live; for blood pollutes the land; and the land can have no expiation for blood that is shed on it, except by the blood of him who shed it. You shall not defile the land in which you live, in which I My-self abide, for I the Lord abide among the Israelite people" (Num. 35:33-34).

19. The double sense of the word clearly poses a problem for translators. I have consulted the following English and German translations: R. H. Charles, *The Book of Jubilees or The Little Genesis* (London: SPCK, 1927); O. S. Wintermute, *Jubilees*, in Charlesworth, ed., *OTP*, vol. 2; C. Rabin, *The Book of Jubilees* in H. F. D. Sparks, ed., *The Apocryphal Old Testament* (Oxford: Clarendon Press, 1984); James C. Van-derKam, *The Book of Jubilees*; and E. Littmann, "Das Buch der *Jubilaen*," in Emil Kautzsch, ed., *Die Apokryphen und Pseudepigraphen des Alten Testaments* (Tubingen: Mohr, 1900 repr. Hildescheim, 1962) 2:31-119. Although none of the translations evidences internal consistency in dealing with the term, the issue is not addressed except by VanderKam, who on one occasion justifies a translation (25:20) on the basis of context.

Given the dual meaning of ארץ in Hebrew and of *terra* in Latin, neither the He-brew translations (A. S. Hartom, ed., *Sefer HaYovlot* in *HaSefarim Hachizonim* [Tel Aviv: Yavneh, 1980] 1:13-139 and Moshe Goldman, trans., *Sefer HaYovlim* in Moshe Kahana, ed., *HaSefarim Hachizonim* [Tel Aviv: Makor, 1936] 1:216-313) nor the edited Latin fragments consulted (R. H. Charles, ed., *The Ethiopic Version of the Hebrew Book of Jubilees* [Oxford: Clarendon, 1895] and H. Ronsch, ed., *Das Buch der Jubilaen oder die kleine Genesis* [Leipzig, 1874, repr. Amsterdam: Rodopi, 1970]) clarify the author's intent.

The Qumran fragments of *Jubilees* which are available include one passage (*Jub.* 21:22) in which the word *h'rs* (*medr*) appears with the problematic dual meaning. However, given the dual meaning of the word in Hebrew as well as in Ge'ez, the fragment, like the Hebrew translations of *Jubilees*, demonstrates rather than illuminates the problem for the translator. See VanderKam, *Textual and Historical Studies*, 54 and by the same author, "The Jubilees Fragments from Qumran Cave 4," in *The Madrid Qumran Congress*, 2:635-48.

While I generally use Wintermute's translation for citations, hereafter I indicate the problematic contexts for *medr* by using both terms, i.e. earth/land, in the text and present the various translation choices in a note. In the passage just examined—Noah's directions to his sons (7:33)—Charles, Rabin, VanderKam, and Littmann use "earth"; Wintermute translates "land."

20. Wintermute, VanderKam, and Littmann translate *medr* here as "earth," perhaps because the prohibition regarding the eating of blood is directed to Noah's sons as well as to the Israelites. However, Charles and Rabin translate it "land." Their rationale may well be the biblical context from which the prohibition is drawn. The prohibition is levitical (Lev. 7:27 and 17:10); the threatened punishment is not. In both passages the punishment is "shall be cut off from his people." The equivalent of this in *Jubilees*—"uprooted/rooted out from the midst of the people/Israel"—appears together with "uprooted from the earth/land" in the stories of Dinah and of Reuben and Bilhah (30:10, 22; 33:13, 17, 19).

21. Charles suggests that last clause may be corrupted (*Ethiopic Version*, note 5, *Jub.* 6:5). Given the connections made between the Noah and Abraham covenants throughout *Jubilees*, I am more inclined to view the clause as a retrojection of part of the blessing of Abraham in Gen. 12:2.

22. 7:27-33; 21:17-20, 22, 24; 36:5-8.

23. 1 Kings 14:15; Isa. 61:3; Jer. 1:10; 11:17; 12:14-15, 17; 18:7; 24:6; 31:28, 40; 32:41; 45:4; Amos 9:15; 2 Chron. 6:20.

24. The metaphor which stresses God's relationship with the righteous (however defined) may reflect Ps. 92:13. See 1 Enoch 10:16; 84:6; 93:5, 10; Pss. Sol. 14:3; and 1 QS 8:5; 11:8. In 1 Enoch 10:16 and 84:6 "righteous plant" refers to the righteous in the generation of the Flood. *Pseudo-Philo* uses the image of Israel as a plant or vine in a number of the speeches which he creates for the various leaders of Israel, e.g., 12:8-9; 23:12; 28:4; 30:4; 39:7; 49:6. In 2 Bar. 84:2, however, the verb "plant" is used in the deuteronomic sense with clear reference to the Land.

25. "And he [Abraham] blessed his Creator who created him in his generation because by his will he created him for he knew and he perceived that from him there would be a righteous planting for eternal generations and a holy seed from him so that he might be like the one who made everything."

26. The verb in the Ethiopic is corrupted here. But even with the corrected verb, the verse at best reads: "And I shall plant them as a plant of righteousness, with all My heart and with all My soul." Charles (note on 1:16) suggests that "it is not improbable that the words 'in this land' have been lost after the verb." However, given a comparable deletion with no question of corrupted text in the *Jubilees* version of the promises made to Jacob at Bethel (32:18-19), there is no support for inserting the words here. For discussion of 32:18-19, particularly for the significance of the deletion in 1:16, see below.

27. In Hebrew Scriptures uprooting from the land is expressed with the verbs נסח (Deut. 28:63) and נתש (Deut. 29:27) and numerous times in prophetic literature, especially Jeremiah. In the one fragment from Qumran which contains the phrase the verb used is הכרית (as in 1 Kings 9:7; Josh. 7:9). On these and other terms used in Hebrew Scriptures to designate exile from the land as punishment for forsaking the covenant, see Weinfeld, *Deuteronomy and the Deuteronomic School*, 346-47.

In the Ge'ez translation of *Jubilees* the word used for "uprooted" is various forms of the intensive verb *sarrawa*, derived from the root *saru* and related to the Hebrew intensive verb שרש, which is found with the connotation of "uprooting" (Ps. 52:7; Job 31:8, 12). In Ps. 52:7 it appears with "from the land of the living." The Latin fragments which contain the phrase (with and without *terra*) use the terms *exterminere*, *aufere*, and *eradicere*. See Charles, ed., *The Ethiopic Version*.

28. All the translations consulted except VanderKam use "land" in 2:27. In the passage prohibiting eating of blood (6:12), Wintermute, VanderKam, and Littmann use "earth," Charles and Rabin, "land."

29. Without using the "pollution" language of Isaiah and Ezekiel, Amos 8:5, Jer. 17:21-27, and Neh. 13:17-18 also connect violation of the Sabbath to destruction of and exile from the Land.

30. Note particularly David's speech in 1 Chron. 28:8, where the modifying phrase "which I swore to your fathers" or "to which I am bringing you" is omitted, much as the author of *Jubilees* omits modifiers which would historically particularize. See also 1 Chron. 16:15-18, 2 Chron. 6:25, and Japhet's comments on the treatment of the Land in *The Ideology of the Book of Chronicles*, 93f., 330f.

31. Endres (*Biblical Interpretation*, 48-49) notes that in presenting the promises to the patriarchs the author subtly shifts attention from the "promissory aspect of the disclosure" to the "demand for covenantal fidelity—an emphasis far more characteristic of the Mosaic covenantal tradition."

32. On the other hand, the writer goes to some lengths to indicate that Terah is unaware of the divine force directing the family history. When Abraham tells his father of his imminent departure, Terah says: "And when you have seen a land pleasant to your eyes to dwell in, come and take me to you" (12:30).

33. The added words are in emphasis. The same phrase appears in the Septuagint version of the second promissory scene (Gen. 13:17), as well as in the Masoretic text preceding Isaac's birth (Gen. 17:8).

34. "For the Lord your God is bringing you into a good land, a land with streams and springs and fountains issuing from plain and hill; a land of wheat and barley, of vines, figs, and pomegranates, a land of olive trees and honey."

35. The author has Abraham use the same terminology in his first address to God in Haran (12:19). The term appears in a description of the priestly character of Melchizedek and as the mode by which the Sodomite king-priest addresses God in prayer in Gen. 14:19. Nothing of that description or prayer are retained in *Jubilees*.

36. *Genesis Apocryphon* has a similar scene, with the patriarch making an offering "to God Most High" in gratitude for having "brought me back to this land in safety" (21:1-3). That author does not, however, include Abraham's pronouncement regarding his relationship with God.

37. There is only an additional metaphor in the promise of numbers. *Jubilees* has both "sands of the sea," and "sands of the earth" (13:20), whereas Gen. 13:16 uses only "dust of the earth."

38. In *Jubilees* and in the Masoretic text, when Abraham is told to view the Land, the promise is "to you and your seed" (*Jub.* 13:20; Gen. 13:15). But when he thereafter is directed to walk in the Land, *Jubilees* has "to your seed" and Genesis "to you" (*Jub.* 13:21; Gen. 13:17). In the Septuagint, however, "I will give it to you and your seed" appears in both verses.

The Masoretic and Septuagint texts both have Abraham commanded to walk in the Land with no implication of possession by touring (i.e., walking and viewing). In contrast, 1QapGen.(21:13-19) includes an expansive geographic description of the tour that is commanded in *Jubilees*.

39. The tithing replaces the tenth Abraham gives to Melchizedek, king of Salem and "priest of God Most High" in the biblical text (Gen. 14:18-20).

40. The additions (emphasized) make the promise essentially the same as in Gen. 17:4-8 which is cited verbatim in *Jub.* 15:7-10.

41. "As for your wife Sarai, you shall not call her Sarai, but her name shall be Sarah. I will bless her; indeed I will give you a son by her. I will bless her so that she shall give rise to nations; rulers of peoples shall issue from her" (Gen. 17:15-16).

"Sarai, your wife, will therefore not be called Sarai because Sarah is her name. And I will bless her and I will give you a son from her. And I will bless him. And he will become a people. And kings of nations will come from *him*" (*Jub.* 15:15-16).

42. In the biblical narrative the clarification comes only after the name changing scene as a response to Abraham's concern for Ishmael's future (Gen. 17:19-21). *Jubilees* retains this scene (15:19-20) and repeats the clarification in two created narratives: an extensive exposition on circumcision following the annunciation of

Isaac (15:30-31) and a dialogue between the visiting angels when Isaac is born (16:17-18).

43. Not named in the text, Passover is indicated by the date of Mastema's challenge "in the first month, in that jubilee, on the twelfth of the month" (17:15).

44. "I swear by Myself, says the Lord, because you have done this thing and you have not denied your firstborn son, whom you love, to me that I shall surely bless you and I shall surely multiply your seed like the stars of heaven and like the sand of the seashore and your seed will inherit the cities of their enemies. And all of the nations of the earth will bless themselves by your seed because you obeyed my word. And I have made known to all that you are faithful to me in everything which I say to you. Go in peace" (Gen. 18:15-16).

45. The author cites Gen. 26:1-5, with the following minor changes to its wording: the singular form is used for "land," and "My covenant" is substituted for "My teachings" (תורתי). As in LXX, the past tense is used in Isaac's proclamation of faith at the successful well digging which elicits elaboration of the covenantal blessings (24:20). See VanderKam's comments on the passage.

46. Moreover, without connecting his merits to any recollection of the the covenantal promises, Abraham begins the testament to Isaac with a description of his own fidelity and obedience (21:2-3).

47. "And you will become a blessing upon the earth, and all the nations of the earth will desire you, and they will bless your sons in my name, so that they might be blessed as I am" (20:10).

48. The reference to Abraham is inserted into the blessing, otherwise cited from Gen. 27:28-29, that Jacob receives when disguised as Esau (26:23-24). It is quoted from Genesis (28:3-4) in the parting blessing when Jacob leaves for Haran (*Jub.* 27:11) and included in a created farewell testament for Jacob and Esau (36:6).

49. Built on his version of the blessing given to Jacob disguised as Esau, "And may all of the blessings with which the Lord blessed me and blessed Abraham, my father, belong to you and to your seed forever" (26:24).

50. I use VanderKam's translation here because he places the final clauses within parentheses.

51. The plan is not effected because Esau immediately tells Isaac that in as much as he had sold his "right of seniority" to Jacob, the property rightly belongs to him (36:14). The favorable characterization of Esau, here followed by the narrative of his reluctant acquiescence to join his sons in attacking Jacob (chap. 37), reflects the complex relationships and territorial conflicts between the Edomites and the Israelites in the Hasmonean period.

Mendels (*The Land of Israel as a Political Concept*, 76) sees the passage as a reference to John Hyrcannus's campaign against Edom, whereas VanderKam points to that of Judas Maccabee (*Textual and Historical Studies*, 229.)

52. The description of Jacob as Abraham's son is rooted in Gen. 28:13, where God reveals Himself to the third patriarch as "God of your father Abraham and the God of Isaac."

53. The translation here is from VanderKam, who, instead of translating the Latin *sanct*, inserts the Hebrew סגולה ("special") to replicate the wording of Deut. 7:6, which the passage otherwise reproduces. On the corruption of the Ethiopic translation, see his notes and Charles on 19:18.

54. All of the translators render *medr* here as earth.

55. The preceding line, "May the nations serve you, and all the nations bow down before your seed" (22:11), is taken from Isaac's blessing of Jacob in Gen. 27:29.

56. Excluding a citation of Gen. 15:7, the word *medr* appears an additional twelve times in the testament (22:9 [twice], 11, 14, 15, 20, 21, 22 [twice], 24 [twice], 30), all but one of which is rendered "earth" by all the translators. The exception is a reference to the house of Abraham which God has built "so that I might cause my name to dwell upon it in the *medr*" (22:24). Here Wintermute and Littmann use "land." Rabin, VanderKam, and Charles, however, translate it as "earth." (See VanderKam's extensive comments on the grammatical structure of the passage in the various manuscripts.) Given the overall tone of the blessing and the Ge'ez, which has the sense of "on the whole" (Rabin), "earth" seems preferable.

57. Noting the Creator awareness here and in the description of Abraham's offering of firstfruits that immediately precedes the testament (22:4), Endres suggests that "both point to the Noachic covenant (6:17, 21, 24) as the primary referent in this section" (*Biblical Interpretation*, 40).

58. The phrase also appears in Sir. 24:8 and in 2 Macc. 1:24-5; 7:22-3.

59. "I am the Lord who brought you from Ur of the Chaldees so that I might give you the land of the Canaanites to possess it forever *and (so that I might) be God for you and for your seed after you*" (14:7). Emphasized words are the addition in *Jubilees*.

60. On Rebecca's special role in *Jubilees*, see Endres, *Biblical Interpretation*, 73-84 and Randall D. Chesnutt, "Revelatory Experiences Attributed to Biblical Women in Early Jewish Literature" in Amy-Jill Levine, ed., *Women Like This: New Perspectives on Jewish Women in the Greco-Roman World* (Atlanta: Scholars Press, 1991), 109-11.

61. Emphasis mine. Charles, Rabin, and Endres (82) translate *medr* here as "earth." Endres's study focuses upon the treatment of the biblical text in *Jubilees*, but neither he nor the two translators comment on the author's unusual development of the second Bethel scene which is predicted here. Wintermute and VanderKam translate the *medr* here as "land" even though they, like all the translators, use "earth" in Abraham's earlier prediction to Rebecca (19:21). VanderKam is sufficiently concerned about the choice as to justify it by the reference to the Land in 25:17. However, his rationale does not explain the larger problem of the relation-

ship between Rebecca's words, the testamental prediction that precedes it, and the author's rewriting of the Bethel scenes which follow. Indeed, neither VanderKam nor any other scholar has explained that rewriting in the overall context of the treatment of the theology of land and covenant in *Jubilees*.

62. The closure recalls the blessing Abraham received at the first covenant-making (Gen. 12:3/*Jub.* 25:22). As Endres points out (*Biblical Interpretation*, 82-83), the addition of "curses you falsely" is a morally sensitive version of the blessing Isaac gives Jacob after being deceived (Gen. 27:29).

63. Interestingly, in later rabbinic literature the contrast between the promise to Abraham in Gen. 13:17 and to Jacob in Gen. 28:14 is the exegetical basis for a similar expansion of the Land promise. Abraham "inherited the world in limited measure" whereas Jacob "inherited the world without measure" (*Gen. Rab.* 11.8). See also *Pesiq. R.* 23.9.

64. Emphasis mine. The alteration is all the more significant because it is the only change made to the first Bethel blessing.

65. VanderKam's translation. The blessing in Gen. 35:9-12 is: "I am *El Shaddai.* Be fertile and increase; A nation, yea an assembly of nations shall descend from you. Kings shall issue from your loins. The land that I gave to Abraham and Isaac I give to you; And to your offspring to come will I give this land."

66. It is intriguing to note the similarity between the prediction in *Jubilees* and the interpretation of Balaam's blessing of Israel ("a people that shall dwell alone," [Num. 23:9]) as "a people who by themselves are destined to possess the world" in *Tg. Onq.* as well as in Josephus' *Antiquities.* On Josephus' interpretation, see below in Chapter 6.

67. The sections deleted in *Jubilees* are indicated in emphasis. In the English translation the deleted clause comes at the end, but in the Hebrew text deletion requires removal of an internal clause:

כל מקום אשר תדרך כף רגלכם בו לכם יהיה מן המדבר והלבנון מן הנהר
נהר פרת ועד הים האחרון יהיה גבלכם.

68. After recollecting the exodus the angel gives Moses instructions regarding the Passover sacrifice that is to be offered "in the days when a house is built in the name of the Lord in the land" (49:19).

69. The narrator simply indicates that Jacob was buried in "Machpelah near Abraham his father, in the tomb which he excavated for himself in the cave of Machpelah in the land of Hebron" (45:14). There is no formal request by Jacob to be buried in the Land (Gen. 47:29-31), and no recollection of the promises as he approaches death (Gen. 48:4). The elaborate description of his burial in the Land (Gen. 50:1-14) is replaced by a created tale of a war between Canaan and Egypt (46:6-13), which serves as the background for a description of the burial of Jacob's bones in Machpelah (46:9) and provides an explanation for the subsequent enslavement of the Israelites in Egypt (46:11-13).

70. Moses' experiences in Midian are covered in one brief sentence (48:1). There is no mention at all of his marriage to a Midianite woman, possibly reflecting the author's abhorrence of intermarriage and esteem for Moses as much as his lack of interest in historical biography.

71. Paralleling Gen. 12:1, 7; 13:15; 15:7; 17:8; 26:3-4; 28:4, 13.

72. Paralleling Gen. 12:7; 13:14: 15:18; 28:14.

73. Not identical to that of Genesis, the *Jubilees* list excludes the Hittites and adds the Phakorites and Hivites.

74. For example, *Jub.* 30:25; 34:5; 39:1; 42:4, 9, 13; 44:4; 45:15; 46:6; 49:18; 50:9.

75. See *Jub.* 13:19-21; 14:4-7; 15:3-4, 8-10. The assurance appears only twice in the covenantal narratives of Genesis (13:15; 17:8).

76. In both cases the commandment is given at the covenantal scene immediately preceding prediction of Isaac's birth, and in both the punishment for violation of the commandment is being "cut off from his people" (Gen. 17:7-14 and *Jub.* 15:9-14).

77. The threat is repeated three times. In the first instance (15:26), the context is particularly unclear. The uncircumcised are called "the children of destruction" who bear no sign that they, like the circumcised angels, "belong to the Lord" and hence they are destined "to be destroyed and annihilated from the land/earth and to be uprooted from the land/earth." Understood as a reflection of the command to Abraham to circumcise both his sons, one could well view *medr* here in the more general sense of "earth." In the second and third threats (15:28, 34) the children of Israel are more directly specified. Consequently, the inclination here is to read *medr* in the context of the Land promise. In the translations consulted, Charles, Rabin, and Wintermute make this contextual distinction ("earth" in 15:26 and "land" in 15:28 and 34). VanderKam and Littmann translate "earth" (*erde*) in all three instances.

78. 30:7, 22; 33:19; 41:27. In the Judah/Tamar story the term appears without the term *medr*; in the Dinah and Bilhah/Reuben narratives the term appears both with and without it.

79. Charles, VanderKam, Littmann, and Rabin translate *medr* as "earth"; Wintermute translates it as "land." Given the context of capital punishment ("blotted out of the book of life and written in the book of those who will be destroyed), "earth" is preferable.

80. Lev. 20:11 is cited in the story of Reuben and Bilhah (33:10ff.), and Lev. 18:15; 20:12 in the story of Judah and Tamar (41:25ff.).

81. "And let them not commit a sin worthy of death because the Lord our God is a judge who does not accept persons or gifts. And say to them these words of the ordinance that they might hear and guard and watch themselves concerning them and they will not be destroyed or uprooted from the earth. For defiled and an

abomination, and blemished, and polluted are all who do them upon the earth before our God" (33:18-19).

VanderKam, Littmann, and Wintermute have "earth." Perhaps basing their choice on the references to Leviticus instead of on the internal context of *Jubilees*, however, Charles and Rabin use "land."

82. VanderKam's translation of 33:11, 20. See also 30:8, 10, 13; 41:26.

83. "All of the Philistine seed is [destined] for destruction and uprooting and removal from the earth....There will not be any name or seed which remains upon the earth for any of the Caphtorim. Because if they go up to heaven, from there they will fall; and if they are set firm in the earth, from there will be torn out; and if they are hidden among the nations, from there they will be uprooted; and if they go down to Sheol, even there their judgment will multiply, and also there will be no peace for them there. And if they go into captivity by the hand of those who seek their life, they will kill them along the way. And neither name nor seed will be left for them in all the earth, because they shall walk in an eternal curse."

All the references to *medr* in the passage are translated "earth" in all the translations consulted.

Unbiblical, the curse is inserted into the narrative immediately following Isaac's receipt of the divine promises at Beer-sheba. Wintermute notes (104, Note h) that the writer's attraction to the Amos passage may be related to the reference to the "way of Beer-sheba" in Amos 8:14.

84. The addressees include "Ishmael and his twelve children, Isaac and his two children and Keturah's six children and their sons" (20:1).

85. Wintermute, Rabin, and Charles translate *medr* here as "land." Given the overall context of the testament, my own preference, like that of Littmann and VanderKam, is "earth."

86. In deuteronomic literature, the terminology of curse and hissing is associated with the destruction of the Land and the exile of its people. See Deut. 28:37; Jer. 19:8; 24:9; 25:9, 18; 26:6; 29:18; 42:18; 44:8, 12, 22.

87. "...so that He might be pleased with you, and grant you his mercy, and bring down rain for you morning and evening, and bless all your works which you have made on the earth and bless your food and your water, and bless the fruit of your womb and the fruit of your land, and the herds of your cattle and the flocks of your sheep" (*Jub.* 20:9).

"...He will love you, and bless you, and multiply you, He will bless the issue of your womb and the fruit of your soil, your new grain and wine and oil, the calving of your herd and the lambing of your flock in the land that He swore to your fathers to give you" (Deut. 7:13).

88. The same phrase with the Hebrew verb שׁרשׁ occurs in reference to Doeg in Ps. 52:7 where it has no relationship to the Land.

89. For "uproot from the land/earth" see Deut. 28:63 and 29:27; on "God hiding His face" see Deut. 31:17, 18. The phrases "uproot/destroy your seed from beneath the sky" and "your name will perish from the land/earth" may be variations on Deut. 9:14 or 29:19.

Charles and Rabin translate *medr* here as "land." Given the broad context of the blessing, the parallels with Noah's testament, and the absence of any other reference to the Land promise, I am inclined to follow Wintermute, VanderKam, and Littmann, who translate it as "earth."

90. "May the Most High God give you all the blessings [with] which he blessed me, and [with] which He blessed Noah and Adam; may they rest upon the holy head of your seed throughout each generation and forever."

91. The context is clearly indicated in the passage: "There is no hope in the land of the living because they will go down into Sheol." All the translations have "earth" for *medr* in 22:22.

92. Referring to the sabbatical legislation of Leviticus 25, the angel makes a point of noting that he had revealed "the sabbaths of the land" and "the years of jubilee in the sabbaths of years" to Moses "on Sinai" (50:2).

93. The projection into a future time is made explicit by the angel's statement that jubilees of years will pass before the Israelites will be purified "from all the sin of fornication, and defilement, and uncleanness, and sin and error" (50:4).

94. *Jub.* 1:7-8 and Deut. 31:19-21, 26-7. Note particularly *Jub.* 1:6/Deut. 30:1; *Jub.* 1:6/Deut. 31:20a, 21, 27.

95. Note the following parallels in language: Sin: *Jub.* 1:8/Deut. 31:20; *Jub.* 1:9/Deut. 7:16; *Jub.* 1:10/Josh. 23:13; *Jub.* 1:11/Deut. 32:17. Punishment: *Jub.* 1:13/Deut. 31:17-18; 32:20; *Jub.* 1:14/Deut. 4:27-28; 28:64. Repentance: *Jub.* 1:15a/Deut. 4:29-31; 30:2. Restoration: *Jub.* 1:15b/Deut. 30:3 (but even more Jer. 29:13-14); *Jub.* 1:16/Deut. 28:13 (The "transplant" theme is from Jer. 32:41 and stands in contrast to the "uprooting" of Deut. 28:63 and 29:27.); *Jub.* 1:17/Deut. 29:12 (also Lev. 26:11-12); *Jub.* 1:18/Deut. 31:6.

96. Gene Davenport (*The Eschatology*, 25, note 3) views Deut. 4:29 as the basic source for the repentance/restoration stages of the paradigm (*Jub.* 1:15-18), with expansions from Deuteronomy 28-30. In contrast, I see the context, structure, and language of the *Jubilees* cycle as closer to the paradigm of Deuteronomy 28-30.

97. The description of Israel's sins goes beyond the Pentateuch, and includes the desecration of feasts, sabbaths, and sanctuary, child sacrifice, and the slaying of God's witnesses. See 1:10-12.

98. "You will search for Me and you will find Me, if only you seek Me wholeheartedly. I will be at hand for you—declares the Lord—and I will restore your fortunes. And I will gather you from all the nations and fro all the places to which I have banished you—declares the Lord—and I will bring you back to the place from which I have exiled you" (Jer. 29:13-14).

99. "I will plant them in this land in truth with My whole heart and with My whole soul" (Jer. 32:41). The Ethiopic text of *Jub.* 1:16, which omits "in this land," is corrupted and has been reconstructed. Charles suggests that the words "in this land" were originally included but were lost (Charles, 5, note on 1:16). However, I believe that the omission reflects a deliberate effort to minimize the eschatological significance of the return from Babylonian exile. Gene Davenport (*The Eschatology*, 25) suggests that the transplanting in v. 16 may be a subtle (inverted) reference to the threat to uproot from the Land in Deut. 28:63 or a paraphrase of Isa. 61:3, where the planting metaphor refers to the spiritual condition of Israel. The two sources support my argument that the author of *Jubilees* purposely takes advantage of the dual use of the term in biblical literature.

100. Describing that relationship in this first chapter, the author uses the biblical phrases that appear throughout the work, e.g., "I shall be their God and they will be my people" (1:12) and in 2:19; 14:7; 22:15 and "I shall plant them as a righteous plant" (1:16) and 7:34; 16:26; 21:24; 36:6.

101. Given the paraphrase of Deut. 9:26, 29, Deuteronomy 9 is the presumed source for the intercession. There, however, as in all the biblical intercessory narratives, there is some reference to the promise of the Land. See Exod. 32:13, Num. 14:16, and Deut. 9:27-28.

102. The repentance must be all inclusive, i.e. "their sin and the sin of their fathers" (l:22). The biblical source for the all-encompassing repentance is Lev. 26:40 rather than the Deuteronomy *tochachot*. In contrast, see *Testament of Moses* 9:4 and analysis of the passage in Chapter 4.

103. None of Moses' intercessory pleas is rejected, and even Abraham's plea bargaining in Genesis 18 softens the divine decree.

104. Although it begins with a description of the perennial condition of man, the presentation (23:14-31) portrays only the period immediately before the eschaton, not all of Israel's future history as in Chapter 1. See G. Davenport's comments on "in that generation" (v. 16) and "in those days," (v. 26) in Davenport, *The Eschatology*, 41.

105. Although אדמה often specifically refers to "soil," in Deuteronomy it is used interchangeably with ארץ, with specific reference to the Land.

106. The modifying phrase I have used here is from Deut. 30:18. I have selected it particularly because the full passage (30:18-20) contains themes that are particularly stressed in *Jubilees* and because the words "that you mayest live" appear therein both with and without the modifying reference to land (Deut. 30:19).

The phrase "that thou mayest live" (למען תחיו) or "prolong your life (למען תאריכו) upon the land which..." or some variant thereof appears with explicit or implicit reference to the Promised Land, repeatedly in Deuteronomy (4:26, 40; 5:16, 30; 6:2; 8:1; 11:9; 16:20; 25:15; 30:20; 31:13; 32:47). The phrase appears twice (Deut. 22:7 and 30:19) without the modifier referring to the Land.

107. The text simply states "after the Flood" (23:9). Noah is not mentioned by name, but he is described in 10:16 as having a lifespan of "nineteen jubilees and two weeks and five years."

108. The similarities are conceptual as well as structural. Note particularly the following common motifs: gentile invaders who have no mercy on young or old (Jub. 23:23/Deut. 32:21, 25); the description of God as Israel's avenger (Jub. 23:20/Deut. 32:35, 41, 43) and as executor of ultimate judgment (Jub. 23:31/Deut. 32:36, 41-43). Nickelsburg notes the tochacha structure, but does not analyze the parallels with Deuteronomy 32 (Jewish Literature, 77ff.).

109. Identifying the particular events referred to in the sin and punishment stages of the cycle has been the subject of much scholarship on Jubilees. See particularly, Davenport, The Eschatology, 41-45; Nickelsburg, Jewish Literature, 78-79; VanderKam, Textual and Historical Studies, 252f.; and Mendels, The Land of Israel as a Political Concept, 57-88. There is agreement that the cycle being described begins in the Maccabean period.

110. In his analysis of the Doppelschema, Karl Baltzer suggests that the doubling may reflect an historical sense of "living in a 'time of disaster' brought on by renewed apostasy" (The Covenant Formulary, 160-61). In the context of the T. 12 Patr. which he is analyzing, the suggestion involves a second redaction and additions to the text. Davenport makes a similar argument for Jubilees 23, suggesting that original author (Maccabean period) "interpreted contemporary events as the beginning of a new day," and a later redactor, for whom the eschatological end has been postponed, inserted 23:21 to account for the return to corruption. See Davenport, The Eschatology, 45.

111. This is the single reference to the Land in Deut. 32:43. Although lacking the exile and return stages, the paradigm in Deuteronomy 31 is notably land-specific. Note vv. 7, 13, 20, 21, 23.

112. Charles, Littmann, Rabin, VanderKam, and Davenport (35, note 2) all see the eschatology as cosmic and translate medr as "earth" throughout the chapter. Wintermute, however, translates it as "land" in verses 14 and 18 and as "earth" in 20 and 23.

113. On the allusions to the Flood story in the eschatology, see Endres, Biblical Interpretation, 54. Destruction of animal life as an aspect of divine punishment and the theme of lack of knowledge, which also appears in Jubilees 23, are found in Hos. 4:1-6. The Hosea passage could well have been the biblical source for 23:18, but if so, the clear context of "this Land" in Hosea was deleted.

114. Charles identifies Jeremiah as the source; Davenport prefers 1 Maccabees and suggests both may be based on Ps. 79:2-3, which also names Jerusalem as the site.

115. The author of Jubilees does not identify the vindicated, God's "servants," "the righteous ones" (23:30), as Israel. At the same time he does not include in his

poem the "historical" background that makes that identification clear in Deuteronomy 32. There also is nothing comparable to the land reference of Deut. 32:43 in *Jubilees* 23.

116. The observation is a theological one which does not resolve the scholarly debate over date of composition or final redaction. One could argue that the mythic, cosmic perspective points to a period of territorial expansion comparable to that of the Hasmonean era. On the other hand, it could also be seen as a reflection of, and/or response to, the cosmopolitan Hellenistic world-view. On the dating of *Jubilees*, see Chapter 1.

117. The redefinition, so crucial to *Jubilees*, is supported by multiple passages in the biblical text, e.g., Exod. 6:7; Lev. 26:12; Deut. 4:20; 26:18; 27:9; 28:9; 29:11-12.

NOTES TO CHAPTER 4

1. Although the *Testament* is often described by scholars as a "rewriting" of Deuteronomy 31-34, in the text as it currently stands there is sparse evidence of Deuteronomy 33-34.

2. A. B. Kolenkow points out that the work has all the characteristics of the "blessing" testament genre: a death scene, revelation of history to the endtime, the response of the person to whom the testament is being given, an affirmation of the future of Israel, and an emphasis on God's ordering of history from the time of creation. See his "The *Assumption of Moses* as a Testament," in Nickelsburg, ed., *Studies*, 71-77.

3. The use of "oath" in 2:7 ("[Four], however, will violate the covenant of the Lord and defile the oath which the Lord made with them") involves understanding the Latin *finem* ("end," "purpose") as a corruption from the Greek (*aron* in place of *arkon*). On the emended text, see Charles, *The Assumption of Moses*; J. Priest's translation and notes in Charlesworth, ed., *OTP* 1:928; and Hartom's comments on the verse in the Hebrew edition.

4. 1:8 and 2:1 specifically recall the promise of the Land to the fathers; 4:2-3, and 5 refer to the covenant with "their fathers," but the land aspect of that covenant is clearly implied in the contexts. 11:11, emended from *araborum* to *atavorum*, simply describes the Land as "land of their forefathers."

5. In the recollections of Deut. 1:8, 6:10, and 30:20 the patriarchs are referred to by relationship and by name; in 34:4 they are named without reference to their status as forefathers. In the *Testament* the patriarchs are referred to by name only in the tribal prayer addressed in direct voice to the "God of Abraham, God of Isaac, and God of Jacob" (3:9).

6. The attitude toward the wilderness generation in the *Testament* is intriguingly contradictory. In the last scene Moses describes his role as intercessor and mediator

"for their sins" (12:6). But in chapter 9, Taxo, the martyr who brings on the eschaton, says to his sons, "Never did [our] fathers nor their ancestors tempt God by transgressing his commandments" (9:4).

7. On the exception, the emended text of 2:7, see note 3 above.

8. In the Latin "covenant and oath" is *testamentum et jusjurandum*. In the *Aqedah* context, "oath" is expressed in the language of נשבע. In Deuteronomy, however, when referring to the the negative stipulations if the covenant is not kept, "oath" is expressed as אלה.

The concept of a divine oath to the patriarchs also appears in *Pseudo-Philo* in the context of a promise never to abandon Israel (30:7). In the *T. 12 Patr.* (*T. Jud.* 22:3) and in the *Pss. Sol.* (17:5), the divine oath refers to the eternality of the House of David.

9. In Ps. 105:9-11 and 1 Chron. 16:15-18 reference is made to God's covenant with Abraham and oath to Isaac regarding promise of the Land. But the only oath mentioned in the promissorial scene with Isaac (Gen. 26:3) is in fact the oath to Abraham at the time of the *Aqedah* (Gen. 22:16) now being transferred to his son.

10. On the date of the epilogue to *Zichronot* liturgy, see Daniel Goldschmidt, *Machzor L'Yamim haNoraim* (New York: Leo Baeck Institute, 1970), 27-29 (Hebrew); Leon J. Liebreich, "Aspects of the New Year Liturgy," *HUCA* 34 (1963): 125-176; and Joseph Heinneman, *Iyunei haT'filah* (Jerusalem: Magnes Press, 1980), 58 (Hebrew).

The association also appears in medieval penitential poetry. See particularly Rabbi Eliezar Bar Natan's "*Et haBrit v'et haShvuah*" in A. M. Habermann, *Sefer Gezerot Ashkenaz we-Sarfat* (Jerusalem: Mosad HaRav Kook: 1945), 107-108.

11. Exod. 6:8; 13:5, 11; 33:1; Deut. 1:8; 6:10; 30:20, among many.

12. The concept of God swearing by himself appears in Jeremiah (22:5; 32:13; 49:13) and in Isaiah (45:23), but in these contexts the oath involves destruction rather than promises of progeny and land.

13. The intercession is made by the tribes on behalf of the new exiles. See below.

14. See Shalom Spiegel, *The Last Trial* (New York: Behrman House, 1967). Spiegel repeatedly notes the antiquity of the aggadic tradition, but does not discuss the *Testament of Moses*.

15. For a similar transformation of an historical event in the biblical narrative into an ongoing condition in Chronicles, see Japhet, *The Ideology of the Book of Chronicles*, 327ff.

16. In early rabbinic *aggadic* literature the *Aqedah* is treated as though Isaac had in fact been martyred and therefore as having atoning value whenever Israel sins. For examples, see *Tg. Ps-J.* on Genesis 22, *Sifra, Behukkotai* 112c; *Lev R.* 36.5; *Gen. R.* 94.5; *b. Ta'an.* 16a, *b. Yoma* 5a, and *Mek.R. Shimon* 4. The tradition is also reflected in *Pseudo-Philo* (18:5; 32:2-4; 40:2). For full development of the theme see Spiegel, *The Last Trial*.

17. "Then, years after they shall have entered *their* land, they shall be ruled by leaders and princes" (2:3). *Emphasis mine.*

18. "In those days a king against them from the east and [his] cavalry will over-run *their land*. And with fire he will burn *their city*...and he will exile all the people and will lead them to his own land....They...have gone as exiles into a foreign land" (3:1-3; 4:3). Emphasis mine.

19. "And in those times he will inspire a king to have pity on them and send them home to their own land" (6:3). Emphasis mine.

20. "Therefore, *their city* (*lit.*, colony) and the full extent of *their dwelling places* will be filled with crimes and iniquities" (5:6). "Then fear of him will be heaped upon them *in their land*" (6:5). "After his death there will come into *their land* a powerful king of the West who will subdue them" (6:8). Emphasis mine.

21. In both passages (3:2 and 5:6) he uses the term "colony," which Priest trans-lates as "city."

22. "Those who truly fulfill the commandments of God will flourish and will fin-ish the good way, but those who sin by disregarding the commandments will de-prive themselves of the good things which were declared before. They, indeed, will be punished by the nations with many tortures" (12:10-11). Collins has described this theology as "thorough-going 'covenantal nomism'" ("Testaments" in Stone, ed., *Jewish Writings* 347.)

23. For biblical sources see 2 Kings 16:3; 21:6; Ezek. 8:8-16; 16:20. The descrip-tion of idolatry includes the presence of carved images of all sorts of animals in the Temple (2:9).

24. The emphasis on Jerusalem and the Temple here is typical of the literature of the Second Temple period, when socially and economically Jerusalem became so central. See Weinfeld, "Inheritance of the Land," 115-37. The transition of focus from land to city and sanctuary in the Second Temple period was a gradual one; both traditions are evident in the *Testament*.

25. The notion that the Judean tribes suffer for the sins of their northern breth-ren also appears in 2 *Bar.* 77:10.

26. "Then all the tribes will lament, crying out to heaven and saying, 'God of Abraham, God of Isaac, and God of Jacob, remember your covenant which you made with them, and the oath which you swore to them by yourself, that their seed would never fail from the land which you have given them'" (3:8-9).

"Remember Your servants, Abraham, Isaac, and Jacob, how You swore to them by Your Self and said to them: I will make your offspring as numerous as the stars of heaven, and I will give to your offspring this whole land of which I spoke, to pos-sess forever" (Exod. 32:13).

27. None of the various analyses of the structural pattern of the *Testament of Moses* attribute significance to the prayer of the tribes. Nickelsburg includes the passage in the stage he labels "turning point," but, like Collins and Harrington, he

has little to say regarding the purpose or significance of this first prayer. See the following in Nickelsburg, ed., *Studies*: Nickelsburg, "An Antiochan Date," 33-37; Collins, "The Date and Provenance," 15-32; and Harrington, "Interpreting Israel's History: *The Testament of Moses* as a Rewriting of Deuteronomy 31-34," 59-71.

28. "Then, in that day, they will remember me, saying from tribe to tribe, even each man to his neighbor, 'Is this not that which was made known to us in prophecies by Moses, who suffered many things in Egypt and at the Red Sea and in the wilderness for forty years (when) he solemnly called heaven and earth as witnesses against us that we should not transgress God's commandments of which he had become the mediator for us? These things which have come upon us since that time are according to his admonition declared to us at that time. And [those words] have been confirmed even to our being led as captives in the land of the East" (3:10-13).

29. "Assemble unto me all the elders of your tribes, and your officers, that I may speak these words in their ears, and call heaven and earth to witness against them" (Deut. 31:28).

"Then, it shall come to pass, when many evil and troubles are come upon them, that this song shall testify before them as a witness, for it shall not be forgotten out of the mouths of their seed" (Deut. 31:21).

30. Experience occasions comparable confirmation of Moses' prophecies in 2 Bar. 84:2-5, in Dan. 9:12-13, and perhaps in 2 Macc. 7:18. In each of these contexts, however, the confirmation is accompanied or followed, as in Deut. 4:28-30 and 30:1-2, by repentance expressed in terms of a confession of sins and/or a call to return to the commandments. See 2 Bar. 84:6-85:4; Dan. 9:7-11, 15-16; 2 Macc. 7:18, 32. The reference to "when all these things happen to them" in Jubilees (1:5-6) is in response to the question raised in Deut. 31:17 and is not part of the cycle. It is presented as an explanation for the Sinai revelation that Jubilees itself portends to be, i.e. the evidence that God had not abandoned them in spite of their sins.

31. This prayer is offered by "one who is over them" (4:1). Ezra or an angel such as in Zech. 1:12 have also been suggested.

32. Licht ("Taxo, or the Apocalyptic Doctrine of Vengeance," 95-103) and Nickelsburg (*Studies*, 33-37) stress the relationship between the *Testament of Moses* and the book of Daniel; Priest argues that the "identification of the prayer with Daniel" is "probable." However, this does not necessarily indicate "that the author of the *Testament* was familiar with the book of Daniel, but rather with certain Danielic traditions" (Charlesworth, ed., *OTP* 1:924).

33. This view is argued by Harrington against Nickelsburg who, as noted above, does not distinguish between the historical patterns of Deuteronomy 28-30 and 31-32 ("Interpreting Israel's History," in Nickelsburg, ed., *Studies*, 66-68.)

34. Collins and Harrington both note that intercession functions as an analogue or counterpart to repentance (Nickelsburg, ed., *Studies*, 15-32, 59-71.)

35. I prayed to the Lord and said, "O Lord God, do not annihilate Your very own people, whom You redeemed in Your majesty and whom You freed from Egypt with a mighty hand. Give thought to your servants, Abraham, Isaac, and Jacob, and pay no heed to the stubbornness of this people, its wickedness, and its sinfulness. Else the country from which You freed us will say, 'It was because the Lord was power-less to bring them into the land that He had promised them, and because He hated them, that He brought them out to have them die in the wilderness.' Yet they are Your very own people, whom You freed with Your great might and Your out-stretched arm" (Deut. 9:26-29).

36. This is one of the two perceptions attributed to the nations in the Deutero-nomy version of the intercession. The argument first appears in the original ac-count of Moses' intercession at Kadesh Barnea (Num. 14:15-16). The related second perception—that God hated the Israelites and brought them to the wilder-ness to kill them (Deut. 9:28)—is the one presented in the Exodus narrative of the Golden Calf (Exod. 32:11-13). The two are compressed into one in Deuteronomy 9, where Moses' recollection of his intercessory role encompasses both occasions.

37. In Exodus a full intercessory scene (the dialogue between God and Moses and acknowledgment of divine acceptance of Moses' appeal) comes after Moses has been told of the worship of the calf but before he has himself witnessed the deed (32:7-14). Yet here, too, there is a doubling. When Moses returns to the mountain after he has destroyed the image, he acknowledges the great sin of the people and urges God to erase him also if He has not forgiven the sin (32:31-32). God re-sponds by urging him to continue leading the people even as He assures him that those who participated in the great sin of the calf will in fact be punished (32:33-34).

38. *Pseudo-Philo* (12:4-9) also uses the Deuteronomy version of the intercession on Sinai, where Moses' response to God comes only after his destruction of the calf.

39. Interestingly, the author of 2 *Baruch* (85:1-4) makes a point of the effective-ness of intercession by "helpers," "prophets," and "holy men" being limited to only so long as "we were...in our country." Once exiled, the Judeans have no recourse but to "direct and dispose" their hearts toward the commandments in order to ef-fect the eschatological return.

40. The *Testament* notes that the returned exiles were not able "to offer sacrifices to the Lord of their fathers" (4:9). Priest argues that the author is asserting no more than the inferiority of the Second Temple to the First (Charlesworth, ed., *OTP* 1: notes to 4:9.) However, such a comparison does not fit the description of the post-exilic period which follows the comment about sacrifices.

41. On the dominance of the deterministic theme in the *Testament*, see Priest's comments in Charlesworth, ed., *OTP* 1:922ff. On apocalyptic determinism generally, see J. J. Collins, "Jewish Apocalyptic Against Its Hellenistic Near Eastern Environment," in *BASOR* 220 (December 1975): 27-36.

42. "*Ut invocetur nomen illius usque in diem paenitentiae in respecta quo respiciet illos Dominos in consummatione exit ius dierum*" (1:18).

43. Neither events nor major characters are specified by name. But the descriptions in chapters five and six are sufficiently clear that scholars generally agree that chapter five describes the Hasmonean period, and six the reign of Herod, his sons, and the invasion of Varus. Chapter eight has been identified with the Antiochan persecution, but that identification, like the historical nature of chapter seven, continues to be the subject of some debate. On the chronological sequence of these chapters, see George W. E. Nickelsburg, *Resurrection, Immortality and Eternal Life in Intertestamental Judaism* (Cambridge: Harvard University Press, 1972), 43ff., and the articles by Collins, Priest, and Rhoads in Nickelsburg, ed., *Studies*.

44. Sin 5:3–6:1/Punishment 6:2-9; Sin 7:3-10/Punishment 8:1-5. If one treats chapters seven and eight as an interpolation, as argued by Licht and Nickelsburg, and places the chapters chronologically, the double sequence of sin/punishment is no longer in order. The pattern found in the work as it stands is the work of the final redactor. For examples of the doubling of the sin/punishment pattern in Deuteronomy, note 28:15-68 (15; 16-57; 58; 59-68) and 31:16-21 (16; 17-18; 20; 21).

45. Exod. 32:11-13; Num. 11:1-3; Deut. 9:8-29; Dan. 9:2-19; 2 Macc. 8:2-3.

46. On the identity of an historical Taxo, see Harold H. Rowley, *The Relevance of the Apocalyptic* (New York: Association, 1963), 149-56 and Solomon Zeitlin, "The *Assumption of Moses* and the Revolt of Bar Kochba," *JQR* 38 (1947-48): 1-45. On Taxo as a messianic figure, see C. J. Lattey, "The Messianic Expectation in 'The Assumption of Moses,'" *CBQ* 4 (1942): 9-21. On the function of the Taxo story, see Licht, "Taxo, or the Apocalyptic Doctrine of Vengeance"; Priest, "Some Reflections on the *Assumption of Moses*"; and the articles by Rhoads ("The *Assumption of Moses* and Jewish History: 4BC–AD48") and Kolenkow ("The *Assumption of Moses* as a Testament") in Nickelsburg, ed., *Studies*.

47. "The messenger who is in the highest place appointed" (10:2) is usually identified as the angel Michael. See Priest's note on 10:2.

48. In the descriptions of the reign of Herod and the invasion of the "powerful king of the West" (6:5, 8), the land is again referred to as "their" land.

49. The specified sins include idolatry ("they will play the harlot after foreign gods" directly cited from Deut. 31:16); pollution of the sanctuary and cult (5:3-6:1); injustice and oppression of the poor (7:3-10). In the Pentateuch and prophetic literature, idolatry (which frequently is described as harlotry) and injustice are sins which result in loss of the Land.

50. "Never did [our] fathers nor their ancestors tempt God by transgressing his commandments" (9:4).

51. In sharp contrast, the author of 2 Maccabees prefaces his tales of martyrs with the assurance that the "misfortunes...were meant not for the destruction of our people, but for their correction" and that Israel's suffering was in fact a mark of God's love (8:12ff.).

52. The reference to the end of the First Commonwealth in 586 is only implicit. Taxo refers to what is happening in his own day as "a second punishment." If one accepts the Nickelsburg thesis that the Taxo narrative is from the Maccabean period, the "second punishment" is understood as a reference to the persecution by Antiochus and the first punishment is the Babylonian exile of 586. If one does not accept that thesis, the "second punishment" could refer to some later oppression, perhaps under Herod, and the first could be 586, the Antiochan persecution, or some later event. See Priest's note on 8:1.

53. With the exception of Priest, who notes that it "may support the view that the chapter had an independent origin" (*"Testament of Moses"* in Charlesworth, ed., *OTP* 1:note d on 9:4), scholars generally have not commented upon Taxo's unusual perspective.

54. If the mounting upon the wings of an eagle (10:8) is understood as a return to God's protective custody, the parallel with Deut. 32:11 is clear. However, if the eagle is identified with Rome and the verse understood as victory over enemies, the parallel no longer functions, for in Deuteronomy 32 it is God, not Israel, who destroys the subjugators of Israel. On the eagle as Rome, see Adela Yarbro Collins, "Composition and Redaction of the *Testament of Moses* 10," *HTR* 69 (1976): 184-86.

55. On the literal interpretation of the verse, see the work of Nickelsburg, particularly, *Resurrection, Immortality*, 28-31; 43-45. Nickelsburg's argument rests heavily on the parallels he sees between the passage here, Dan. 12:3 and 1 *Enoch* 104:2-7, as well as later descriptions of the endtime in 2 *Bar.* 51:5-12.

56. Abraham's seed "shall possess the gate of his enemies."

57. In Exod. 6:8 the oath is transferred through the merit of the fathers to the Israelites, whom Moses is to lead. In Exod. 32:13 it becomes the basis upon which Moses bases his plea on behalf of the Israelites who have constructed the Golden Calf.

NOTES TO CHAPTER 5

1. See James, *Biblical Antiquities*, 45-46.

2. 12:8; 23:12; 28:4; 30:4; 39:7. On the use of the plant metaphor in 1 *Enoch* and the Damascus Document, see John J. Collins, *The Apocalyptic Imagination* (New York: Crossroad, 1987), 56-57; 60-61, 116.

3. On references to Noah and the Flood, see *Pseudo-Philo* 3; 7:4; 13:8; 19:11; 25:11. On the introduction of Abraham in a prepatriarchal context, see 4:ll; 7:4. On the cosmic perspective, see passages such as 9:3; 11:1; 13:7; 15:7.

4. On Pseudo-Philo's enhancement of God's role in the biblical narrative, see Frederick Murphy, "God in Pseudo-Philo," *JSJ*, 19 (1988): 1-18 and by the same author, *Pseudo-Philo*, 223-29.

5. 10:2; 12:4. The only later patriarch mentioned by name in a covenant-making context is Jacob, who is described as being the "third one called firstborn" and as one to whom God will reveal everything as he had to Abraham (18:6). Although Isaac is not mentioned by name in this passage, his significance to the election of Israel is noted in 18:5.

6. Created passages foretell the covenant with Abraham in 4:11 and 7:4, a covenant-making scene is presented in 8:3, and the promises to Abraham are recollected in 9:3-4; 18:5; 23:5.

7. The technique is comparable to that of Gen 5:6-7, 11:6-7, and 18:17-21, but whereas entry into God's mind is unusual for the biblical writer, it is a frequently adopted perspective in *Pseudo-Philo*'s creative additions. On this technique of rewriting, see Murphy, "God in Pseudo-Philo," 7-9.

8. Note that in *Pseudo-Philo* God refers to the departure as from *their* land, whereas, pointedly emphasizing the alienation required of the patriarch, Genesis has "from *your* native land and from *your* father's house" (Gen 12:1).

9. Murphy does not comment on the tonal shifts in his commentary on the passage. He emphasizes the correspondence between the description of the Land as untouched by the Flood and the righteousness of Abraham, which he sees as "a correspondence between land and people...that is essentially biblical" (*Pseudo-Philo*, 49).

10. God to Balaam: "Is it not regarding this people that I spoke to Abraham in a vision, saying, 'Your seed will be like the stars of the heaven.'"

11. Gen. 12:7 is cited in Exod. 33:1-2 and paraphrased in Deut. 34:4. On *Pseudo-Philo*'s subsequent use of the verse, see 10:2; 12:4; 21:9; 23:5.

12. See Gen. 13:15; 15:7; 17:8; 26:3; 28:4, 13; 35:12. The major exception is Gen. 12:7. The stress on seed in Gen. 15:18 and 48:4 is justified by the contexts.

13. The possession of the Land is described as eternal in Gen. 17:8; 48:4; Lev. 25:34. The covenant *per se* as eternal appears in Gen. 9:16; 17:7, 13, 19; Exod. 31:16; Lev. 24:8; 2 Sam. 23:5; Isa. 24:5; 55:3; 61:8; Jer. 32:40; 50:5; Ezek. 16:60; 37:26; Ps. 105:10. Significantly, neither אחזת עולם nor ברית עולם appears in Joshua or Judges.

14. Murphy notes the change in placement of the adjective in his commentary, but neither here nor elsewhere does he relate such changes to the author's reinterpretation of biblical land theology (*Pseudo-Philo*, 50).

15. See Exod. 3:6-8, 16-17; 6:2-4, 8. In these passages God identifies himself as the God of Abraham, Isaac, and Jacob, refers to the promise of the Land, and affirms that he will bring the Israelites out of Egypt to that land.

16. In rabbinic literature, the plan is Amram's (*b. Sota* 12a; *Mek.R. Shimon* 3; *Pesiq. R.* 43, 180a-b; *Exod. Rab.* 1.13).

17. *Pseudo-Philo*'s birth narrative for Moses has a number of parallels with the one he creates for Abraham. Both are miracle stories, both contain annunciation scenes, and both involve leaders whose heroic dimension involves going against the will of compatriots in suffering. On the development of the leadership theme in *Pseudo-Philo*, see Nickelsburg, "Good and Bad Leaders in *Pseudo-Philo's Liber Antiquitatum Biblicarum*," in Nickelsburg and Collins, *Ideal Figures*, 49-65 and Frederick Murphy, "Divine Plan, Human Plan: A Structuring Theme in Pseudo-Philo," *JQR* 77 (1986): 5-14.

18. Exod. 32:10ff. (recalled in Deut. 10:10) and Num. 14:11-12.

19. In Num. 14:30 the promise is recollected as having been sworn directly to the Israelites rather than to the forefathers, as here.

20. He does include Moses' vision of the Land in Deut. 34:1-4 in his summary review, but deletes the recollection of God's oath to the forefathers as well as all the references to territorial boundaries in the biblical scene. In their place he has: "Then the Lord showed him the land and all that is in it and said, 'This is the land that I will give to my people'" (19:10).

21. Lev. 23:29-30 contains only the warning that God would destroy anyone who violated the fast ("self-denial") and the prohibition against work on that day.

22. Three manuscripts include "*et non in corde suo*" after "*et constituam eos in terra sua confidenter*," thereby contrasting God's constancy over against Israel's inconstancy. See Feldman's "Prolegomenon," xcviii.

23. Depending on the context, promises to "the fathers" in these passages may refer to the patriarchs or to the wilderness generation.

24. In contrast, see Josh. 1:2-4, 11-12, 15; 11:23; 18:3; 23:3, 5, 15-16; 24:13. It is significant that when *Pseudo-Philo* cites from the last verse, he describes God "bringing to" (*induxi*) as opposed to "giving" (נתן) the Land (23:11).

25. *Pseudo-Philo* very briefly mentions only the conquests of Jericho, of the Amorites (20:7, 9), and the allocation of territory to Caleb (20:10).

26. In the biblical book the scene at Mounts Ebal and Gerizim takes place immediately after the destruction of Ai (not mentioned in *Pseudo-Philo*) and before the encounter with the Amorites and the apportionment of the Land (Josh. 8:30-35). *Pseudo-Philo* places the scene at the end of the conquest years and mentions only Mount Ebal. On the deletion of Mount Gerizim, see further.

27. The description is structured around a midrashic interpretation of the various animals offered at the *Brit ben Ha-Betarim*.

28. Recollection of the exodus and the wilderness experience are central to the review in Joshua (24:5-10) which contains no reference at all to Sinai. In contrast, *Pseudo-Philo* devotes only half of one verse to the Egypt story (23:9b) and makes no mention at all of the saving acts in the wilderness.

29. "I took you into the land which I had promised on oath to your fathers. And I said,'I will never break My covenant with you.'"

30. "But I will recall that time that was before the creation of the world...when I said that...I would plant a great vineyard, and from it I would choose a plant; and I would care for it and call it by by mine, and it would be mine forever."

31. "The Lord will take pity on you today, not because of you but because of his covenant that he established with your fathers and the oath that he has sworn not to abandon you forever" (30:7).

32. "For if the ordinances that you have established with our fathers are true, saying, 'I will multiply your seed,' and they will experience this, then it would have been better to say to us, 'I am cutting off your seed,' than to neglect our root."

33. In his narrative description of the battle (31:2) *Pseudo-Philo* uses v. 20 of the song in Judges 5—"The stars fought from heaven, From their courses they fought against Sisera"—as a literal description.

34. *Pseudo-Philo* uses the technique of a report to the souls of the fathers on several occasions, c.f., the narrative of Kadesh Barnea (15:5) and in the celebration of the covenant at Gilgal (21:9).

35. See Japhet's analysis of the Chronicler's problem with the exodus as a singular historical event in *The Ideology of the Book of Chronicles*, 80ff.

36. Note that *Pseudo-Philo* substitutes fulfillment of God's promise of redemption from Egypt for fulfillment of the promise to give them the Land (Num. 14:23) in his rewriting of Moses' intercession at Kadesh Barea (15:5).

37. The phrase is retrojected into the unbiblical description of the initial call to Abraham from the description of the Land in Deut. 11:12.

38. See *b. Zebah.* 113a and *Shir Hashirim Rab.* 1:15 for the same theme in rabbinic literature.

39. The description which appears once has no parallel in the Torah or early prophets books. It is found in Zech. 2:16, 2 *Bar.* 63:10, 4 Ezra 13:48, and 2 Macc 1:7.

40. In a midrashic development of Deut. 34:1, 4, *Pseudo-Philo* describes how God takes Moses on a heavenly journey from which he shows him the sources of earth's waters and "the place from which the holy land drinks" (19:10). The idea that the Land of Israel has its own particular source of water also appears in rabbinic literature (cf. *b. Ta'an.* 1).

41. Specifically, he never refers to the Land as "the land of the Canaanites, Hittites, Amorites, Hivites, Jebusites," as in Exod. 3:8, 17; 13:5, nor as "the land of" any one of those nations as in Exod. 13:11; Deut. 1:7; 4:47; 11:30, nor as "their"

land when the pronoun refers back to such nations as in Deut. 4:38; 9:5; 12:29; 19:1.

42. Note the absence of "land of the Canaanites, etc.," as in Josh. 1:4, 13; 13:4; 24:8; Judg. 1:36; 10:8; 11:21 and of "their" land as in Josh. 24:8, 15; Judg. 6:9, 10.

43. In the parallel narrative of Joshua 22, there are several references to "the land of Canaan" (vv. 9, 10, 11). Moreover, in the scriptural narrative the Israelites refer to the territory east of the Jordan as "the land of your holding" and to the west as "the land of the Lord's own holding" (Josh. 22:19). *Pseudo-Philo* uses the possessive pronoun to substitute Israelite for divine ownership.

44. Josh. 23:2 and Judg. 4:2, the parallel biblical verses, contain no references to the Land.

45. On contemporary relevance of the Land theology embedded in this biblical narrative, see Schwied, 20-21.

46. A dissonant universal perspective is inserted into the legislation. The Ten Commandments are introduced as "a light to the world," a "covenant with the sons of men," by which "the whole world" will be judged (11:1-2). Similarly, the rains associated with Succot are for "the whole earth" and will serve as "an everlasting sign" explicitly associated with Noah and the Flood (13:7). In contrast, Deut. 11:11-12 notes the promised land's particular dependence on rain for its water supply. God's control over the rain and hence the fruitfulness of the Land frequently appear in *tochachot* contexts, e.g., Lev. 26:19-20; Deut. 11:13-15; 28:12, 23-24, which *Pseudo-Philo* tends to avoid. There are, however, parallels to *Pseudo-Philo*'s universal perspective in rabbinic literature (cf., *b. Rosh Hash.* 16a). See James's comments on 13:4-7 and Feldman's notes in his "Prolegomenon," xcviii.

47. *Pseudo-Philo* refers to an offering of "your fruits" in connection with Shvuot (13:6) and associates Succot with rain, but in neither instance does he make an association with the Promised Land.

48. The biblical context also suggests that ארץ could refer to the property holding of the individual Israelite making the pilgrimage.

49. *Pseudo-Philo*'s version is closer to that of Deut. 5:16, where a dual consequence is described: "that you may long endure, and that you may fare well in the land that the Lord your God is giving you." However, the language in Deuteronomy, as in Exodus, is still the conditional one that is not present in *Pseudo-Philo*'s command.

50. I have followed the James translation in using the imperfect form of the verb for *derelictum est*. Harrington uses "has been abandoned," but the more literal translation does not fit the sense of the passage.

51. "I will grant peace in the land, and you shall lie down untroubled by anyone; I will give the land respite from vicious beasts, and no sword shall cross your land. You shall give chase to your enemies, and they shall fall before you by the sword.

Five of you shall give chase to a hundred, and a hundred of you shall give chase to ten thousand; your enemies shall fall before you by the sword" (Lev. 26:6-8).

52. In Deut. 31:18 the "yet" is expressed with the conjunctive "vav" of ואנכי. In *Pseudo-Philo* 13:10 it is expressed by "*tamen.*"

53. Compare Moses' speeches in Deut. 4:25-31; 28-30 which not only threaten exile from the Land, but also offer no comparable assurance without repentance on the part of the Israelites.

54. Given *Pseudo-Philo's* interest in minimizing the connection between the Land and the Law, I do not agree with Ginzberg's suggestion that the text of 11:7 is a mistranslating of the Hebrew and should read as "that My roads (i.e., the roads of My land) become not desolate." The rabbinic interpretation he cites (*b. Sabb.* 33a) in fact would be the one *Pseudo-Philo* would avoid. See Louis Ginzberg, *The Legends of the Jews* VI (Philadelphia: JPS, 1968), 40-41.

55. On the absence of the theme of repentance and *Pseudo-Philo's* development of the surety of the covenantal promises, see F. Murphy, "The Eternal Covenant in *Pseudo-Philo, JSP* 3 (1988): 43-57.

56. "You shall apportion to this people the land that I swore to their fathers to give them. But you must be very strong and resolute to observe faithfully all the Teaching that My servant Moses enjoined upon you."

57. 23:12 is a restructured version of Deut. 4:6.

58. "And behold now, all you leaders, know today that if you proceed in the ways of your God, your paths will be made straight. But if you do not heed his voice and you become like your fathers, your affairs will be spoiled and you yourselves will be crushed and your name will perish from the earth" (20:3-4).

59. "*Iuxta habundantiam misericordie sue hereditatis sue.*"

60. "*Et ecce nunc Dominus inviscerabitur vobis in hodierna die.*" A variant text (*Editio Princeps*) has "*reconciliabitur.*" See Guido Kisch, ed., *Pseudo-Philo's Liber Antiquitatum Biblicarum* (Notre Dame: University of Notre Dame, 1949), 200.

61. "*Sed ipse misericors sicut nemo miseretur generi Israel, etiam si non propter vos vel pro eis quie dormierunt.*"

62. "*a longanimitate sua*"

63. "*sed misericordia eius implevit terram*"

64. 31:2 is a midrashic development of Judg. 5:20. 35:3 involves an addition to the dialogue between Gideon and the angel in Judg. 11:12ff. The insertion of the mercy motif into the Jephthah dialogues (39:4-6) is an expansion of the biblical description of Judg. 10:16.

65. In their prayer of repentance before the appearance of Deborah (30:4), the people complain that "we cannot dwell in our own land and our enemies have power over us." But even here, sovereignty over the Land is perceived as a consequence of being the "plant of God's vineyard," "more blessed than other nations," not of the covenantal promise of Land per se.

66. "But he will not destroy his inheritance by my death" (27:7). "Now therefore spare those of your household and your children, and stay in the paths of the Lord your God lest the Lord destroy his own inheritance" (28:2). "And who knows, perhaps God will be reconciled with his inheritance so as not to destroy the plant of his vineyard" (30:4). "For we would prefer to be handed over to death once and for all than for his people to be punished thus over a period of time" (35:2). "Look, Lord, upon the people that you have chosen, and may you not destroy the vine that your right hand has planted" (39:7). "For if the ordinances that you have established with our fathers are true, saying, 'I will multiply your seed,' and they will experience this, then it would have been better to say to us, 'I am cutting off your seed,' than to neglect our root" (49:6).

67. The activating of divine mercy is expressed in various ways: in the Kenaz narrative God shows mercy "because he has toiled so much among us" (28:5). Deborah attributes it to recollection of the covenant with the fathers (30:7; 32:13-14), particularly to the role of Isaac (32:4). Gideon describes God as showing mercy "on account of those who have fallen asleep" (35:3). And Jephthah presents divine mercy as restraint (39:5). In contrast, in Judges God's intervention is presented as a response to Israel's cries, e.g., Judg. 3:15; 4:3; 6:7; 10:10-16.

68. Harrington (note on 33:5) views the two passages, 33:5 from Deborah's final speech and 35:3 from the angel's dialogue with Gideon, as contradictory. However, the first deals with intercession and the second with patriarchal merit, two concepts that are not necessarily connected to each other. Harrington's reading may be influenced by an editor's gloss in the margin of the *Editio Princeps*. See Feldman's, "Prolegomenon," cxix.

69. It is significant that the biblical description of the intercession also makes no reference to repentance.

70. For *Pseudo-Philo* the connection between the intercession at Sinai and the *Aqedah* is problematic because it involves restatement of the promise of eternal possession of the whole Land.

71. See also 12:13; 13:10; 16:3; 19:4, 7, 12-15; 25:7; 26:13; 32:17; 48:1 and James's enumeration of passages in *Biblical Antiquites*, 34ff. On the overall treatment of eschatology in the work, see Perrot's comments in *Pseudo-Philon: Les Antiquities Bibliques*, D.J. Harrington, J. Cazeaux, C. Perrot and P. Bogaert, eds. (Paris: Cerf, 1976), 2:53-57.

72. Although it is never specifically stated, *Pseudo-Philo* appears to include only Israelites among the "just."

73. *Pseudo-Philo* attributes Moses' death prior to the conquest to God's desire to keep him from seeing the idols which the Israelites will worship.

74. The exception is in the introductory chapter (Judg. 2:20-22). But even here the issue is expulsion of the indigenous population, which is related to but not identical with acquisition of the Land. Moreover, in the subsequent narratives the

Israelites's appeal is for divine assistance against oppression at the hands of these nations rather than for aid in conquest or retention of the Promised Land. The typological biblical model for redemption from oppression is, of course, the Egyptian bondage when Israel's survival as a nation is threatened.

75. In addition to the absence of any reference to the destruction of the Second Temple, a point other scholars have made in support of a pre-70 date, I suggest that *Pseudo-Philo* would not have shown so little interest in exile had he written the work after 70. On the exile of Judeans after the fall of Jerusalem, see Josephus, *War* VI.418-21.

NOTES TO CHAPTER 6

1. On Josephus' description of the program for *Antiquities*, see Louis H. Feldman, "Hellenizations in Josephus' *Jewish Antiquities*: The Portrait of Abraham," in Louis H. Feldman and Gohei Hata, eds., *Josephus, Judaism and Christianity* (Detroit: Wayne State University Press, 1987), 133-35.

2. Although the work is primarily intended for gentile readers, Feldman notes that the allusions to the moral lessons to be learned from Jewish history points to a Greek-speaking Jewish audience as well. See Feldman, "Hellenizations in Josephus' *Jewish Antiquities*: The Portrait of Abraham," 135.

3. On Josephus' biblical sources, see A. Schalit, *Yosef ben Mattityahu (Flavius Josephus), Quadmoniyot ha-Yehudim*, 2d ed. (Jerusalem: Mosad Bialik 1967), xxvii-xxxi (Hebrew) and Harold Attridge, *The Interpretation of Biblical History in the Antiquitates Judaicae of Flavius Josephus*, HDR 7 (Missoula, Mont.: Scholars Press, 1976), 29-38.

4. "A disposition of property, especially by will and testament." H. Jastrow, *Dictionary of the Targumim, the Talmud Babli and Yerusalmi* (New York: Traditional Press, 1975), 294.

5. The term does appear later in *Antiquities* (Books XIII-XVIII), but is never used anywhere in Josephus as the equivalent of ברית. I am grateful for Louis Feldman for this notation as well as numerous other helpful suggestions.

6. Writing as an historian, Josephus tends to summarize and paraphrase biblical dialogues. When he permits a character to make a direct speech, it indicates an "important moment" to which he wishes to draw particular attention. On his use of direct speech in *Antiquities*, see Willem C. Van Unnik, "Josephus' Account of the Story of Israel's Sin with Alien Women in the Country of Midian," in M. S. Heerma van Voss, et. al., eds., *Travels in the World of the OT: Studies Presented to Professor M. A. Beek*, Studia Semitica Neerlandica 16 (Assen: Van Gorcum, 1974), 241-61.

7. The appearance of birds of prey is an indication of acceptance of Abraham's sacrifice rather than a sign of covenant-making. For the significance of birds of prey in antiquity, see Livy, *History of Rome*, Book I, ch. 7.

8. The phrase אחזת עולם or its equivalent does not appear in each of the Genesis covenantal encounters. Serving as a natural preface and conclusion to the patriarchal land promises, it is used when Abraham is told of Isaac's forthcoming birth (Gen. 17:8) and again in Jacob's blessing of Joseph's children (48:4). The first of these narratives is included in *Antiquities* without any reference to the land promise (I.191); the second is omitted.

9. The author of *Jubilees* also develops the theme of Jacob's fear. However, there the fear is rooted in the revelation at Bethel that he would die in Egypt (*Jub*. 44:2, 5-6). The focus on fear in the two texts is invited by the "Fear not to go down to Egypt" which appears in Gen. 46:3 without any prefacing description of the patriarch's state of mind. The more significant similarity between *Jubilees* and *Antiquities* here lies in the fact that in each case development of the passage is somehow related back to one of the Bethel scenes. In *Jubilees* it is the encounter on the patriarch's return to Canaan; that encounter having been omitted in *Antiquities*, the passage points back to the first encounter at Bethel.

10. Compare Gen. 48:4, 21; 50:24.

11. In *Pseudo-Philo* Miriam has the dream vision announcing Moses' future (9:10), and Amram, not God, recollects the patriarchal history (9:3-4). Like the recollection in *Antiquities*, that one focuses on numbers and fertility, but the patriarchal covenant construct is retained by *Pseudo-Philo*. On the similarities between *Pseudo-Philo* and *Antiquities*, see Feldman, "Prolegomenon."

12. Gen. 25:6 simply states that Abraham sent the sons of his concubines "away from his son Isaac eastward, to the land of the East."

13. For example, Exod. 32:13; Num. 14:22-23; 32:10-11; Deut. 1:8, 35; 4:37-38; 8:18; 9:5; 10:11; 11:9; 30:20; 34:4; Josh. 5:6. Josephus does not include a divine oath (*horkos*) either in his patriarchal narratives or in any recollections.

14. The theme of God as "ally" or source of "succor" runs throughout *Antiquities*. In addition to the passages cited, note also II.349; III.19, 45, 98, 217, 302; IV.45, 182; V.39, 60.

15. In his narration of the Kadesh Barnea story Josephus does have God promise "to give" the Land (III.315), but he uses the Greek *paradidomi*, "to hand over," "deliver up," "surrender," rather than the gift language of *doreo* (*dosis*).

16. III.306, 309/Num. 14:8; IV.315/Deut. 31:7; IV.168/Num. 32:7-9; V.115/Josh. 24:2-13.

17. On Josephus' embellishment of the Joshua narrative of the two and a half tribes, see Louis H. Feldman, "Josephus' Portrait of Joshua," *HTR* 82:4 (1989): 372-73.

18. Attridge argues that Josephus attempts to normalize God's relationship with Israel by developing a concept of God as ally in a relationship that is specifically conditional in nature. Attridge focuses heavily on Abraham and Moses, leaving unexplained the basis of God's relationship with Jacob, who is not such a model hero. Moreover, Attridge's argument does not account for Josephus' neglect of many land-focused passages which would have demonstrated the conditional character of God's alliance with Israel. Lastly, the thesis does not explain why Josephus avoids the promise of covenanted land far more than that of numbers and peoplehood.

19. The same idea of God as ally appears in *The Jewish War*. But there it is Agrippa who discourages revolt against Rome with whom God is allied (*War* II.390) and Josephus, who urges surrender because fortune and God have passed the "rod of empire" to Rome (*War* V.366-69). Titus also urges his troops onward to the siege with the assurance of having a divine ally (*War* VI.38-41).

20. On the distinctions between Palestine, Canaan, and Judea in Josephus, see Louis H. Feldman, "Some Observations on the Name of Palestine," *HUCA* LXXI (1990): 11-12.

21. "They would overcome their foes, vanquish the Canaanites in battle, and take possession of their land and cities."

22. Explaining that he is hellenizing the form of proper names for the "pleasure" of his readers, Josephus notes that this is not the form that "is used in *our* country" (I.129). Because of the disorder of the Hebrews in the period of the Judges, the Ammanites and Philistines "ravaged *their* (i.e., the Judeans') country" (V.255). The Babylonian attack on Judea in the time of Manasseh "ravaged *their* country" (X.40), and Zedekiah's alliance with Egypt resulted in Nebuchadnezzar's armies "ravaging *his* country" (X.109). (Emphasis mine.)

23. Attribution of the fruitfulness of a land to a deity is a common treatment of land in ancient paganism. See Davies, *The Gospel and the Land*, 1ff.

24. The same phrasing is used in earlier descriptions of the levitical cities (IV.67) and of the cities of refuge to be established in the Land (IV.172-73).

25. The enumeration includes the establishment of a central place of worship, described in *Antiquities* as "one holy city in that place in the land of Canaan that is fairest and most famous for its excellence" (IV.200), the annual pilgrimage festivals, firstfruits and tithing, the laws regarding kingship, and certain prohibited sexual unions.

26. Two passages about the burial of a corpse reflect Deut. 21:22-23. In both "You shall not defile the land that the Lord your God is giving you to possess" is omitted. Similarly, in an earlier passage describing the cities of refuge to be established after the conquest, Josephus omits all references to blood polluting the Land. See IV.172-73 and Num. 35:33-34.

27. "…render thanks to God for having delivered his race from the insolence of the Egyptians and given them a good land and spacious to enjoy the fruits thereof."

28. In the biblical narrative the assumption is that since the altar has been constructed in "unclean" land, the two and a half tribes intend to use it for the worship of other gods (Josh. 22:16-20). The tribes defend themselves against the charge "that we have built us an altar to turn away from following the Lord; or if to offer thereon burnt offering of meal offering or if to offer sacrifices of peace-offering thereon" (Josh. 22:23).

29. See Feldman, "Josephus' Portrait of Joshua," 372-73.

30. Context justifies Thackeray's translation of *ge* as "earth" rather than "land." Had he been referring specifically to Canaan, to avoid confusion Josephus would have indicated the country by name as he does earlier in III.87.

31. The Greek here is *edoke* from *didomi*.

32. Moses tells the Israelites that if they follow the laws they will be "blessed and envied of all men" (IV.180) "more glorious than foreign races" and "uncontested renown with future generations" (IV.183). He seems to make a point of not directly mentioning acquisition of the Land. Instead, hinting at it with "your possession of those good things which ye have already will rest assured, and those yet absent will soon be present in your hands," he affirms the aid God provides to the faithful when they enter into combat (IV.181).

33. In Deuteronomy 31-32, God also is the initiator of a restoration that is not preceded by repentance. That paradigm could have served as a model for Josephus' version here. But given the freedom the historian takes overall in interpreting biblical narratives, the similarity does not necessarily indicate a source model.

34. Noting that Josephus' later descriptions of the end of the First Commonwealth later in *Antiquities* refer to the "removal of the people" (X.149), "the captivity of the Israelites" (X.185), the "deportation of the two tribes" (X.185), and that a passage in *The War* describes the Babylonian bondage as "exile" (*War* V.389), A. Shochat argues that the absence of exile here indicates that the passage refers not to the destruction of the First Temple, but rather to that of the Second ("The Views of Josephus on the Future of Israel and its Land" in Michael Ish Shalom, et. al., eds., *Yerushalayim* [Jerusalem: Mosad HaRav Kook, 1952] [Hebrew], 43-50).

More convincing is Shochat's argument that Josephus uses the language of dispersion for the Roman period and that of exile, uprootedness, for the earlier Babylonian one. However, that distinction is not helpful in this passage where neither terminology is employed.

35. Such interweaving is a concomitant of Josephus' philosophy of God's role in history, a philosophy he sets forth explicitly in *The War*: "God has a care for men, and by all kinds of premonitory signs shows His people the way of salvation, while they owe their destruction to folly and calamities of their own choosing" (*War* VI.310). To buttress this philosophy, Josephus rewrites scriptural passages in *Antiquities* so that they clearly show "premonitory signs." See X.277-80 for another statement on God and history.

For Josephus' attitude toward prophetic oracles, an aspect of the same issue, see Frederick Bruce, "Josephus and Daniel," *Annual of the Swedish Theological Institute* 4 (1965): 148-62; and on the relationship between prophet and historian, prophecy and history in Josephus, see Louis H. Feldman, "Prophets and Prophecy in Josephus," *JTS*, NS 41, Pt. 2 (1990): 397-400.

36. On Josephus' development of the passage, see Shochat, "The Views of Josephus on the Future of Israel and its Land," 47.

37. On Josephus' attitude toward Rome, see Menahem Stern, "Josephus and the Roman Empire as Reflected in *The Jewish War*," in Feldman and Hata, eds., *Josephus, Judaism and Christianity*, 71-80, and Shochat, "The Views of Josephus on the Future of Israel and its Land," 43-50.

38. In *The Jewish War* (II.399) and in *Against Apion* (II.282) Josephus also comments favorably on the dispersion of the Jews in his own day.

39. In his study of the portrait of David, Feldman notes that Josephus stresses David's distinguished ancestry as well as his personal virtues, but makes a point of omitting any reference to the tradition of David as ancestor of the Messiah. See "Josephus' Portrait of David," *HUCA* 60 (1989): 129-174.

40. In his account of the Tower of Babel, Josephus has God commanding Noah's descendants "to send out colonies," "to cultivate much of the earth and enjoy an abundance of its fruit." It is specifically their failure to do so that precipitates the building of the ill-fated tower (I.110-111). Feldman has noted that the command to send out colonies due to an increase in population is "reminiscent of Herotodus's description of the founding of Etruria by Lydians." See his "The Portrait of Noah in Josephus, Philo, Pseudo-Philo's *Biblical Antiquities* and Rabbinic Midrashim," *Proceedings of the American Academy for Jewish Research* 55 (1988): 53.

Bibliography

Alexander, Philip. "Retelling the Old Testament." In *It Is Written: Scripture Citing Scripture*, edited by D. A. Carson and H. G. Williamson, 99-121. Cambridge: Cambridge University Press, 1988.

Alter, Robert and Peter Kemode, eds. *The Literary Guide to the Bible*. Cambridge, Mass.: Harvard University Press, 1987.

Attridge, Harold. *The Interpretation of Biblical History in the Antiquitates Judaicae of Flavius Josephus*. HDR 7. Missoula, Mont.: Scholars Press, 1976.

————. "Josephus and His Works." In *Jewish Writings of the Second Temple Period*, edited by Michael Stone, 185-232. Assen: Van Gorcum and Philadelphia: Fortress, 1984.

Avigad, N. and Y. Yadin, eds. *A Genesis Apocryhon: A Scroll for the Wilderness of Judea*. Jerusalem: Magnes, 1956.

Baltzer, K. *The Covenant Formulary in the Old Testament, Jewish and Early Christian Writings*. Philadephia: Fortress, 1971.

Bloch, Rene. "Midrash." In *Approaches to Ancient Judaism: Theory and Practice*, edited by William S. Green. Brown Judaic Studies I, 29-50. Missoula, Mont.: Scholars Press, 1978.

Brandenburger, E. *Himmelfahrt Moses*. JSHRZ 52. Gutersloh: Mohn, 1976.

Bruce, Frederick. "Josephus and Daniel." *Annual of the Swedish Theological Institute* 4 (1965): 148-62.

Buber, Martin. *Israel and Palestine: The History of an Idea*. London: East and West Library, 1952.

Charles, R. H., ed. *Apocrypha and Pseudepigrapha of the Old Testament*. Vol. 2. Oxford: Clarendon, 1913.

————., ed. *The Assumption of Moses Translated from The Sixth Century Manuscript*. London: Black, 1897.

————., ed. *The Book of Jubilees or the Little Genesis*. London: SPCK, 1927.

————., ed. *The Ethiopic Version of the Hebrew Book of Jubilees*. Oxford: Clarendon, 1895.

Charlesworth, James, ed. *Old Testament Pseudepigrapha*. 2 vols. Garden City, N. Y.: Doubleday, 1983-85.

Chestnutt, Randall. "Revelatory Experiences Attributed to Biblical Women in Early Jewish Literature." In *Women Like This: New Perspectives on Jewish Women in the Greco-Roman World*, edited by A. J. Levine, 109-11. Atlanta: Scholars Press, 1991.

Cohn, Leopold. "An Apocryphal Work Ascribed to Philo of Alexandria." *JQR, Old Ser.* 10 (1898): 277-332.

Collins, Adela. "Composition and Redaction of the *Testament of Moses 10*." *HTR* 69 (1976): 184-86.

Collins, John J. *The Apocalyptic Imagination*. New York: Crossroad, 1987.

————."The Date and Provenance of the Testament of Moses." In *Studies*, edited by G. Nickelsburg, 15-32. SBLSCS 4. Missoula, Mont.: Scholars Press, 1973.

————. "Jewish Apocalyptic Against Its Hellenistic Near Eastern Environment." *BASOR* 220 (1975): 27-36.

————. "The Testamentary Literature in Recent Scholarship." In *Early Judaism and Its Modern Interpreters*, edited by R. Kraft and G. Nickelsburg, 268-278. Philadelphia: Fortress, 1986.

Davenport, Gene L. *The Eschatology of the Book of Jubilees*. Leiden: Brill, 1971.

Davies, Philip R. "Calendrical Change and Qumran Origins: An Assessment of VanderKam's Theory." *CBQ* (1983): 80-89.

Davies, W. D. *The Gospel and the Land*. Berkeley: University of California Press, 1974.

————. *The Territorial Dimension of Judaism*. Berkeley: University of California Press, 1982.

De Guglielmo, A. "The Fertility of the Land in the Messianic Prophecies." *CBQ* 19 (1957): 306-11.

Dimant, Devorah. "Qumran Sectarian Literature." In *Jewish Writings of the Second Temple Period*, edited by Michael Stone, 483-550. Assen: Van Gorcum and Philadelphia: Fortress, 1984.

————. "Use and Interpretation of *Mikra* in the Apocrypha and Pseudepigrapha." In *Mikra: Text, Translation, Reading and Interpretation of the Hebrew Bible in Ancient Judaism and Early Christianity*, edited by M. J. Moulder, 379-419. Assen/Maastricht: Van Gorcum and Philadelphia: Fortress, 1988.

Dinaburg, B. "Zion and Jerusalem: Their Role in the Historic Consciousness of Israel." *Zion* 16 (1951): 1-17. (Hebrew)

Eisen, Arnold. *Galut*. Bloomington: Indiana University Press, 1986.

Endres, John. *Biblical Interpretation in the Book of Jubilees*. CBQMS 18. Washington, D.C.: Catholic Biblical Association, 1987.

Feldman, Louis. "Epilegomenon to Pseudo-Philo's *Liber Antiquitatum Biblicarum*." *JJS* 25 (1974): 305-312.

————. "Hellenizations in Josephus' *Jewish Antiquities*: The Portrait of Abraham." In *Josephus, Judaism and Christianity*, edited by L. Feldman and G. Hata, 133-53. Detroit: Wayne State University Press, 1987.

————. "Josephus as Biblical Interpreter: The *Aquedah*." *JQR* 75 (1985): 212-52.

————. "Josephus' Portrait of David." *HUCA* 60 (1989): 129-174.

————. "Josephus' Portrait of Joshua," *HTR* 82:4 (1989): 351-76.

————. "The Portrait of Noah in Josepus, Philo, Pseudo-Philo's *Biblical Antiquities*, and Rabbinic Midrashim." Proceedings of the American Academy for Jewish Research 55 (1988): 31-57.

————. "Prolegomenon." In *The Biblical Antiquities of Philo*, edited by M. R. James, vii-clxix. New York: Ktav, 1971.

————. "Prophets and Prophecy in Josephus." *JTS* 41 (NS) (1990): 397-400.

————. "Some Observations on the Name of Palestine," *HUCA* 61 (1990): 1-23.

————. "Use, Authority and Exegesis of *Mikra* in the Writings of Josephus." In Mikra: Text, Translation, Reading and Interpretation of the Hebrew Bible in Ancient Judaism and Early Christianity, edited by M. J.

Moulder, 455-518. Assen/Maastricht: Van Gorcum and Philadelphia: Fortress, 1988.

Fishbane, Michael. *Biblical Interpretation in Ancient Israel*. Oxford: Clarendon, 1985.

Fitzmyer, Joseph. *The Genesis Apocryphon of Qumran Cave I: A Commentary*. Rome: Biblical Institute, 1971.

Ginzberg, Louis. *The Legends of the Jews*. Philadelphia: Jewish Publication Society, 1968.

Goldman, Moshe, trans. *Sefer HaYovlim*. In *Hasefarim Hachizonim*, edited by Moseh Kahana. Vol 1., 216-313. Tel Aviv: Makor, 1936.

Goldstein, Jonathan. "The Date of the Book of Jubilees." *PAAJR* 50 (1983): 78-83.

Goldschmidt, Daniel. *Machzor L'Yamim HaNoraim*. New York: Leo Baech Institute, 1970. (Hebrew)

Habermann, M. *Sefer Gezerot Ashkenaz we-Sarfat*. Jerusalem: Mosad HaRav Kook, 1945.

Halkin, Abraham. "Zion in Biblical Literature." In *Zion in Jewish Literature*, edited by Abraham Halkin, 18-37. New York: Herzl, 1961.

Halpern-Amaru, Betsy. "Land Theology in Josephus' *Jewish Antiquities*." *JQR* 71 (1980-81): 201-229.

Harrington, Daniel. "The Biblical Text of Pseudo-Philo's *Liber Antiquitatum Biblicarum*." *CBQ* 33 (1971): 1-17.

———. "Interpreting Israel's History: The Testament of Moses as a Rewriting of Deuteronomy 31-34." In *Studies*, edited by G. Nickelsburg, 59-71. SBLSCS 4. Missoula, Mont.: Scholars Press, 1973.

———. "The Original Language of Pseudo-Philo's *Liber Antiquitatum Biblicarum*." *HTR* 63 (1970): 503-14.

———. "Palestinian Adaptations of Biblical Narratives and Prophecies." In *Early Judaism and Its Modern Interpreters*, edited by Robert Kraft and George Nickelsburg, 239-58. Philadelphia: Fortress and Atlanta: Scholars Press, 1986.

———. "Pseudo-Philo." In *Old Testament Pseudepigrapha*, edited by James Charlesworth. Vol 2., 297-377. Garden City, N. Y.: Doubleday, 1988.

Harrington, D. J., J. Cazeaux, C. Perrot, and P. M. Bogaert, eds. *Pseudo-Philon, Les Antiquities Bibliques*. Vol. 2. Paris: Cerf, 1976.

Hartom, A. S., ed. *Sefer HaYovlot* in *Hasefarim Hachizonim*. Tel Aviv: Yavneh, 1980. (Hebrew)

Heinemann, I. "The Relationship Between the Jewish People and Their Land in Hellenistic-Jewish Literature." *Zion* 13-14 (1948-49): 1-9. (Hebrew)

Heinemann, J. *Iyunei ha T'filah*. Jerusalem: Magnes, 1945. (Hebrew)

Hoffman, Lawrence, ed. *The Land of Israel: Jewish Perspectives*. Notre Dame: University of Notre Dame Press, 1986.

James, M. R. *The Biblical Antiquities of Philo*. London, 1917; reissued New York: Ktav, 1971.

Japhet, Sarah. *The Ideology of the Book of Chronicles and Its Place in Biblical Thought*. Jerusalem: Mosad Bialik, 1977. (Hebrew)

Jastrow, H. "Dictionary of the Tarqumim, the Talmud Babli and Yerusalmi." New York: Traditional Press, 1975.

Josephus, Flavius. *Works*. Edited by H. St. John Thackeray. Cambridge, Mass.: Harvard University Press and London: Heinemann, 1926-34.

Kisch, Guido. "The Editio Princeps of Pseudo-Philo's *Liber Antiquitatum Biblicarum*." In *Alexander Marx: Jubilee Volume on the Occasion of His Seventieth Birthday*, edited by S. Lieberman, 425-46. New York: Jewish Theological Seminary, 1949.

―――. "A Note on the New Edition of Pseudo-Philo's Biblical Antiquities." *Historia Judaica* 12 (1950): 153-58.

Kish, Guido, ed. *Pseudo-Philo's Liber Antiquitatum Biblicarum*. Notre Dame: University of Notre Dame Press, 1949.

Kolenkow, A. B. "The *Assumption of Moses* as a Testament." In *Studies*, edited by G. Nickelsburg, 71-77. SBLCS 4. Missoula, Mont.: Scholars Press, 1973.

Kraft, Robert and George Nickelsburg, eds. *Early Judaism and Its Modern Interpreters*. Philadelphia: Fortress and Atlanta: Scholars, 1986.

Krensky, Tikvah Frymer. "The Atrahasis Epic and Its Significance for Our Understanding of Genesis 1-9." *BA* (1977): 147-55.

Lattey, C. J. "The Messianic Expectation in *The Assumption of Moses*." *CBQ* 4 (1942): 9-21.

Liebreich, Leon. "Aspects of the New Year Liturgy." *HUCA* 34 (1963): 125-76.

Licht, Jacob. "Taxo, or the Apocalyptic Doctrine of Vengeance." *JJS* 12 (1961): 95-103.

Littmann, E., ed. "Das Buch der *Jubilaen*." In *Die Apokryphen und Pseudepigraphen des Alten Testaments*, edited by Emil Kautzsch, vol. 2, 31-119. Tubingen: Hildescheim, 1962.

Livy. *The History of Rome*. Translated by B.O.Foster. New York: Putnam and London: Heinemann, 1919-59.

Lustig, Ian. *For the Land and the Lord*. New York: Council on Foreign Relations, 1988.

Marquardt, W. *Die Juden und ihr Land*. Hamburg: Siebenster Taschenbuch, 1975.

Mendels, Doron. *The Land of Israel as a Political Concept in Hasmonean Literature*. Tubingen: Mohr, 1987.

Milgrom, Jacob. "Atonement in the Old Testament." In IDB Sup., 81.

Murphy, Frederick J. "Divine Plan, Human Plan: A Structuring Theme in Pseudo-Philo." *JQR* 77 (1986): 5-14.

―――. "The Eternal Covenant in Pseudo-Philo." *JSP* 3 (1988): 43-57.

―――. "Retelling the Bible: Idolatry in Pseudo-Philo." *JBL* 107 (1988): 275-87.

―――. *Pseudo-Philo: Rewriting the Bible*. New York, Oxford: Oxford University Press, 1993.

―――. "God in Pseudo-Philo." *JSJ* 19 (1988): 1-18.

Nickelsburg, George. "An Antiochan Date for the *Testament of Moses*." In *Studies*, edited by G. Nickelsburg, 33-37. SBLSCS 4. Missoula, Mont.: Scholars, Press, 1973.

―――. "The Bible Rewritten and Expanded." In *Jewish Writings of the Second Temple Period*, edited by Michael Stone. Assen:Van Gorcum and Philadelphia: Fortress, 1984.

———. "Good and Bad Leaders in Pseudo-Philo's *Liber Antiquitatum Bibli-carum.*" In *Ideal Figures in Ancient Judaism: Profiles and Paradigms*, edited by George Nickelsburg and John Collins, 49-65. Chico, Calif.: Scholars Press, 1980.

———. *Jewish Literature Between the Bible and the Mishnah: A Historical and Literary Introduction.* Philadelphia: Fortress, 1981.

———. *Resurrection, Immortality, and Eternal Life in Intertestamental Judaism.* Cambridge, Mass.: Harvard University Press, 1972.

———, ed. *Studies on the Testament of Moses.* SBLSCS 4. Missoula, Mont.: Scholars Press, 1973.

Orlinsky, Harry. "The Biblical Concept of the Land of Israel: Cornerstone of the Covenant Between God and Israel." In *The Land of Israel: Jewish Perspectives*, edited by L. Hoffman, 27-65. Notre Dame: University of Notre Dame Press, 1986.

Priest, J. "Some Reflections on the Assumption of Moses." *Perspectives on Religious Studies* 4 (1977): 92-111.

———. "Testament of Moses." In *Old Testament Pseudepigrapha*, edited by James Charlesworth, vol. 1, 919-926. Garden City, N.Y.: Doubleday, 1988.

Pummer, R. "The Book of *Jubilees* and the Samaritans." *Eglise et Theologie* 10 (1979): 147-78.

Rabin, C. *The Book of Jubilees.* In *The Apocryphal Old Testament*, edited by H. Sparks. Oxford: Clarendon, 1984.

Ravitzky, Aviezer. *Messianism, Zionism, and Jewish Religious Radicalism.* Tel Aviv: Am Oved, 1993. (Hebrew)

Rendtorff, R. *Israel und sein Land.* Munchen: Kaiser, 1975.

Ronsch, H., ed. *Das Buch der Jubilaen oder die kleine Genesis.* Leipzig: 1874, repr. Amsterdam: Rodopi, 1970.

Rhoads, D. M. "*The Assumption of Moses* and Jewish History: 4 B.C.-A.D. 48." In *Studies*, edited by G. Nickelsburg, 53-58. SBLSCS 4. Missoula, Mont.: Scholars Press, 1973.

Rowley, Harold. *The Relevance of the Apocalyptic.* New York: Association, 1963.

Sanders, E. P. "The Covenant as a Soteriologial Category and the Nature of Salvation in Palestinian and Hellenistic Judaism." In *Jews, Greeks, and Christians: Studies in Honor of W. D. Davies*, edited by R. Hamerton-Kelly and R. Scroggs, 11-44. Leiden: Brill, 1976.

———. *Paul and Palestinian Judaism*. Philadelphia: Fortress, 1977.

Sanders, James A. "Text and Canon: Concepts and Method." *JBL* 98 (1979): 5-29.

Schalit, A. *Yosef ben Mattityahu, Quadmoniyot ha-Yehudim*. 2nd ed. Jerusalem: Mosad Bialik, 1967. (Hebrew)

Schuerer, Emil. *The History of the Jewish Peoople in the Age of Jesus Christ*, edited by F. Millar and G. Vermes. Edinburgh: Clark, 1986.

Schwartz, J. "Jubilees, Bethel and the Temple of Jacob." *HUCA* 56 (1985): 63-85.

Schweid, E. *The Land of Israel: National Home or Land of Destiny*. Cranbury, N.J.: Associated University Presses, 1985.

Shochat, A. "The Views of Josephus on the Future of Israel and its Land." In *Yerushalayim*, edited by Michael Ish Shalom, et. al., 43-50. Jerusalem: Mosad HaRav Kook, 1952. (Hebrew)

Spiegel, Shalom. *The Last Trial*. (New York: Behrman House, 1967.

Stern, Menahem. "Josephus and the Roman Empire as Reflected in *The Jewish War*." In *Josephus, Judaism and Christianity*, edited by L. Feldman and G. Hata, 71-80. Detroit: Wayne State University Press, 1987.

Stone, Michael, ed. *Jewish Writings of the Second Temple Period: Apocrypha, Pseudepigrapa, Qumran Sectarian Writings, Philo, Josephus*. Assen: Van Gorcum and Philadelphia: Fortress, 1984.

———. "Reactions to Destruction of the Second Temple." *JSJ* 12 (1981): 195-204.

Strecker, G., ed. *Das Land Israel in biblischer Zeit*. Gottingen: Vandenhoechk and Ruprecht, 1983.

Strugnell, John. "Philo (Pseudo-) or *Liber Antiquitatum Biblicarum*." In *EncJud*, vol. 13, 408-409.

VanderKam, James, ed. *The Book of Jubilees*, vol. 1. Louvain: E. Peeters, 1989.

————. "The Jubilees Fragments from Qumran Cave 4." In *The Madrid Qumran Congress*, vol. 2, 635-648, edited by Julio Trebolle Barrera and Luis Vegas Montaner. Leiden, New York, Koln: Brill, 1992.

————. "The Putative Author of the *Book of Jubilees*." *JSS* 26 (1981): 209-217.

————. "The Righteousness of Noah." In *Ideal Figures in Ancient Judaism: Profiles and Paradigms*, edited by George Nickelsburg and John Collins. SBLSCS 12, 13-33. Chico, Calif.: Scholars, 1980.

————. *Textual and Historical Studies in the Book of Jubilees*. HSM 14. Missoula, Mont.: Scholars Press, 1977.

van der Woude, A. S. "Fragmente des Buches Jubilaen aus Qumran Hohe XI (11QJub)." In *Tradition and Glaube: Das fruhe Christentum in seiner Unwelt: Festgabe fur Karl George Kuhn*, edited by G. Jeremias, H. W. Kuhn, and H. Stegemann. Gottingen: Vanderhoeck and Rubrecht, 1971.

van Unnik, Willem. "Josephus' Account of the Story of Israel's Sin with Alien Women in the Country of Midian." In *Travels in the World of the OT: Studies Presented to Professor M. A. Beek*, edited by M. Heerma van Voss, et. al. *Studia Semitica Neerlandica* 16. Assen: Van Gorcum, 1974.

Vermes, Geza. *Post-Biblical Jewish Studies.* Vol.8 of *Studies in Judaism in Late Antiquity*, edited by Jacob Neusner. Leiden: Brill, 1975.

————. *Scripture and Tradition in Judaism: Haggadic Studies.* Leiden: Brill, 1961.

Weinfeld, Moshe. "The Covenant of Grant in the Old Testament and in the Ancient Near East." *JAOS* 90 (1970): 184-203.

————. *Deuteronomy and the Deuteronomy School*. Oxford: Oxford University Press, 1972.

————. "Inheritance of the Land—Privilege versus Obligation: The Concept of the Promise of the Land in the Sources of the First and Second Temple Periods." *Zion* 49 (1984): 115-37. (Hebrew)

————. "Universalism and Particularism in the Period of Exile and Restoration." *Tarbiz* 33 (1963-64): 229-42. (Hebrew)

Wintermute, O. S. "*Jubilees*." In *Old Testament Pseudepigrapha*, edited by James Charlesworth, vol. 2, 35-51. Garden City, N.Y.: Doubleday, 1988.

Zeitlin, Solomon. "*The Assumption of Moses* and the Revolt of Bar Kochba." *JQR* 38 (1947): 1-45.

————. "The *Book of Jubilees* and the Pentateuch." *JQR* 48 (1957): 218-35.

————. "The *Book of Jubilees*, Its Character and Significance." *JQR* 30 (1939-40): 1-31.

Index of Texts